Introduction to
Cataloging and Classification

Introduction to Cataloging and Classification

with 45 Exhibits *and* 15 Figures

SIXTH EDITION

Mildred Harlow Downing

David H. Downing

*Revised and greatly enlarged
in accordance with AACR2R88
and the 20th edition of the
Dewey Decimal Classification*

McFarland & Company, Inc., Publishers
Jefferson, North Carolina, and London

Grateful acknowledgment is made for permission to use certain copyrighted materials from the following organizations:

American Library Association. *Anglo-American Cataloguing Rules*, 2nd edition, 1988 revision. Chicago, 1988.

Gale Research, Inc. *Library of Congress Classification Schedules Combined with Additions and Changes*. Detroit, 1989.

Innovative Interfaces, Inc. Screen displays from *INNOPAC System*. Berkeley, California, 1991.

OCLC Forest Press, *Dewey Decimal Classification*, 20th edition. Albany, New York, 1989. By permission of Forest Press, a division of OCLC Online Computer Library Center, owner of copyright.

OCLC Online Computer Library Center. Screen displays of bibliographic description records and name authority records. Dublin, Ohio, 1991.

British Library Cataloguing-in-Publication data are available

Library of Congress Cataloguing-in-Publication Data

Downing, Mildred Harlow, 1929–
    Introduction to cataloging and classification / Mildred Harlow
Downing, David H. Downing. — 6th ed.
    p. cm.
    Includes bibliographical references and index. ∞
    ISBN 0-89950-720-4 (lib. bdg. : 50# alk. paper)
    1. Cataloging. 2. Classification — Books. I. Downing, David H.,
1959–   . II. Title.
Z693.D684 1992
025.3 — dc20   91-51210
                                                  CIP

Manufactured in the United States of America

McFarland & Company, Inc., Publishers
Box 611, Jefferson, North Carolina 28640

Acknowledgments

This textbook, encompassing as it does the broad field of cataloging and classification, involved contributions from various individuals, representing a number of institutions. We especially want to thank the many persons whose help and support were invaluable. Among them are:

Ms. Janice Donahue, head of the Collection Organization Department and director of Technical Services at Florida Atlantic University's S. E. Wimberly Library, who set a standard of dedicated professionalism which inspires emulation. Ms. Donahue provided both access to the Collection Organization Department's resources, and several of the practical suggestions appearing throughout this book;

Dr. Edward G. Holley, dean emeritus and professor of the School of Information and Library Science at the University of North Carolina at Chapel Hill, who not only acted as liaison for us with the OCLC Online Computer Library Center, but has, over the years, provided intellectual stimulation, encouragement and support;

Dr. Jerry D. Saye, associate professor at the aforementioned School of Information and Library Science, whose kindness and generosity in permitting us full access to equipment and materials in the Cataloging Research Laboratory of the University of North Carolina, and the value of his many helpful comments and suggestions, cannot be overestimated;

Mrs. Elizabeth Laney and Mrs. Elizabeth Grey, librarians of the Library of the School of Information and Library Science at the University of North Carolina, who provided invaluable assistance in gaining access to specialized material, and in locating obscure references;

Mrs. Linda Folda and Mrs. Stacey Hagerty, of the Technical Services Department of the Chapel Hill, North Carolina, Public Library, who gave generously of their time and expertise in discussing cataloging, access, and retrieval of materials in a public library environment;

Mr. Gerald M. Kline, of Innovative Interfaces, Inc., for his enthusiastic permission to reproduce screens from the INNOPAC system used in the Chapel Hill Public Library;

Mr. Lawrence Souder, who, in his capacity as instructor in the Technical and Science Communication Program at Drexel University, critiqued portions of the manuscript, providing comments and recommendations which served as overall guidance;

Dr. Alexander C. Friedlander, assistant professor, and director of the Technical and Science Communication Program at Drexel University, who enlightened us on a number of important principles concerning document design and effective communication;

Dr. Jacques Catudal, assistant professor in the Technical and Science Communication Program at Drexel University, who provided the opportunity to examine several ethical questions pertaining to certain matter discussed in this textbook;

Dr. Eva Thury, associate professor in the Technical and Science Communication Program at Drexel University, whose thoughts on the relationship between technical and fiction writing served to augment our discussion of the issues involved in classifying literature;

Mrs. Denise Singleton, permissions associate, and Ms. Sandra C. Davis, text permissions supervisor, for allowing us to reproduce material from the Gale Research, Inc., editions of the Library of Congress Classification schedules;

Mr. David P. Lighthill, vice president of OCLC Online Computer Library Center, Inc., who, in granting permission to use copyrighted OCLC materials, expressed a gracious wish for our success;

Mr. Peter Paulson, executive director of OCLC Forest Press, publishers of the *Dewey Decimal Classification*, who not only allowed us to cite short excerpts from the DDC, but kindly said that such usage was encouraged, for educational purposes, since it promoted use of the classification and helped the users thereof.

Table of Contents

8. Dewey Decimal Classification: Number Building in the 400 and 800 Classes: Language and Literature

9. Library of Congress Classification: An Overview

List of Figures

List of Sample Catalog Records in Appendix I

Preface to the Sixth Edition

There have been numerous changes in the field of cataloging and classification since the fifth edition appeared in 1981. The second edition of the *Anglo-American Cataloguing Rules* now exists in a 1988 revision, as does Maxwell's *Handbook for AACR2*. The year 1989 saw the publication of the 20th edition of the *Dewey Decimal Classification*, with its significant changes and additions from earlier editions. There have been many revisions to the Library of Congress Classification, including the recent updating of several entire schedules and the renumbering of the auxiliary tables for Class P. Nonbook media have established an important position in many collections, and several new types of nonbook materials have appeared.

Most importantly, the online shared cataloging system has become central to the practice of preparation of bibliographic records. While many libraries and information centers still maintain manual card catalogs, most cataloging departments no longer type catalog cards by hand. Rather, their employees create and edit machine-readable catalog records which serve as the basis for printed materials.

The basic principles of cataloging and classification have not, however, changed. In fact, they have not changed since humankind first saw the need to arrange all recorded knowledge in some logical fashion. Whether you are inputting bibliographic data at a computer terminal, typing it onto a catalog card, or carving it into a stone tablet, you must develop and sharpen the same two skills. You must be able to determine and communicate:

(a) those details of an item which will distinguish it from all others with which it might be confused, and

(b) those details which serve to create useful links between similar items.

Therefore, we have attempted, in this sixth edition, not only to chronicle the changes in the field, but to give you a clear picture of what has not changed. Furthermore, we have attempted to explain why the computer makes competence on the part of the human cataloger more, rather than less, important.

In addition to updating the book to reflect today's orientation toward online cataloging, we have made several other changes aimed at providing a more complete introduction to cataloging and classification. To begin with, we have added numerous discussions of practical issues with which you will likely have to deal in an actual working environment. These discussions grew out of our experiences in such environments.

We have also reorganized the chapters on the Dewey Decimal Classification. Material which the fifth edition presented in four chapters appears here in two longer ones. By presenting certain concepts together in one chapter, we have attempted to emphasize applicability of certain principles throughout the whole of the Dewey Decimal Classification.

We have expanded the overview to the Library of Congress Classification, providing a more detailed description of call numbers and their component parts. We have added more graphic displays to this and many of the other chapters.

Finally, although this is an introductory textbook, we have provided a more detailed discussion of some of the advanced problems in the field. While this section does not emphasize step-by-step instructions, it will alert you to many issues with which you must be conversant if you wish to become a professional cataloger and excel in your position.

1

Introduction

The usefulness of a collection of materials depends almost entirely on the ease with which potential users can locate desired items therein. The cataloger's purpose is to facilitate the retrieval process, and thus maximize the collection's value. In order to achieve this purpose, the cataloger must perform two contrasting tasks;

(1) Prepare a description of each item which emphasizes those attributes *unique* to it — those which distinguish it from other items with which it might be confused. This is what we mean by *cataloging*.

(2) Group both these descriptions and the items themselves according to attributes they *share* — such that a user can locate *all* items that fit *any* specified criteria. This is what we mean by *classification*.

Much of the cataloger's job involves crucial value judgments regarding the most relevant unique characteristics of an item and the proper "shared characteristics" group in which to place that item. No aspect of librarianship or of any of the information handling professions is potentially more intellectually challenging than cataloging, or more demanding, in many situations, of initiative and imagination.

As a neophyte cataloger, you should learn the essential concepts underlying all aspects of cataloging and classification. A grasp of fundamentals will enable you to identify in any system of cataloging and classification those problems common to all schemes whose purpose it is to effect the coherent organization of a heterogeneous collection of materials.

This chapter will therefore discuss broad, generally applicable principles of descriptive cataloging, will offer a brief survey of the history of classification and cataloging, will point out the need for a

1

methodical approach to cataloging and classification and for competent catalogers, and will touch upon the implications of standardization and automation.

The purposes of descriptive cataloging

The cataloger must always ask the question, how will the user look for this work? The purpose of descriptive cataloging is to insure that users can tell any item apart from all others in the collection with which it might be confused. This involves providing those details of an item which make it unique, and presenting these elements in a record format that can be integrated with entries of the same type for all other items in the collection.

Chapter 2, following, will describe in detail the methods by which catalogers prepare a descriptive cataloging record. You will find exhibits, exemplifying all instructions given, in Appendix I, "Sample Catalog Records." The point you must remember here is that the need of the user must determine the decision of the cataloger. This objective has never been more clearly stated than by Charles A. Cutter (1904). According to Cutter—whose words we have augmented slightly with the phrases in brackets—a catalog's purpose is:

1. To enable a person to find a book [or other item] of which either
   (A) the author
   (B) the title   } is known
   (C) the subject
2. To show what the library [or information center] has
   (D) by a given author
   (E) on a given subject
   (F) in a given kind of literature
3. To assist in the choice of a book [or other item]
   (G) as to its edition (bibliographically)
   (H) as to its character (literary or topical)

By adding a few phrases to this quote from Cutter, we have made his objectives pertinent to the modern age of information science. The physical medium of the catalog is now in the process of changing from cards to online displays, but the function of the bibliographic description is still to provide users with information about the collection.

The history of cataloging and classifications, summarized in the following two sections, demonstrates the gradual recognition over time of the problems of cataloging, and the development of attempts at solutions.

Early systems of cataloging and classification

To think in a sane and coherent manner, human beings must be able to categorize their ideas about their environment. Likewise, to create a readily comprehensible record of their collective thought, human beings must be able to organize any accounts of their perceptions, knowledge, beliefs and reactions which they set down.

Attempts at such categorization, or classification, began almost as soon as tangible records of human thought became important enough to warrant gathering. The earliest known librarian was Amilanu, a Babylonian who lived over a thousand years before the founding of the library at Ninevah in 700 B.C. The first library of the Babylonians was built in the 17th century B.C., and its arrangement, when unearthed, suggested that these ancient libraries had behind them many years of experience in matters of classification and cataloging (Norris 1939). Other ancient civilizations seem to have had libraries equally old; the oldest library catalog known is that of the library of Edfu in Upper Egypt. This catalog was engraved on the walls of the library and probably consisted of a bare list of books. Of these ancient catalogs, Norris says, "Long before we reach 700 B.C., cataloging was such a commonplace thing that no one thought it worthwhile either to make or preserve any records as to the methods of compiling catalogs then in use."

The books of these ancient libraries were in the form of clay tablets. Four centuries after the founding of the library at Ninevah, when the libraries of the Ptolemies at Alexandria came into being, books had taken the form of rolls of papyrus and letters written in ink had supplanted cuneiform characters. Callimachus, the poet and second librarian of the Alexandrian library, devised a classified catalog having 120 classes. The main divisions of this scheme were:

1. Epic writers	5. Historical writers
2. Dramatic writers	6. Oratorical works
3. Writers on law	7. Rhetorical works
4. Philosophical writers	8. Miscellaneous works

Callimachus included in his catalog not only the title of the work but a brief analysis of it and a biographical note of its author. As Norris states, "The year 240 B.C., then, can give us a work which was a classified catalogue, a bibliography, and a biographical dictionary all in one."

Over the centuries, hundreds of individual classification schemes for recorded materials have sprung up. Richardson (1930, 1964), in his work *Classification*, after commenting that "The historical tradition ... begins with Callimachus," lists over 120 "practical systems of classification" devised between that of Callimachus in 260–240 B.C. and the first publication of the Dewey Decimal Classification.

The monastic libraries of the Middle Ages followed the patterns established by Cassiodorus and the abbey of Monte Cassino, founded by St. Benedict, both in the 6th century. Collections consisted of theological and biblical works, canon and civil law, standard classical texts, and some medical, historical, and other miscellaneous works. Arrangement was by location symbol and the books, which were limited to a few hundred volumes, were often chained to prevent loss.

The pioneers of book classification by *subject* were not librarians but booksellers and bibliographers. Among these individuals were the 16th century Swiss doctor Konrad von Gesner and an 18th century group known as the "Paris booksellers." When, by the end of the 19th century, college and public libraries began permitting unrestricted or "open" access into their collections, a need for detailed subject classification schemes arose, which led to the development of such schemes as that of the Library of Congress and Melvil Dewey's Decimal Classification, which he developed for Amherst College in 1872.

If in addition to these "practical schemes" consideration is given to such theoretical systems as that of Plato, Aristotle, and Zeno, the list of classification schemes becomes too lengthy for discussion in this brief survey; if you wish to learn more about the history of classification, refer to the sources listed at the end of this chapter. You should be aware that present day attempts to organize, codify, and classify information have behind them a long history of human effort. As Richardson points out, "Human thought ... seems to lie in just this power of binding things together in a group according to their likeness and unlikeness and keeping clearly discriminated on these lines."

The beginnings of modern cataloging

Today, every cataloging agency dealing with a comprehensive collection in the United States, Canada, Great Britain, and Australia is expected to perform descriptive cataloging according to the *Anglo-American Cataloging Rules*. We shall discuss the current version of these rules, the 1988 revision of the second edition, in the next chapter. This code has, among its ancestors, the code developed by Panizzi in 1839 (Strout 1957). Panizzi, a lawyer by profession, was appointed in 1831 to the library of the British Museum. With the publication of his "91 Rules," in 1839, modern cataloging may be said to have begun.

The cataloging problems which faced Panizzi and the British Museum 150 years ago are still with us today. Consider, for example, the following questions: "Have you ever heard it proposed that each book should be catalogued under the form of name appearing on the title without regard to the different forms of name adopted by the author, or arising from the different languages in which works by the same may be printed?" This question came, in 1849, from the Earl of Ellesmere, then chairman of the group that produced the *Report of the Commissioners Appointed to Inquire into the Constitution and Government of the British Museum* (Strout 1957). The Earl's question concerns a branch of cataloging commonly termed *name authority control*, which we shall discuss in Chapter 3. Must a library catalog have a single, correct entry for any given author, to which it refers everyone who searches under other possible forms of that author's name? Does such an arrangement serve a valid need? Is it, in fact, always desirable? As a professional cataloger, this is the kind of fundamental question you must be prepared to consider. Furthermore, you will have to deal with questions like this in light of the widespread use of centralized services and national cataloging networks. What is *your* responsibility in *your* individual library?

Standardization, mechanization, computerization and cataloging

Although computers can perform many tasks much more quickly and efficiently than human beings, the computer will never replace the cataloger. However powerful any computer might be, it can only function when and if a human being gives it commands. Furthermore, it will obey those commands even if they prove not to be the ones which the human operator or programmer meant to issue. Therefore, the effectiveness of any computer depends almost entirely on the competence of whoever is controlling it at the moment. One especially important implication of this is that a computer can do a great deal of damage in the wrong hands, just as an automobile can.

We can translate these general cautions into many specific warnings regarding the use of computers in the cataloging process. We will provide some of these warnings in later chapters, but will offer several general observations now.

There is no doubt that large online centralized bibliographic networks are changing the management, organization, and personnel of cataloging and technical service departments. Two such networks are OCLC (Online Computer Library Center) which is located in Dublin, Ohio, and RLIN (Research Libraries Network) based at Stanford University in California. Other new technologies are freeing technical service personnel from routine tasks, saving time, money, and effort, and are allowing many institutions to undertake projects which formerly would have been impossible.

But these networks and other technologies actually require *more* competence than ever before on the part of the cataloger. This is because a computer cannot evaluate the data it receives, and will thus record, reproduce, and transmit, without question, even data which contain errors. Data, in the case of an online bibliographic network, can consist of the work of one cataloger, which many institutions throughout the country will use. If the cataloger has made errors, all of those institutions will have to deal with them.

Therefore, a corps of highly trained cataloging specialists are required both at the national and local level. Networks perform more and more cataloging of both American and foreign works. Tendencies toward international standardization of cataloging codes and practices, as exemplified in manuals, the *I.S.B.D.(M)*, *I.S.B.D.(S)* (1974), *I.S.B.D.(G)* (1977), means that catalogers must remain aware of up-to-the-minute developments. The trend toward common, standardized ways of dealing with the already overwhelming and steadily growing mass of published materials is increasing rather than diminishing. This trend could eventually centralize all American cataloging in one huge, national pool with the Library of Congress as the final authority. At present, however, it seems more likely that several large bibliographic networks will continue to coexist as they do now, with regional organizations such as SOLINET, PALINET, and NELINET continuing to act as communication brokers. In any case the individual cataloger still is, and always will be, required to perform thoughtful, accurate work. All catalogers interacting with an online bibliographic network will also have to modify their own copy of any existing bibliographic record which either contains errors or is not suitable for their institutions.

Thus, if you are a cataloger in an individual local library, you have a serious commission, particularly if your library contributes original cataloging to the central bibliographic system. If you make an error, thousands of institutions may suffer for it. Databases are only as good as the items they contain and each item is only visible to searchers if it contains the access points they will be using to locate it. If you input an author's name as it appears on the title page, and that form of the name proves not to be the one most people will search under, the work in question may be extremely difficult to retrieve. If you add a record from OCLC or RLIN to your local catalog, but do not properly modify it to suit your library's needs, you may end up failing to communicate essential information. We cannot overstress the importance of understanding basic principles of cataloging and classification.

Sources cited and suggestions for further reading or study

Anglo-American Cataloguing Rules, 2nd ed., 1988 revision, edited by Michael Gorman and Paul W. Winkler. Ottawa: Canadian Library Association; Chicago: American Library Association, 1988.

Cutter, Charles A. *Rules for a Dictionary Catalog,* 4th ed., rewritten. Washington, D.C.: U.S. Gov. Printing Office, 1904. Republished in 1962 by the Library Association, Chaucer House, Malet Place, London, W.C.I.

International Federation of Library Associations. *ISBD(G): International Standard Bibliographic Description,* annotated text prepared by the Working Group on the General International Standard Bibliographic Description set up by the IFLA Committee on Cataloguing. London: IFLA International Office for UBC, 1977.

_____. *ISBD(M): International Standard Bibliographic Description for Monographic Publications,* 1st standard ed. London: IFLA Committee on Cataloguing, 1974.

_____. *ISBD(S): International Standard Bibliographic Description for Serial Publications,* 1st standard ed. London: IFLA Committee on Cataloguing, 1974.

Norris, Dorothy May. *A History of Cataloguing and Cataloguing Methods, 1100–1850: With an Introductory Survey of Ancient Times.* London: Grafton, 1939.

Richardson, Ernest Cushing. *Classification,* 3rd ed. Hamden, Conn.: Shoe String Press, 1964 (Copyright 1930.)

Strout, Ruth French. "The Development of the Catalog and Cataloging Codes." In her *Toward a Better Cataloging Code,* 4-25. Chicago: University of Chicago Graduate Library School, 1957.

2

Bibliographic Description I:
Basic Concepts

Retrieval of any item in a collection depends on a full and accurate description of the work. If, as stated in Chapter 1, one purpose of cataloging is to differentiate the individual item from all others with which it might be confused, how can you accomplish this objective? What are the data, regardless of medium, you must record about any book, sound recording, film, software package, painting or other conveyance of information or inspiration?

Elements of bibliographic description will include attributes whose particulars can vary—e.g., authorship, place of origination, size, etc.— yet which are each sufficiently common to a large body of material to permit differentiation to be made among the items being described. From the elements contained within the description of a book or other item, certain key characteristics, often termed "access points," may be selected for indexing and retrieval. These access points will be attributes of the work least likely to change and elements by which the user is most likely to seek out the item.

A description of a book or other item serves as a surrogate for the work itself. This chapter will deal with the creation, standardization and organization of such surrogates. These may take the form of a display at a computer terminal, a catalog card, a frame of microfiche or an entry in a book catalog. Whatever their form, the principles of bibliographic description and the need for standardization, uniformity and quality control of the bibliographic descriptive unit must obtain throughout the cataloging system.

Therefore, if you are a cataloger preparing data for entry into an online bibliographic database, you must be as mindful of standard cataloging rules and practices as if you were preparing copy for a set of catalog cards. Form of entry, items of bibliographic description, the order in which the items are presented and their identification by means of prescribed punctuation will be governed by principles intended to produce a concise, exact, full and unambiguous record for the work being described. By producing a standardized and uniform display of data elements, you can achieve the second objective of cataloging—presenting intelligible entries that can be integrated with entries of other items and that respond to the needs of the user.

We have based instructions in this chapter about the production of a catalog record on the second edition of the *Anglo-American Cataloging Rules*. This edition first appeared in 1978, then in 1988 in a revised form. We have chosen this code, hereafter referred to as AACR2R88, for exemplification because, as we stated in the previous chapter, it is the standard cataloging tool of American, Canadian and British libraries.

This chapter will identify, define and describe the elements of bibliographic description. However, we will begin with a brief discussion of one method of assembling descriptive data into a bibliographic record. We do this in the hope that you may better understand this chapter's information if you can see it in terms of concrete operations.

Since it is likely that you, as a cataloger, will be working with an online shared cataloging system which uses MARC (MAchine-Readable Cataloging) records, this is the method we will describe. We will do this in two sections. First we will describe one particular online shared cataloging system. We have chosen the OCLC system because it is the one with which we have had the most experience. We will then discuss the MARC record apart from any particular system. Please keep in mind that a full understanding of the material we present in the next two sections is separate from a thorough comprehension of cataloging itself.

Use of the OCLC online shared cataloging system

The following is a general overview of OCLC. To avoid distracting you from the main point of this chapter, we will not cover particulars of OCLC protocol and syntax. The reader who wishes more information should consult the instructional materials available from OCLC.

It is quite common for many libraries to acquire a copy of a particular book (or other type of item). However, if each such library is a member of the same online shared cataloging system, such as OCLC, only one need prepare a bibliographic description of the book. Located in Dublin, Ohio, the OCLC system contains, to date, over 21 million records. About one million are added each year. Originally, "OCLC" was an acronym for the Ohio College Library Center. However, as the system expanded, this appellation became inappropriate. The present corporate name is "OCLC Online Computer Library Center."

Participating libraries originally used computer terminals constructed solely for the OCLC system. These, bearing model numbers M100 and M105, contained a standard typewriter keyboard augmented by keys for various OCLC symbols and commands. The M300 and M310 workstations arrived in the mid–1980s. Each was essentially an IBM-PC with OCLC symbol/command keys added to its keyboard. These machines could function as either OCLC terminals or personal computers, and could combine these two functions in various ways.

A more recent workstation, the M386/16, uses an IBM-PC keyboard which does not contain special OCLC keys. The user must learn and remember which keys correspond to which system commands. Workstations pre-dating the M386/16 are not compatible with the new OCLC subsystem PRISM, introduced in 1991. The PRISM is an expanded, powerful system for editing on line, allowing, for example, word-processor-like "cutting and pasting." While many searching strategies remain the same on PRISM, there are two new search capabilities. A title browse feature allows easier access to particularly difficult searches, such as proceedings and journals. The combined key search permits two searches to be joined with the Boolean operator "and." See Lee (1990) for further discussion.

Whenever a library's size and budget permit, it is standard procedure to assign the actual data retrieval and entry operations to technical assistants. They begin the cataloging process by searching new books in the OCLC database. If the Library of Congress, generally regarded as the final cataloging authority in the United States, has cataloged the book, the library will probably accept that institution's bibliographic record as is. High (1990) has assembled statistics which show the percentage of libraries which accept Library of Congress records, and various portions thereof.

A technical assistant who finds a record input by another member library prints it, then routes book and printout to a cataloger. The cataloger edits the printout, in accordance with local policy and proper cataloging practice, then returns it to the technical assistant, who keys in the additions and changes. (Technical assistants who, through experience, have learned something of cataloging practice may make editing suggestions. It may also be part of their job to spot anomalies in Library of Congress records.)

Note that a bibliographic record's presence in the OCLC database provides no assurance of its quality. Although the system rejects records which fail to meet certain requirements, it cannot evalute the actual cataloging.

After altering the record online per the cataloger's instructions, the technical assistant commands OCLC to produce the record. This includes storing it on magnetic tape and printing cards for any manual catalogs the library maintains. The library may add the record to its local online catalog from the tape, or by one of several other means.

For a book that has not already been cataloged by another OCLC member, the library follows a procedure similar to the one we have just described. The one significant difference is that the cataloger must create, rather than edit, a bibliographic record. Returning to the above discussion of quality, observance of proper cataloging practice is especially important in a shared system, given that, as we said in Chapter 1, every member must deal with any library's mistakes.

The cataloger creates a bibliographic record by recording the elements of description — along with other data discussed below — on a local workform. An example is shown in Figure 1. The completed local workform goes back to the technical assistant, who transfers the information to an OCLC workform, shown in the upper half of Figure 2.

The result is a complete record such as that shown in the lower half of Figure 2. This is added to the master database, then recorded on magnetic tape and used to print cards in the same manner as an edited preexisting record. At this point, the system assigns an OCLC control number to the record, which, from then on, will appear in place of the word "NEW" in the display.

As we mentioned above, both the local and OCLC workforms contain other data besides the actual description. These are part of the MARC record format, the subject of the next section.

The MARC record

The OCLC, RLIN, and other online shared cataloging systems receive, store, manipulate, and transmit bibliographic data in the form of MARC (MAchine-Readable Cataloging) records. A MARC record is a

Figure 1. *Local Workform*

Type: a   Bib lvl: m   Govt pub _b_ Lang: _ita_ Source: _d_ Illus: _b_

Repr: _b_ Enc lvl: I   Conf pub _∅_ Ctry: _it_ Dat tp: _S_ M/F/B: _l ∅ b_

Indx: _∅_ Mod rec: _b_ Festschr: _∅_ Cont: _b_

Desc: _i_ Int lvl: _b_ Dates: _1852_, _bbbb_

010

040   NOC   ‡c NOC

020

041

090   PQ4683.B5 ‡b A19   1852

049 ● NOCC

1 0 0 1 ∅   Berchet, Giovanni, ‡d   1783-1851

24 5 1 ∅   Poesie di Giovanni Berchet

250

260 ∅   Milano: ‡b [s.n.], ‡c [1852?]

300   158 p. ; ‡c 16 cm.

4 _ _ _ _

5 _ _ _ _   "Unica edizione completa...italiane"

6 _ _ _ _

7 _ _ _ _

8 _ _ _ _

Figure 2. *OCLC Workform and New Record*

```
OCLC: NEW            Rec stat: n Entrd: 790710        Used: 790710 ¶
▶Type: a Bib lvl: m Govt pub:   Lang: ███ Source: u Illus:
 Repr:     Enc lvl: █ Conf pub: 0 Ctry:  xx  Dat tp: n M/F/B: 00
 Indx: 0 Mod rec:    Festschr: 0 Cont:
 Desc: █ Int lvl:    Dates:      ,      ¶
 ▶ 1 010       ¶
 ▶ 2 040       ‡c XXX ¶
 ▶ 3 020       ¶
 ▶ 4 041 █     ‡b ¶
 ▶ 5 050       ‡b ¶
 ▶ 6 090       ‡b ¶
 ▶ 7 049       XXXM ¶
 ▶ 8 1██ ██    ‡d ¶
 ▶ 9 24█ █     ‡b  ‡c  ¶
 ▶10 250       ¶
 ▶11 260 █     ‡b  ‡c  ¶
 ▶12 300       ‡b  ‡c  ¶
 ▶13 4██ ██    ‡d ¶
 ▶14 5██ █     ¶
 ▶15 590       ¶
 ▶16 6██ ██    ¶
 ▶17 7██ ██    ‡d ¶
 ▶18 8██ ██    ¶
```

```
OCLC: NEW            Rec stat: n Entrd: 800729        Used: 800729 ¶
▶Type: a Bib lvl: m Govt pub:   Lang: eng Source:   Illus: a
 Repr:     Enc lvl: I Conf pub: 0 Ctry:  nyu Dat tp: s M/F/B: 10
 Indx: 1 Mod rec:    Festschr: 0 Cont: b
 Desc: i Int lvl:    Dates: 1977,    ¶
 ▶ 1 010       77-77941 ¶
 ▶ 2 040       DLC ‡c XXX ¶
 ▶ 3 020       0525171940 : ‡c $17.95 ¶
 ▶ 4 050 0     GN31.2 ‡b .L43 1977 ¶
 ▶ 5 082       573.2 ¶
 ▶ 6 090       ‡b ¶
 ▶ 7 049       XXXM ¶
 ▶ 8 100 10    Leakey, Richard E. ¶
 ▶ 9 245 10    Origins : ‡b what new discoveries reveal about the
emergence of our species and its possible future / ‡c Richard E. Leakey
and Roger Lewin. ¶
 ▶10 260 0     New York : ‡b Dutton, ‡c c1977. ¶
 ▶11 300       264 p. : ‡b ill. (some col.) ; ‡c 25 cm. ¶
 ▶12 504       Bibliography: p. 257. ¶
 ▶13 500       Includes index. ¶
 ▶14 650 0     Anthropology. ¶
 ▶15 650 0     Human evolution. ¶
 ▶16 700 10    Lewin, Roger, ‡e joint author. ¶
```

bibliographic record transcribed in a form and medium which a computer can read and manipulate. The MARC records have a standardized form, independent of the various online shared cataloging systems. Therefore, all online shared cataloging systems can accept and manipulate MARC records from any agency which produces them and adheres to the correct form.

Although there are several versions of the MARC record, bearing names such as USMARC, LCMARC, and UKMARC, these are all extensions or minor alterations of the standard form. At worst, an online shared cataloging system dealing with an alternate version of the MARC record will have to contend with pieces of missing or extraneous data. The different versions of MARC have enough in common that, for our purposes, we will use the one term to refer to them all.

Because our purpose is not to teach you about the data-processing operations involved in online cataloging, we will not discuss the structure of the MARC record. Our goal is to show you how to input the data properly so that OCLC, or whatever system you are working with, can manipulate it. For a more detailed discussion of computer storage techniques, see Appendix III. For a comprehensive discussion of the MARC format, see Crawford (1989).

As you can see from figures 1 and 2, the local and OCLC workforms, along with the completed online records, contain other data in addition to the bibliographic description. In a MARC record, the bibliographic description is divided into sections, each of which begins with a numeric, three-digit label, a *tag*—100, 245, 260, etc. Some of these tags are followed by one or two additional digits, the *indicators*. In our example, the indicators following both tags 100 and 245 are 1 and 0. Each distinct tagged section of the description is a *variable field*.

Within most of these variable fields are *subfields* designated by a "‡"plus a lowercase letter, a *subfield delimiter*—‡b, ‡c, etc.

The five lines at the top of the workform are the *fixed fields*. With the exception of the "Desc:" these do not affect the appearance of the bibliographic record, but rather help an online system to store and index it. Every MARC record contains additional fields, also used for storage and indexing, which do not show up in an online display. For more on these fields, see Appendix III or Crawford (1989).

Not every record uses all variable fields which the MARC format defines. This is because these fields correspond to the various elements of the bibliographic description, not all of which apply to every record. A fuller explanation follows in the discussion of bibliographic description.

Access points and the concept of main entry

An access point is any attribute of a book which a library patron is expected to use in locating it. The term "main entry heading" refers to the principle access point the cataloger chooses for the basic catalog record. Other access points chosen for the same record are known as "added entries." But in cataloging a work, which attributes should you choose as access points? In reflecting upon this question, you should recall the manner in which you yourself have searched for a desired item. Exactly what did you want? Which elements of the item's description did you believe were most likely to lead you to the exact work you were after?

Consider a hypothetical example. In searching for a book on biology by Lewis Rudolphson, would you fare better searching under "Rudolphson" or "biology"? Would you fare better searching through all books on biology or all red books 600 to 700 pages in length?

Why distinguish between main entry and added entries? In the case of a manual card catalog, there is one rather obvious reason. The cards must stand in some logical order, which means that one access point must represent each card for filing purposes. Granted, a library may have multiple copies of each card, one for each of the bibliographic record's access points. In fact, most libraries with manual catalogs do this, providing author, title, and subject cards for each item they own. However, although such an arrangement is desirable, it is optional. If there were no main entries, it would be obligatory.

However, the above argument does not apply to an online catalog, since any of the bibliographic record's access points may represent it, for purposes of sorting and retrieval, at a given moment. (For a more detailed discussion of why this is so, see Appendix III.) Therefore, only one copy of a record need exist, even if none of its access points has been designated the main entry.

Does it then make sense for libraries to place the same emphasis on main entry which they have in the past? In fact, AACR2R88 has somewhat reduced this emphasis (as did the original 1978 version). The 1949 and 1967 cataloging codes both opened with a long series of rules for entry headings. In contrast, Part 1 of AACR2R88 has to do with "description," leaving "Headings, uniform titles and references" to Part 2. The AACR2R88 does retain the concept of main entry, although with some qualifications:

0.5 In Part II the rules are based on the proposition that one *main entry* is made for each item described, and that this is supplemented by *added entries*. The question of the use of *alternative entry headings* (i.e., sets of equal entries for each item described) was discussed but not embodied in the rules. It is recognized, however, that many libraries do not distinguish between the main entry and other entries [page 2].

The AACR2R88 does not, in every instance, give precise directions for main entry (for example with nonbook materials). When a specific rule does not exist, the cataloger is expected to interpret the provisions of a more general rule. Rule 0.9 states, "These rules recognize the necessity for judgement and interpretation by the cataloger. Such judgement and interpretation may be based upon the requirements of a particular catalogue or upon the use of the items being catalogued."

We believe the concept of main entry remains valid, partly because the manual card catalog is unlikely to pass completely out of existence for some time. More importantly, the main entry is not simply a filing device; it conveys information about the work being cataloged and the culture that produced the work. For example, in Western cultures, main entry heading is usually made under the last name of the authors, since the author's name is not only the most important identifying attribute for a book but is the feature most likely to endure unchanged. The practice represents, in part, the Western philosophy of the importance of the individual and of consequent attribution to the creator of a work. In the Orient, books are usually entered under title; in the Arab world, lack of family name is often cited as a reason for the use of a title unit entry rather than a main author entry (Hamdy 1973 and el-Sheniti 1962).

Sir Thomas Bodley, founder of the Bodley Library at Oxford in 1602, issued in 1620 the first general catalog of a European library arranged in alphabetical order according to the surnames of the authors. That a consistent and authoritative form of author entry should be employed was the concept of Panizzi, who in 1841 published the first English code of cataloging rules (Norris 1939).

Each of the editions of the code of American cataloging rules published by the American Library Association, starting with the 1908 *Catalog Rules: Author and Title Entries* and continuing to AACR2R88 has stated as a primary cataloging principle that main entry should be made under principle author, composer, artist, cartographer, etc., when one can be determined. Entry under title, however, is becoming increasingly more common, a practice reflected in the provisions and point of view of AACR2R88. Chapter 3 will deal with the problem of and methods of determining the full, correct form of author entry. See Appendix I for examples of correct main entry heading under author. For further discussion of the history of the concept of "main entry," see Tait (1970).

The components of a basic catalog record

A catalog record acts as a surrogate for the book itself. In so doing, the record must supply sufficient bibliographic information for readers adequately to evaluate the pertinence of the book to their needs. We list, in the pages following, the items appearing on the basic catalog record, with appropriate rules cited from AACR2R88 in support of the statements made. Appendix I presents various catalog records, each provided in both catalog card and MARC form. These records will illustrate the practices described in this and subsequent chapters.

While AACR2R88 gives precise directions as to the order, capitalization, abbreviation and punctuation of the elements of bibliographic description, it prescribes no overall format that one must follow in creating a document surrogate. The arrangement of information on a catalog card or online public catalog screen display will be determined by the individual library or the producers of various automated cataloging and retrieval systems.

Choice of format must take into account general guidelines provided by AACR2R88 along with established practices which have proven to produce neat, clear, uniform, easily read and unambiguous catalog records. For example, AACR2R88 Rule 0.6 states: "Distinguish a name heading and or uniform title assigned to a description from the descriptive data either: a) by giving them on separate lines above the description *or* b) by separating them from the description by a full stop and two spaces."

In dealing with various libraries' catalogs, you have probably become accustomed to alternative "a," which is often chosen for catalog cards. Many online public catalog screen displays also use this format, essentially emulating the catalog card.

The various indentations used on cards and the screen displays patterned after them are neither recommended nor prohibited by AACR2R88; they represent conventions which have been found to be efficient and clear. The AACR2R88's general comment (Rule 0.14) is:

The examples used throughout these rules are illustrative and not prescriptive. That is, they illuminate the provisions of the rule to which they attached rather than extend those provisions. Do not take the examples *or the form in which they are presented* as instructive unless specifically told to do so by the rules [emphasis added].

Following are the items appearing in a basic catalog record, each given with its MARC tag(s). Where appropriate, MARC subfield designations are also given. Note that every MARC field contains a subfield "a" (‡a) which in the OCLC system need not be explicitly designated if it comes first—which it usually does. We will not refer to it explicitly in the following list unless it is one of several subfields to be discussed.

Call Number—050, 082, 090, 092. This consists of a classification number (‡a)—i.e., Dewey or Library of Congress—followed by a book number (‡b). We will discuss call numbers and classification systems more fully in later chapters. What you should know about the call number at this point is that it serves to locate the book on the shelves, and to place the bibliographic record in the catalog contiguous to others which describe works of the same type. It appears on catalog cards in the upper lefthand corner. Its position on screen displays varies with the system in question. It may or may not appear in the upper left corner of a display patterned after a catalog card.

The tags 050 and 082 represent Dewey and Library of Congress classification numbers, respectively, which have been assigned by the Library of Congress. The tags 090 and 092 represent Dewey and Library of Congress classification numbers, respectively, which have been assigned by other OCLC member libraries.

Author Main Entry Heading—100. The AACR2, even in its original 1978 edition, has made significant changes with respect to author headings. Chapter 3, "Personal Name Authority Control," will discuss this matter in more detail. For the present, you should note one major change from earlier rules. Formerly, works by a given author were entered under the fullest available form of his or her real name. A work was entered under a pseudonym only if no one knew the author's real name. In contrast, AACR2R88 Rule 22.1A—which is essentially the same as the corresponding 1978 rule—directs the cataloger to enter an author under "the name by which he or she is commonly known."

Title and Statement of Responsibility Area—245. Include here:

(1) The title proper, parallel titles and subtitles (‡a, ‡b), transcribed exactly as they appear on the title page of the book except as otherwise indicated. See AACR2R88 rules 1.1, 2.1, 3.1, etc. (Note that books are

sometimes published in a form consisting of two or more works bound together. These are known as "works without a collective title.")

(2) The statement of responsibility (‡c), in contrast to earlier rules, must always be included, even if the name therein is exactly the same as the main entry. The AACR2R88 uses the term "statement of responsibility" rather than "statement of authorship" because this area includes editors, illustrators, translators, et al., in addition to actual authors.

Under AACR2R88, you are not permitted to add such words as "by" or "and" in square brackets to a statement of responsibility if they do not appear in the work you are cataloging. Rule 1.1F8 does allow you to add an explanatory word or phrase if the relationship between the title and the person or group named in the statement of responsibility, "is not clear." However, you should read, "is not clear," to mean, "is other than that of author and is not explicitly stated as such."

Edition Statement — 250. Under AACR2R88, you must transcribe an edition statement appearing in an item, even in the case of a first edition. If an item other than a first edition lacks an edition statement, you may supply one enclosed in square brackets ([ ]). In any case, give ordinal numbers in standardized form and use the abbreviations in Appendix B of AACR2R88. The statement of responsibility and the edition statement are separated by a period-space-dash-space (. --). (In typewriter script the dash is normally represented by two hyphens.) Further details concerning the edition statement may be found in AACR2R88 rules 1.2, 2.2, 3.2, etc. Also, chapters 4, "Series, Notes, Analytics and Other Issues," and 12, "Nonbook Materials," will treat different kinds of editorship.

Publication, Distribution, etc. Area — 260. This contains three elements, the place of publication (‡a), the name of the publisher (‡b) and the date of publication (‡c), listed in this order. In some cases, you may also include the name of the distributor. For some works, you will be forced to substitute a date of manufacture or copyright for a publication date.

Unless a large and well-known city (such as New York, London or Paris) is the place of publication, you must provide additional identifying details, using abbreviations set forth in Appendix B of AACR2R88. If two cities are listed, record the one that either comes first or by virtue of large printing or special positioning is indicated in the work to be the primary place of publication. For books bearing a foreign and American imprint, omit the foreign imprint whenever it is obviously subsidiary to the American one.

Record the name of the publisher in the shortest possible form which will not be ambiguous (observing the use of the ampersand, "&," when employed). Eliminate terms such as "Inc.," "and Sons," "Ltd.," etc., but retain the word "Press" in most cases. When a publisher's name consists of a personal name given in direct order and using initials, omit the initials unless this would cause confusion.

Take the data for this area from the title page, the verso of the title page, or other primary sources within the item you are cataloging. If the copyright date differs from the date of printing, include both; cite the copyright date as such, e.g., "c1984."

Enclose imprint data taken from a source other than the title page, the preliminaries, or the colophon in square brackets. Between the edition statement and the imprint data appear another period-space-dash-space. For punctuation between the various parts of the imprint, see AACR2R88 Rule 1.0C, "Punctuation," for general instructions and then rules 1.4A1, 2.4A1, 3.4A1, etc. See also Appendix I, "Sample Catalog Records."

Physical Description Area — 300: The descriptive data which must appear in this area are:

(1) (‡a) Extent of the work as to pages, volumes, or other physical units. This area also includes the temporal extent of sound recordings, videorecordings, and other items which have a running time.

(2) (‡b) Illustrative matter, when present.

(3) (‡c) Size, expressed as the height of a book in centimeters, to the next centimeter up. Width is also given if it is either greater than, or less than half, the height.

(4) (‡e) Accompanying material, when present. This consists of maps, sound cassettes, floppy disks, etc., issued as part of the book, and intended to be used in conjunction with it. These items are frequently housed in pockets physically attached to the book.

The AACR2R88 rules covering this area are numbered 1.5, 2.5, 3.5, etc., and all abbreviations used in this portion of the description are found in AACR2R88 Appendix B. We will discuss the physical description of nonbook materials more thoroughly in Chapter 12.

We will return to bibliographic description in Chapter 4, where we will discuss the "series" and "notes" areas of the bibliographic record. First, however, we must discuss an issue which we have, thus far, touched on only lightly — the proper form of an author's name to be used as an entry element. The rules and methods for determining this are the subject of our next chapter.

Review questions for Chapter 2

1. Does a "main" entry serve any purpose in the present-day card catalog?

2. Does a "main" entry serve any purpose in an online catalog?

3. Discuss situations in which the choice of main entry for a work is debatable.

4. What attributes of a work might be used as access points?

5. Of these, which would best serve to locate the *specific* work desired? Why?

6. Describe the relationship between the elements of a bibliographic description and the fields of a MARC record.

7. Explain why a bibliographic description which contains errors might be more likely to appear in an online catalog than in a card catalog.

Sources cited and suggestions for further reading or study

Anglo-American Cataloguing Rules, 2nd ed., 1988 revision, edited by Michael Gorman and Paul W. Winkler. Ottawa: Canadian Library Association; Chicago: American Library Association, 1988.

Ayres, F.H. "The Code, the Catalog, and the Computer." *Library Journal* 105 (1980): 775–780.

Crawford, Walt. *MARC for Library Use: Understanding Integrated USMARC,* 2nd ed. Boston: G.K. Hall, 1989.

Hamdy, M. Nabil. *The Concept of Main Entry as Represented in the Anglo-American Cataloguing Rules.* (Research Studies in Library Science Series, No. 10.) Littleton, Colo.: Libraries Unlimited, 1973.

High, Walter Martin, III. *Editing Changes to Monographic Cataloging Records in the OCLC Data Base: An Analysis of the Practice in Five University Libraries.* Dissertation, Ph.D. Chapel Hill, N.C., 1990.

Lee, Deborah. Pre-order searching and the OCLC PRISM system. Thesis, MSLS, Chapel Hill, N.C., 1990.

Library of Congress Rule Interpretations for AACR2: A Cumulation from Cataloging Service Bulletin Numbers 11–, compiled by Lois Lindberg, Alan Boyd, and Elaine Druesedow. Oberlin, Ohio: Oberlin College Library, 1982–.

Maxwell, Margaret F. *Handbook for AACR2: Explaining and Illustrating the Anglo-American Cataloguing Rules, 1988 Revision.* Chicago: American Library Association, 1989.

Norris, Dorothy May. *A History of Cataloguing and Cataloguing Methods, 1100–1850: With an Introductory Survey of Ancient Times.* London: Grafton, 1939.

OCLC. *Books Format,* 3rd ed. Dublin, Ohio: OCLC, 1986–.

el-Sheniti, Mahmoud. "Cataloging and Classification of Arabic Books: Some Basic Considerations." *UNESCO Bulletin for Libraries* 14 (1960): 105. F.L. Kent and F. Abu Haidar. "Library Development in the Arab World." *Revue Internationale de la Documentation* 29 (1962).

Tait, James A. *Authors & Titles.* Hamden, Conn.: Shoe String Press, 1970.

3

Personal Name Authority Control

In the last chapter, we said that in addition to the rules of description there exist rules for setting an author up as either a main or added entry. The purpose of this chapter is to familiarize you with these rules. However, we shall begin by explaining the need for them and discussing past attitudes toward them. We shall then describe the work situation you are likely to encounter, in which you will probably not always be the one applying the rules.

The definition and purpose of personal name authority control

We can illustrate both the concept of and the need for personal name authority control by describing a situation you have probably encountered often. You have no doubt received, in the mail, multiple copies of many brochures, newsletters, circulars, and similar items, each bearing a slightly different form of your name. If your full name is John Bernard Wilson, the address labels of these various copies might read as follows:

> J. Wilson
> J.B. Wilson
> John Wilson
> John B. Wilson
> J. Bernard Wilson
> John Bernard Wilson

Some companies have sent letters something like the following to all names on their mailing lists:

Dear Customer:
If you are receiving multiple copies of our mailings, each addressed to a slightly different form of your name, please let us know and tell us which form you wish us to use. This will allow us to send only one copy of our materials to each customer and so keep our costs down. Thank you.

Such a letter is an attempt at personal name authority control—the practice of establishing one name in one form as the sole, definitive means of denoting a particular individual. Personal name authority control is one of several types of authority control. In later chapters, we will discuss the need for a definitive form of subject headings, corporate body names, and, in some cases, titles. For a comprehensive discussion of authority control in general, covering personal and corporate names, subject headings, and series and uniform titles, see Clack (1990).

The purpose of personal name authority control for the companies discussed above is to minimize expenses and wastage. For a library or information center, the purpose of personal name authority control is to establish one preferred heading under which to gather all works by a given author. This heading should distinguish the author from any others with which he or she could be confused. The library must also establish some type of *syndetic structure*—a logical network of connections between variant forms and the preferred form. In a manual card catalog, syndetic structure usually takes the form of "see" references—i.e.:

Clemens, Samuel, 1835–1910.
see Twain, Mark, 1835–1910.

In an online catalog, syndetic structure takes the form of linkages in the database which allow a user to search under "Clemens, Samuel" and retrieve bibliographic records for works by Mark Twain. The first online catalogs lacked syndetic structure. Many still do, but many others are adding it.

Past approaches to personal name authority control

According to Auld (1982), concern for and practice of personal name authority control waxed and waned from 1900 to 1980, with some of the more interesting work having been done by Sharpe et al. for *Chemical Abstracts*. Auld points out that the last edition of ALA cataloging rules to devote a special section to the "how-to" of authority work was published in 1941, and was aimed at the library book cataloger.

The automation of cataloging has focused attention of the problem of authority control. The following is a comment made in the announcement of the institute held on May 21–23, 1979, at Atlantic City, New Jersey, entitled, "Authority Control: The Key to Tomorrow's Catalog":

> Authority control—one of the librarian's most important bibliographical tools—is also one of the most overlooked and underworked devices in libraryland. Automation is, however, bringing it to the forefront as one of the most important cataloging and searching tools that is required to establish and maintain order in our processing and user worlds. The closing-the-catalog vogue, the advent of on-line terminals, COM, and other developments have brought the realization that we cannot hide incorrect entries, old fashioned terms, and outmoded concepts in our modern, easily accessible public catalogs. Authority control is a must if chaos is to be kept out of our modern bibliographical and searching systems [ALA 1979].

Several large libraries or institutions that did appreciate the magnitude of the problems described above developed sophisticated computer-based systems in answer to their own needs. Among the more interesting are those of the New York Public Library, a pioneer of automated authority control system (Malinconico 1979); the National Library of Canada, which had to develop capabilities for controlling *equivalent* access point in two languages, French and English (Buchinski 1979, Fournier 1978); the online system of the Washington Library Network (WLN) (Calk 1978); and the specialized work of Sharpe (1978) and others in establishing preferred-term names of authors for the *Chemical Abstracts* indexes.

Personal name authority control today

The AACR2R88, along with its 1978 predecessor, has caused serious conflicts between formerly used and newly established forms of entry headings. Because the new rules differ radically from earlier ones, many formerly valid headings are now incorrect. For example, "Pennsylvania, University" has become "University of Pennsylvania" and "Eliot, Thomas Stearns" has become "Eliot, T.S. (Thomas Stearns)."

At the same time, it is becoming standard practice for a member of an online bibliographic network, such as OCLC, RLIN, or a smaller regional system, to adopt whatever heading for a given author that appears first within that network. This has created a need for a centralized, national authority which can be trusted to establish headings according to the rules. Not surprisingly, the accepted authority is the Library of Congress. Today, many cataloging institutions' authority work consists primarily of locating Library of Congress authority records. A cataloger can search for these manually in the *Library of Congress Name Headings with References* (1974–), or online as MARC records. We shall discuss the MARC authority format further on.

This means that you are unlikely to be doing your own authority work a great deal of the time. Rather, you will use whatever heading the Library of Congress has created for a particular author. Of course, the Library of Congress will not have established a heading for every author you encounter. In these cases, if your library is part of a network, you may be directed to use whatever form of the author's name has been established within the network.

Your interpretation of the rules may lead you to question the validity of a heading, even a Library of Congress heading. If this happens, you may discover that you must give primary consideration to conformity with other network libraries. Chan (1983) discusses the disparity between the ideal and the actual practices and principles of uniform headings.

Whatever your work environment, you will occasionally encounter a new author for whose name you can find no externally produced authentication. When this happens, you must do your own authority work. Since the thrust of this book is toward original cataloging, it is this situation with which we are primarily concerned. Even if you never need to create an authority record, you must be competent to judge records you work with. For these reasons, we now present the rules and methods for establishing an acceptable entry.

Choosing the correct name

In many cases, the correct choice of name is obvious. If someone named William Edmund Rhodes has written five books, all of whose title pages bear the name "William Edmund Rhodes," you should enter this author's works under "Rhodes, William Edmund." But what if the title pages read "William E. Rhodes," yet you knew his middle name? What if he wrote three books under "William Edmund Rhodes," and three more under "William E. Rhodes"? Furthermore, how do you handle George Orwell, Mark Twain, or anyone else who wrote—or writes—under a pseudonym?

The initial answer of AACR2R88 to such questions, given in Rule 22.1A, is: "Choose, as the basis of the heading for a person the name by which he or she is commonly known." Rule 22.1B explains that you should determine what that name is "from the chief sources of information of works by that person issued in his or her language." The chief source of information for a book is the title page. We have listed the chief sources of information for the various nonbook materials in Chapter 12. In cases where no such chief source is available, you must determine the name, "from reference sources issued in [the person's] language or country of residence or activity."

In the case of persons known by several names, none of which is a pseudonym, you must, according to Rule 22.2A1:

> Choose the name by which the person is clearly most commonly known, if there is one. Otherwise, choose ... according to the following order of preference:
> a) the name that appears most frequently in the person's work.
> b) the name that appears most frequently in reference sources
> c) the latest name.

If a person always writes under a single pseudonym, that will be the name by which he or she is most commonly known. Therefore, enter all of that author's works under the pseudonym, even if you know his or her real name.

Rules 22.2B2 and 22.2B3 cover persons whose works appear under several pseudonyms or under both their real names and pseudonyms. Both rules sanction the practice of dividing author's works among the various pseudonyms, or pseudonyms and real names, under which they have written. You are to do this for older authors who have "established two or more bibliographic entities," and for all contemporary authors using several pseudonyms or their real names and one or more pseud-onyms.

You will note that these two rules are at odds with what we have said is an important aim of personal name authority control — to gather all of an author's works together under one heading. We shall discuss arguments for and against the practice of splitting an author's works among several heading later in this chapter.

Constructing the complete heading

Determining the correct name for the individual, including the proper fullness of form, is only the first step in constructing a heading. You must then arrange the elements in the proper order and make any additions permitted or required by the rules.

In the majority of cases, the order of elements will present no special problem. You will simply use the "Last, First Middle" form which has become almost a universal standard for formal listing of names. However, compound surnames or surnames with prefixes present special problems, and are handled differently depending on the language of the name or the nature of the surname. There are also cases in which entry under given name is required, along with various other special cases. Rules 22.4–22.11 of AACR2R88 cover the order of entry elements.

The most common additions to a name are years of birth and death and spelled out forms of names given only as initials. We will discuss these in more detail below. Other additions include titles of nobility, designations of rank, office, status, etc. Rules 22.12–22.20 cover additions to names, with 22.17–22.20 specifically covering additions to distinguish identical names.

Dates, covered by Rule 22.17, follow the name, preceded by a comma — i.e.:

Jones, William, 1890–1976.

When the heading is for a person still living, the dash following the year of birth is the last mark of punctuation:

Wallace, Susan, 1954–

If it is necessary to give a person's birth date to the day, give the year first followed by the day with *no comma* between them:

Wallace, Susan, 1954 Jan. 5–

See AACR2R88 Rule 22.17 for instructions on designating various types of uncertain or unknown dates.

Spelled out forms of names appear in parentheses immediately after the name, before any dates, if they are present:

Rogers, William R. (William Robert), 1934–
Baxter, C. Martin (Charles Martin), 1965–

The entire portion of the heading which contains the name to be spelled out is included within parentheses. This is in contrast to the practice, used in some reference sources, of simply adding the remainder of the name in parentheses: "Rogers, William R(obert), 1934–".

Note that the only names which you may add solely at your discretion are those represented by initials (or some other abbreviation) in the chosen form of the complete name. You are permitted to add first or middle names completely omitted in the chosen form—i.e.:

Wallace, Susan (Susan Stockman)
Miller, David (George David)

only when you *must* do so to distinguish between headings which would otherwise be identical. Again, you must include within the parentheses the entire portion of the complete name to which you are adding the first or middle name (or initial, if only that is available).

In fact, AACR2R88 considers the adding of *all* spelled out names and dates of birth and death necessary only when they are needed to distinguish headings which would otherwise be identical. You will see this reflected in many Library of Congress headings, a fact which we shall return to at the end of this chapter.

If you examine AACR2R88 closely, you will see that, despite its extensive instructions on constructing headings for persons, it makes explicit reference neither to personal name authority control nor to authority control in general. Both terms are absent from the entire text, including the glossary. This is because AACR2R88 (along with its 1978 predecessor) does not discuss in detail one of the most important aspects of personal name authority control. This is the research needed to establish a heading, along with the documentation of that research — the topic of the next section.

Researching headings and documenting your research

Construct an individual workform for each name you research. This is where you will record details of your search. An example of a template for such a workform is given in Figure 3. Establish a name using the following three sources:

A. The book cataloged:

1. Record the name as it is given in the book.

2. Examine the book for any information that seems of potential use in your search, such as the period in which the author probably lived, the author's nationality, subject field, etc.

3. Record these items on the workform.

B. Reference works. Begin with those most likely to contain the name—i.e., those covering persons in your author's field. If the *Biography and Genealogy Master Index* and the *Almanac of Famous People* are available, consult them first, as they are both comprehensive indexes to biographical sources. A list of biographical sources, including these two, is provided in Appendix II.

When you find your author, record the following on the workform:

1. The exact form of the name which appears in the reference work.

2. Every variant of the name found, including prefixes or compound surnames.

3. Any pseudonyms used.

4. Every *cross reference* to the name. A cross reference is a variant form of the name—or, in the case of an author who uses one or more pseudonyms, an alternate name—which a reference source deems invalid, but prints along with an instruction to search under the "correct" form.

5. Dates of birth and death.

6. Any other item that might be of use in establishing the official form of the name. Possibilities include the fact that the person in question was a member of the nobility, was canonized, holds or held an official government position, etc.

In choosing reference sources, remember that you must support your choice of "preferred name" by proving it to be "the name that appears most frequently in the person's works." Since you may only have one or two works in hand, you may have to consult such sources as *Books in Print,* or the statements of responsibility found (a) on the card

Figure 3. *Authority Workform*

WORK BEING CATALOGED: _____

NAME ON TITLE PAGE: _____

n/d/o   SOURCE CONSULTED   DATA FOUND

_____

_____

_____

_____

_____

_____

_____

_____

SUBSTANTIATION OF NAME ON TITLE PAGE:

_____

_____

images in the Library of Congress *National Union Catalogs,* and (b) in the bibliographic records found online in OCLC, RLIN, or whatever shared cataloging system you have at your disposal.

    C. *The AACR2R88 rules in Chapter 22,* many of which we have already discussed.

        1. Following the rules pertinent to the name you are search-ing, establish the entry in its official form.

        2. Record the official form and all of the cross references

which the rules advise. Remember that your search must substantiate all of the variant forms as well the preferred form.

 3. Record, on the workform, the numbers of the rules you used.

Keep in mind, as you search, that all biographical reference sources have limitations, some of which may invalidate a particular source for your purposes. Ascertain, by examining the work's preface, introduction, chapter headings, title page, etc., the following:

When and *where* was this source published, and *by whom*?

Is it multivolume? If not, how many pages does it have? For example, you may need only a hand-holdable, easy-to-deal-with single volume, such as Bohdan Wynar's *ARBA Guide to Biographical Dictionaries* for certain relatively easy searches.

What is the work's scope with regard to: Language; Nationality; Subject fields; Degree of specificity; Time period covered; Kind of person included?

Is it an ongoing, continuing source, or is it retrospective, with a closed date of publication?

Is each new edition cumulative?

No one source is necessarily superior to another, just possibly more pertinent to the purpose you have in mind. Michael Grant's *Greek and Latin Authors, 800 B.C.–A.D. 1000* will have neither worldwide nor current coverage, but may supply exactly the information you need to identify an obscure, little-known Greek poet.

A sample search

The following example will take you step by step through a typical instance of establishing a personal name.

Step 1. Examine the book. We will examine *The Cat-Nappers, a Jeeves and Bertie Story,* by P.G. Wodehouse (New York: Simon & Schuster, 1974). (In fact, the Library of Congress has established a heading for Wodehouse, but for the purposes of our discussion, we shall assume you are working in a library that prefers its own authority work to that of the Library of Congress.) You can obtain other potentially useful details from both the book and its dust jacket. For example, the dust jacket contains the sentence, "On January 1, 1975, the Queen of England knighted Pelham Grenville Wodehouse, and Sir Plum, K.B.E. was born, ninety-three years after he made his first appearance in the world." Also noted on the dust jacket, bordered in black, is the comment, "P.G. Wodehouse died in his sleep on February 14, 1975." The book is a work of fiction published in New York; it had been previously published in London under the title *Aunts Aren't Gentlemen*. Jot all such information down on your work slip, directly under the name "P.G. Wodehouse" as it appears on the title page.

Step 2. Select relevant reference sources, such as those listed in Appendix II. Note the main entry used in each reference work, the variants of the name, the dates of birth and death, the references from other forms of the name, honors bestowed, marriages, pseudonyms, etc. (See Figure 4, "Completed Authority Work Slip for Agatha Christie.") Write all these items down. If a reference source contains nothing about P.G. Wodehouse, write, "not found" to avoid accidentally rechecking the same source.

Keep in mind that you must establish the name your author most often used on the title pages of his or her works. In the case of P.G. Wodehouse, for example, you will find early works published under "Pelham Grenville" rather than "P.G." Also, find out to what extent Wodehouse used the title. Will you need to retain the *Sir*?

Step 3. Apply the appropriate AACR2R88 rules. You will have now obtained, from an examination of *The Cat-Nappers, a Jeeves and Bertie Story*, and from all pertinent reference sources, all the details you need to make a choice of entry for Wodehouse. You should then turn to the relevant AACR2R88 rules from Chapter 22, establish the name in its official form in accordance with such rules, and, finally, establish the authority record and the necessary "see" and "see also" references.

The authority record

A library should make a permanent authority record to substantiate the choice of personal name heading established for use in its public catalog. The record gives the name in its official form, provides a brief record of the search made to establish the name, and lists all "see" and "see also" references made from variant forms of the name or alternate names. Whenever possible, symbols and abbreviations are used on this card, as follows:

n   Name was found; date(s) were not.

nd   Name and date(s) were found.

Figure 4. *Completed Authority Work Slip for Agatha Christie*

WORK BEING CATALOGED: <u>The Mysterious Affair at Styles</u>

NAME ON TITLE PAGE: <u>Agatha Christie</u>

[Put down comments as suggested.]

nd   *Pre '56 Imprints*, v. 108: "Christie, Mrs. Agatha (Miller), 1891–"
nd   *NUC 1973-1977*, v. 23: "Christie, Agatha Miller, Dame, 1891-1976."
o   *Biography Index 1946-1949*
nd   *Biography Index 1955-1958:* "Christie, Agatha (Miller) (Mary West-macott, pseud.), 1891–"
nd   *CBI 1970:* "Christie, Agatha (Miller) (Mrs. Max Edgar Lucien Mal-lowan), 1891–"
nd   *Pre '56 Imprints*, v. 357: "Christie, Agatha (Miller), 1891-
     × Mallowan, Agatha Christie"
nd   *NUC 1953-1957*, v. 26: "Christie, Agatha (Miller), 1891-
     × Westmacott, Mary, pseud."
n   *20th Century Authors:* "Christie, Mrs. Agatha (Miller)"
nd   *The Times Index*, April–June 1976: "Christie, Agatha (Dame) – death January 13, 1976; funeral January 14, 1976"
n   *Readers Guide*, March 1975-Feb. 1976: "Christie, Dame Agatha"
n   *Current Biography 1940:* "Christie, Agatha – father's name was Frederick Alvar Miller"
nd   *Encyclopaedia Brit.* (Macropaedia), II, 1978 ed.: "Christie, Dame Agatha (Mary Clarissa) (b. Sept. 15, 1890, Torquay, Devon – d. January 12, 1976, Wallingford, Oxfordshire)"
d   *The Times*, Sept. 17, 1890: under *Births*: "On the 15th of September, at Ashfield Torquay, the wife of Frederick Alvar Miller, of a daughter"
nd   *Encyc. of Mystery and Det.:* "Christie, Agatha (Mary Clarissa Miller), 1890–"
n   *The Detective Short Story: A Bibliography,* "Christie, Agatha"
nd   *Longman's Comp. to 20th Cent. Lit.,* "Christie, Agatha (née Agatha Mary Clarissa Miller, 1891–; married (1) Archibald Christie, 1914; (2) Max Mallowan, 1930)"
nd   *Contemporary Authors*, v. 19-20: "Christie, Agatha (Mary Clarissa) 1890– (Mary Westmacott)"
nd   *Chamber's Biographical Dictionary:* "Christie, Agatha Mary Clarissa, née Miller (1891–)"
nd   *Biographical Dictionary Master Index 1975-1976:* "Christie, Agatha, 1890–"
nd   *Facts on File 1976:* "Agatha Christie, 85, died Jan. 15, 1976; named a Dame of the British Empire in 1971"

Substantiation of name on title page: **BIP** – Agatha Christie 128, Westmacott 9. **NUC** (statement of responsibility or authority file): *Pre '56 Imprints* – Christie 87, Westmacott 6; **NUC** (most recent edition – Christie, 46, Westmacott 6).

o   Name was not found.

×   Used in a citation, means that a "see" reference, exactly as recorded after the " × " was found in the source cited.

×   Used after all citations, indicates a "see" reference to be made for main catalog and authority file.

--   (Dash made of two typed hyphens) used after an initial letter means that the name — i.e. first, middle, last — so represented is exactly the same as it appears in the official heading. For example: Name in the official heading is Crow, Donald Lester; if one reference source listed the name as Crow, Donald, you could cite the name given as C--, D--. The use of this shortcut is optional.

Figure 5 shows how the final authority record will look. Figure 6 shows how "see" and "see also" references will appear in a manual card catalog.

In an online catalog, "see" references may be hidden. If you search under "Clemens, Samuel Langhorne," the system may respond exactly as if you had searched under "Twain, Mark."

An online catalog can also display these references. In the situation described above, the system can display a message such as:

The heading CLEMENS, SAMUEL LANGHORNE is invalid.
The correct heading is: TWAIN, MARK, 1835-1910.

immediately preceding the list of records under "Twain, Mark, 1835–1910."

When, in performing authority work, you observe carefully the procedures we have outlined, you will accomplish three objectives. First, you will better enable users to find works by the author in which

Figure 5. *Final Authority Record*

Christie, Agatha, 1890-1976.

nd Pre '56 Imprints, v. 108, <u>Christie, Mrs.
 Agatha (Miller)</u>, 1891-

nd NUC 1973-1977, v. 23, <u>Christie, Agatha
 Miller, Dame, 1891-1976.</u>

o Biography Index 1946-1949

nd Biog. Index 1955-1958. <u>Christie, Agatha
 (Miller) (Mary Westmacott, pseud.),
 1891-</u>

(continued)

Christie, Agatha, 189--1976.   (Card 2)

nd C. B. I. 1970, <u>Christie, Agatha (Miller)
 (Mrs Max Edgar Lucien
 Mallowan)</u>, 1891-

nd Pre '56 Imprints, v 357, <u>Christie, Agatha
 (Miller), 1891-   .</u>
 x <u>Mallowan, Agatha Christie</u>

nd NUC 1953-1957,v. 26, <u>Christie, Agatha
 (Miller), 1891-   . x West-
 macott, Mary, pseud.</u>

(continued)

Figure 5. *Final Authority Record (Continued)*

Christie, Agatha, 1890–1976.   (Card 3)

n Read. Gde. Mar. '75–Feb. '76, Christie,
                Dame Agatha

n Current Biography 1940, Christie,
                Agatha: father's name
                was Frederick Alvar
                Miller.

n 20th Cent. Au., Christie, Mrs. Agatha
                (Miller)
                      (continued)

Christie, Agatha, 1890–1976.   (Card 4)

nd Biographical Dictionary Master
        Index 1975–1976, Christie, Agatha,
            1890–

nd Chamber's Biographical Dictionary,
                Christie, Agatha Mary
                Clarissa, née Miller,
                (1891–   )

                      (continued)

Figure 5. *Final Authority Record (Continued)*

Christie, Agatha, 1890-1976.   (Card 5)

nd Contemp. Au., v. 19-20, <u>Christie, Agatha</u>
               <u>(Mary Clarissa) 1890-</u>
               <u>(Mary Westmacott)</u>

nd Encyclopedia of Mystery and Det., <u>Christie,</u>
               <u>Agatha (Mary Clarissa Miller),</u>
               <u>1890-</u>

n The Detective Short Story: a Bibliog.,
               <u>Christie, Agatha</u>

               (continued)

Christie, Agatha, 1890-1976.   (Card 6)

nd Longman's Comp. to 20th Cen. Lit.,
               <u>Christie, Agatha (nee</u>
               <u>Agatha Mary Clarissa Miller,</u>
               <u>1891-</u>   ; married (1)Arch-
               ibald Christie, 1914; (2)
               Max Mallowan, 1930).

n The Times Index April-June 1976, <u>Christie,</u>
               <u>Agatha (Dame)</u>: memorial fund
               set up Ap. 27 by Sir Max
               Mallowan.

               (continued)

Figure 5. *Final Authority Record (Continued)*

Christie, Agatha, 1890–1976.   (Card 7)

nd The Times Index Jan.-Mar. 1976, Christie,
          Agatha (Dame): death Jan. 13,
          1976; funeral Jan. 14, 1976.

nd Facts on File 1976, "Agatha Christie, 85,
          dies Jan. 13, 1976; named a
          Dame of the British Empire
          in 1971."

                              (continued)

Christie, Agatha, 1890-1976.   (Card 8)

nd Encyclopaedia Britannica (Macropaedia), II,
          1978 ed., Christie, Dame Agatha (Mary
          Clarissa) (b. Sept. 15, 1890, Torquay,
          Devon.--d. Jan. 12, 1976, Wallingford,
          Oxfordshire).

                              (continued)

Figure 5. *Final Authority Record (Continued)*

Christie, Agatha, 1890-1976.   (Card 9)

d The Times Sept. 17, 1890, Under "Births":
   "On the 15th of September, at
   Ashfield, Torquay, the wife of
   Frederick Alvar Miller, of a
   daughter."

Substantiation of name on title page:
   BIP: Agatha Christie, 128
         Westmacott, 9
   NUC Statement of Responsibility or

O   (continued)

Christie, Agatha, 1890-1976.   (Card 10)

Authority File:
   Pre '56 Imprints: Agatha Christie, 87
                      Westmacott, 6
   NUC (most recent ed.): Christie, 46
                           Westmacott, 6

x Westmacott, Mary
x Mallowan, Agatha Christie
x Mallowan, Mrs. Max Edgar Lucien
(AACR 2 Rules: 22.1A; 22.2A; 22.4A;
                22.5A; 22.12B; 22.18)

Figure 6. *"See" and "see also" Cards*

Westmacott, Mary

see

Christie, Agatha, 1890–1976

Wright, Willard Huntington
see also Van Dine, S. S.

Van Dine, S. S.
see also Wright, Willard Huntington

they are interested; if they do not know the correct heading under which to search, the "see" references will take them to it. Second, you will group together all works by an individual instead of dispersing them throughout the catalog (except in cases where you feel it is appropriate to invoke AACR2R88 Rule 22.2B2 or 22.2B3). Third, you will prevent duplication and proliferation of entries.

As we have mentioned several times, many libraries, rather than doing their own authority work, simply accept Library of Congress headings. This is partly because they are caught in the budget crunch of the 1990s and partly because they and other libraries in a local or regional network must be consistent with each other. Once again, however, this does *not* mean that there is no need for you to learn how to perform authority work. The Library of Congress may not have established a heading for the author of a new, obscure, very old, or foreign work.

You should also be in a position to assess the quality of any heading you encounter which you are not required to accept as is.

However, you should expect to be using Library of Congress headings most of the time. Because you are likely to be using them in the form of MARC authority records, we shall now discuss these records in more detail.

The MARC authority file

Since this book is not about automation per se, we shall present only a brief, general discussion of the MARC authority format. For a more detailed treatment, see Crawford (1989). The MARC authority records used as figures 7 and 8 are shown as they appear in OCLC.

While development of the MARC bibliographic record began in the 1960s, the first version of the MARC authority record, prepared by Lenore S. Maruyama, did not appear until 1976 (LC 1976). This format was used until 1983, when the Library of Congress completed work on a revised version of the MARC authority record (LC 1983). The latest documentation for the current format (USMARC 1989) is a one-volume, looseleaf work designed to allow easy updating.

A MARC authority record uses the same type of fields and subfields as a MARC bibliographic record. The MARC authority format accommodates not only personal names, but corporate body names and uniform titles, both of which are discussed in Chapter 14. The most impor-

Figure 7. *Pair of MARC Authority Records*
for Author with Several Headings

```
                 ¶
ARN: 2598516   Rec stat: c      Entrd: 890915        Used: 900206
Type: z        Geo subd: n      Govt agn: •  Lang:   Source: c
Roman: •       Subj: a          Series: n   Ser num: n  Head: aab
Ref status: a  Upd status: a    Auth status: a       Name: a
Enc lvl: n     Auth/Ref: a      Mod rec:             Rules: c
  ¶
▶ 1 010      no 89013215  ¶
▶ 2 040      MnHi ‡c MnHi ‡d MnHi ¶
▶ 3 053      PR6005.H66 ¶
▶ 4 100 10   Westmacott, Mary, ‡d 1890-1976 ¶
▶ 5 500 10   Christie, Agatha, ‡d 1890-1976 ‡w nnnc ¶
▶ 6 663      Works by this author are entered under the name used in the item.
For a listing of other names used by this author, search also under ‡b
Christie, Agatha, 1890-1976 ¶
▶ 7 670      Her Absent in the spring, 1944: ‡b t.p. (Mary Westmacott) ¶
▶ 8 670      NUC pre-56 ‡b (hdg: Christie, Agatha Miller, 1891-  ; usage: Mary
Westmacott) ¶


Screen 1 of 2      ¶
ARN: 271932    Rec stat: c      Entrd: 840818        Used: 900206
Type: z        Geo subd: n      Govt agn: •  Lang:   Source: •
Roman: •       Subj: a          Series: n   Ser num: n  Head: aab
Ref status: a  Upd status: a    Auth status: a       Name: a
Enc lvl: n     Auth/Ref: a      Mod rec:             Rules: c
  ¶
▶ 1 010      n  79038407  ¶
▶ 2 040      DLC ‡c DLC ‡d MnHi—¶
▶ 3 053      PR6005.H66 ¶
▶ 4 100 10   Christie, Agatha, ‡d 1890-1976 ¶
▶ 5 400 10   Christie, Agatha Miller, ‡c Dame, ‡d 1891-1976 ‡w nnaa ¶
▶ 6 400 10   Christie, Agatha Miller, ‡d 1890-1976 ¶
▶ 7 400 10   Christie, Agatha Mary Clarissa Miller, ‡d 1890-1976 ¶
▶ 8 500 10   Mallowan, Agatha Christie, ‡d 1890-1976 ‡w nnnc ¶
▶ 9 500 10   Westmacott, Mary, ‡d 1890-1976 ‡w nnnc ¶
▶10 663      For works of this author entered under other names, search also
under ‡b Mallowan, Agatha Christie, 1890-1976; Westmacott, Mary, 1890-1976 ¶
▶11 670      Her The mysterious affair at Styles, 1920. ¶


Screen 2 of 2      ¶
▶12 670      Fitzgibbon, R.H. The Agatha Christie companion, c1980: ‡b t.p.
(Agatha Christie) p. 15 (b. 9/15/90) ¶
▶13 670      Contemp. auth., 1976 ‡b (Christie, Agatha, b. 1890) ¶
▶14 670      NUC pre-56 ‡b (hdg: Christie, Agatha Miller, 1891-  ; usage:
Agatha Christie; Agatha Christie Mallowan; Mary Westmacott; full name: Agatha
Mary Clarissa Miller Christie) ¶
```

tant fields for you to recognize in a *personal* name authority record are:

100: Official heading established for the person in question.

400: Invalid heading for the person in question. In a manual card catalog,
this heading would be connected to that in the 100 field with a "see"
reference. Any number of 400 fields may appear in an authority
record.

500: Other usable heading for the person in question. In a manual card
catalog, this heading would be connected to that in the 100 field with
a "see also" reference. For every 500 field in an authority record, there
should be a corresponding record in which that field and the 100 field
are reversed (See Figure 7). Such pairs or groups of authority records
are the result of invoking AACR2R88 rules 22.2B2 and 22.2B3.

Figure 8. *MARC Authority Record Using ‡q and ‡d*

```
                     ¶
ARN: 448636    Rec stat: c    Entrd: 840819      Used: 900209
Type: z        Geo subd: n    Govt agn: • Lang:  Source:
Roman: •       Subj: a        Series: n   Ser num: n Head: aab
Ref status: a  Upd status: a  Auth status: a    Name: a
Enc lvl: n     Auth/Ref: a    Mod rec:          Rules: c
  ¶
▶ 1 010       n 80067088  ¶
▶ 2 040       DLC ‡c DLC ‡d DLC ¶
▶ 3 053       PR6007.A95 ¶
▶ 4 100 20    Day Lewis, C. ‡q (Cecil), ‡d 1904-1972. ¶
▶ 5 400 10    Lewis, Cecil Day-, ‡d 1904-1972 ¶
▶ 6 400 10    Lewis, C. Day ‡q (Cecil Day), ‡d 1904-1972 ¶
▶ 7 400 20    Day-Lewis, Cecil, ‡d 1904-1972. ‡w nnaa ¶
▶ 8 400 20    Day Lewis, Cecil, ‡d 1904-1972 ¶
▶ 9 500 10    Blake, Nicholas, ‡d 1904-1972 ¶
▶10 670       Oxford poetry ... 1927. ¶
▶11 670       His A question of. proof, 1990: ‡b CIP t.p. (Nicholas Blake) ¶
▶12 670       Dic. of Irish lit., 1969 ‡b (Day-Lewis, Cecil, 1904-1972; pseud.:
Nicholas Blake) ¶
```

The three fields listed above — along with the 100, 600, and 700 fields of a bibliographic record — use most of the same subfields. The two you are likely to encounter most often are ‡q, which contains names appearing in a parenthetical qualifier, and ‡d, which contains dates. Figure 8 illustrates the use of both.

Another which appears less frequently is ‡c. This contains data such as the "distinguishing terms" described in AACR2R88 Section 22.19. One example of ‡c is:

Wilson, Joseph, ‡c Ph. D.

You will see, from figures 7 and 8, that MARC authority records also have fixed fields. One of these, labeled "Rules" in the OCLC system, warrants brief discussion here. Only records containing a "c" or "d" in this field are considered valid under AACR2. A "c" means that the heading was actually established according to AACR2. The heading in a "d" record is pre–AACR2 but has been judged by the Library of Congress to be "AACR2-compatible." That is, it may coexist with AACR2 headings without causing problems. This means that if you are working in a library which accepts Library of Congress headings, you are only required to accept "c" and "d" headings.

We have now covered all of the essential points of personal name authority control. Having done so, we wish to discuss further two issues we alluded to earlier.

Splitting an author's works among
two or more headings: should it be allowed?

We said earlier that AACR2R88 rules 22.2B2 and 22.2B3 sanction the practice of dividing authors' works among two or more headings. You will note that this practice is at odds with what we have said is an important aim of personal name authority control — to gather all of an author's works together under one heading. This suggests that either the validity of this practice or the universal importance of the aim is questionable. On the one hand, you may argue that a library patron who wants to read Lewis Carroll's *Alice in Wonderland* will probably not be interested in Charles L. Dodgson's works on mathematics and logic, and vice versa. Furthermore, some authors have goals they wish to achieve by using pseudonyms — goals which could be undermined by a cataloging agency's gathering their works under one heading. For several authors' statements on this matter, see "What's in a Pen Name," *The Writer* (1982) and King (1985).

On the other hand, separating an author's works obscures the truth — that one individual produced several different types of works under several names. (Both rules instruct catalogers to connect the various heading with explanatory references, but patrons cannot always be relied upon to take proper notice of these.)

Granted, by raising this point, we invite two questions. First, would patrons benefit from knowing the whole truth about an author? There is one set who definitely would — those who are doing research about that author. For example, someone trying to gather information about mystery writers might be very interested to know that Nicholas Blake, author of the mystery novel *The Beast Must Die,* was also Cecil Day Lewis, poet laureate of England from 1967 to 1972.

Even a patron who simply wants to read a mystery novel might be especially interested in one by an author with this distinction. Of course, there are many patrons who simply want to find a desired work by a desired author, and thus may not care about such details. However, these people may feel cheated if they subsequently discover the truth, and thus realize that their library did not provide it for them.

The second question that needs an answer is: would the extra time and effort involved in conveying this truth outweigh the benefits of doing so? The answer depends to some extent on the particular case. There is, for example, one situation in which a library would expend *less* time and effort electing not to separate an author's works. A library might have all of Charles Dodgson's works under his real name because they were cataloged under pre–AACR2 rules, which directed catalogers to use an author's real name if it was known. If that library elected to use Dodgson's real name for all of his works, it would not have to redo any of its old cataloging. Many libraries may have older authors' works cataloged in this fashion.

Of course, there are other occasions on which *separating* the works would require less time and effort because the multiple headings have already been established, and someone would have to decide which was to be the official heading.

Please note that we are *not* suggesting that you choose a particular course of action *because* it would involve less time and effort. Rather, we are pointing out that the AACR2R88 rules in question would not always involve less time and effort.

There is a third question which we ask you to consider: would a library which elected not to consolidate an author's works be laying itself open to problems worse than those involved in consolidating them? We believe that the answer to this might be yes. A primary intention of personal name authority control is to solve the problem of an author's works' being scattered throughout the catalog. A cataloging agency which routinely divides an author's works among several headings might be laying the foundation for a reemergence of that problem. We may once again have to answer the Earl of Ellesmere's 1849 question (see page 5) about uniformity and collocation.

Personal name conflicts:
how rigid should the definition be?

We must begin with a somewhat vague definition of a *personal name conflict* in order to encompass two existing definitions which differ significantly. A personal name conflict arises from a group of name headings, or instances of one heading which creates confusion over whether all of its members represent the same person, or in some cases, a combination of both problems.

A cataloger *resolves* this conflict by first researching the situation, then taking the appropriate action. If all *instances of a heading* prove to represent the same person, they are left unchanged. If all *headings in a group* represent the same person, a cataloger decides which one to use and all instances of the others are corrected. (Because these decisions can be difficult and affect large portions of the catalog, there may be only one senior member of a library's cataloging department empowered to make them.) If all headings or instances of a heading in a group represent different people, the cataloger adds clarifying elements to those headings which need them.

According to what has been called the "technical definition," headings are in conflict whenever they could potentially represent the same person; for example:

> Smith, M.S.
> Smith, M.S. (Mary S.), 1956–
> Smith, Mary S.
> Smith, M. Susan

Under the technical definition, the only way to resolve the above conflict is to augment these headings such that any two of them will contain contradictory data. Following are two possible resolutions:

> Smith, M.S. (Melanie S.)   Smith, M.S. (M. Stern)
> Smith, M.S. (Mary S.), 1956–   Smith, M.S. (Mary Starr), 1956–
> Smith, Mary S., 1945–   Smith, Mary S. (Mary Steele)
> Smith, M. Susan (Martha   Smith, M. Susan
>   Susan)

The Library of Congress uses a much narrower definition, which states that a conflict exists only when:

> (a) Multiple headings appear for one person.
> (b) One heading appears for two or more people.

Under this definition, the headings

> Smith, M.S.
> Smith, M.S. (Mary S.), 1956–
> Smith, Mary S.
> Smith, M. Susan

are in conflict only if they represent the same person; if the cataloger determines that each represents a different person, they may all stand as is. Additions to a heading are only necessary to distinguish two headings which would otherwise be *completely identical*. Furthermore, the Library of Congress requires that an addition be made only to *one* of the headings, thus rendering them no longer completely identical.

Both the technical and Library of Congress definitions assert that there should be a unique heading for each individual, which should distinguish that person from anyone else with whom he or she might be confused. However, the Library of Congress definition asks end users of a catalog to assume that *two headings which differ in appearance represent different people*. This difference need not be in the form of the name. The headings

Smith, Roger
Smith, Roger, 1934–

are, according to the Library of Congress, not in conflict because one includes a date and one does not.

Therefore, the Library of Congress adds birthdates, spelled-out names in parentheses, etc., only to newly established headings which would otherwise be identical to existing headings. The existing headings are left unchanged. If you examine the Library of Congress authority file, either in print or online, you will find many pairs of headings similar to the "Smith, Roger" example above.

There are two significant problems involved in adhering to the technical definition of a personal name conflict. First, the amount of time and effort involved is likely to be prohibitive. Second, any library or information center which chooses the technical definition will derive only limited benefit from Library of Congress authority records. The form of an individual's name will be correct, but many Library of Congress records will lack the full names or dates which the technical definition requires.

However, the less rigorous approach to personal name conflicts results in many headings containing very little information. Also, patrons may not be aware of the assumption they are being asked to make — that any two headings different in appearance signify different people. Furthermore, if someone should transcribe a heading incorrectly, omitting a date or qualifier, and this error showed up in the public catalog, it could lead to the same type of confusion that results in the multiple mailings we discussed at the beginning of this chapter. If such an error appeared in a catalog which used the technical definition, patrons would immediately spot and question it. For these reasons, we encourage you to be aware of the technical definition of a personal name conflict and to use it whenever you are at liberty to set up your own headings.

Having familiarized you with personal name authority control and the various issues it raises, we can now discuss the series and notes areas of the bibliographic description. We shall deal with these and several other topics in the next chapter.

Review questions for Chapter 3

1. Give three examples of the kinds of problems that may arise if the cataloger takes the author's name from the title page without doing authority work to establish the correct form of that author's name.

2. Cite two relevant sources, from among those listed in Appendix II, of information about the following categories of author: (a) an anonymous writer, (b) a scientist who writes science fiction, (c) a saint of the Roman Catholic Church, (d) a writer of best-selling murder mysteries, (e) a British knight or dame.

3. Would you be willing to accept, as your established main entry, a name heading contained in a MARC record found in a bibliographic database such as OCLC? (Assume that the Library of Congress has not established the heading.) Why or why not? What factors might enter into your decision? (Note that one piece of information readily available in a MARC bibliographic record is the symbol of the library which input it.)

4. Why is it necessary to supply "see" references from variant forms of an author's name?

5. What is the difference between "see" and "see also" references?

6. Discuss the importance of personal name authority control in an online catalog.

7. When patrons search under invalid name headings in an online catalog, do you believe they should be given (a) the results they would have gotten if they had used the valid headings, (b) an instruction to search under the correct headings, (c) both the results they would have gotten if they had used the valid headings and a message informing them that they have been taken from the invalid to the valid heading? What are your reasons for your choice?

8. Discuss the advantages and disadvantages of having one centralized source, such as the Library of Congress, for national authority control.

Sources cited and suggestions for further reading or study

American Library Association. Library and Information Technology Association. Notice: "Authority Control: The Key to Tomorrow's Catalog." Conference held May 21–23, 1979, at Atlantic City, New Jersey.

Anglo-American Cataloguing Rules, 2nd ed., edited by Michael Gorman and Paul W. Winkler. Chicago: American Library Association; Ottawa: Canadian Library Association, 1978.

————, 1988 revision, edited by Michael Gorman and Paul W. Winkler. Ottawa: Canadian Library Association; Chicago: American Library Association, 1988.

Buchinsky, Edwin J. *Initial Considerations for a Nationwide Data Base.* (Network Planning Paper, No. 3; ISSN 0160-9742.) Report of a study performed under the direction of the Library of Congress Network Development Office, 1978.

————, William L. Newman and Mary Jane Dunn. "The National Library of Canada Authority Subsystem: Implications." *Journal of Library Automation* 10 (March 1977): 28–39.

Calk, Jo. "On-Line Authority Control in the Washington Library Network." In *What's in a Name? Control of Catalogue Records through Automated Authority Files.* Toronto: University of Toronto, 1978. 135–161.

Chan, Lois Mai. "The Principle of Uniform Heading in Descriptive Cataloging: Ideal and Reality." *Cataloging & Classification Quarterly* 3 (Summer 1983): 21–35.

Clack, Doris Hargrett. *Authority Control: Principles, Applications, and Instructions.* Chicago: American Library Association, 1990.

Crawford, Walt. *MARC for Library Use: Understanding Integrated USMARC,* 2nd ed. Boston: G.K. Hall, 1989.

Fournier, Michel. "Le Repertoire de Vedetts-Matière de la Bibliothèque de l'Université Laval." In *What's in a Name? Control of Catalogue Records through Automated Authority Files.* Toronto: University of Toronto, 1978. 135–161.

King, Stephen. "Why I Was Bachman." In *The Bachman Books: Four Early Novels.* New York: New American Library, 1985.

Library of Congress. MARC Development Office. *Authorities: A MARC Format.* Washington, D.C.: Library of Congress, 1976.

————. MARC Development Office. *Authorities: A MARC Format.* Washington, D.C.: Library of Congress, 1981; updated 1983.

————. *Monographic Series.* Washington, D.C.: Library of Congress, 1974–.

————. *Name Headings with References.* Washington, D.C.: Library of Congress, 1974–.

Library of Congress. Network Development and MARC Standards Office. *USMARC Format for Authority Data: Including Guidelines for Content Designation.* Washington, D.C.: Cataloging Distribution Service, Library of Congress, 1989– (looseleaf).

Malinconico, S. Michael. "The Library Catalog in a Computerized Environment." *Wilson Library Bulletin* 4 (September 1979): 36–45.

Maxwell, Margaret F. *Handbook for AACR2: Explaining and Illustrating the Anglo-American Cataloguing Rules,* 1988 revision. Chicago: American Library Association, 1989.

Sharpe, Richard B., John B. Fox and Silas E. Hammond. "Computer-Based Editing of Personal and Corporate Author, Inventory and Patent Assignee Names for Publication in CA Author Indexes." American Society for Information Science. *Proceedings of the ASIS Meeting* 15 (1978): 304.

"What's in a Pen Name?" *The Writer* 95 (1982): 24–28.

4

Bibliographic Description II: Series, Notes, Analytics, and Other Issues

In Chapter 2, we discussed those elements of a bibliographic description which must appear in either all or a clear majority of bibliographic records. For all items you catalog you must provide a title, publication details, and a physical description. For most items, you must also provide an author main entry, a statement of responsibility, and an edition statement. The descriptive elements covered in this chapter, series, notes, and ISBN number, appear in many bibliographic records, but are not a standard part of every, or almost every, record.

In addition to discussing these, we will explain the process of "analysis," that is, the preparation of a bibliographic record which describes a part (or parts) of an item. We will also provide a few more historical facts regarding the origin of AACR2, and discuss an issue which has arisen because of online cataloging.

The series area

Many monographs — items such as books which are complete in themselves — appear that, while bibliographically independent, are part of a larger collective entity known as a *series*. The series has a collective title applying to all the items which comprise it.

Series, serials, and sets

You must keep in mind the distinction between a series and a *serial*, which is a continuing publication, appearing (ideally) at regular intervals, the individual issues of which do not usually stand alone.

The distinction between a series and a serial is not always clearcut, especially in instances of numbered series. For example, corporate bodies often publish "yearbooks" and "annuals" whose contents deal with one unified subject not necessarily related to that of the previous year's annual or yearbook. The *Yearbook of Agriculture,* dealing with such various subjects as nutrition and consumerism, is one example.

Another possible source of ambiguity is the distinction between a series and a *set*, known as a *multipart item*. The AACR2R88 defines a multipart item as a "monograph complete, or intended to be completed, in a finite number of separate parts." In a true set, the individual items do not stand alone but must be considered as part of a bibliographic whole. For example, it would make little sense to catalog Volume 12 of an encyclopedia separately.

Yet, in some cases, particularly wherein the successive parts of the set are published sequentially, and each part treats relatively autonomous subject matter, it is not always clear whether the cataloger is dealing with a bibliographic unit or a series of separate monographs. Consider, for example, the groups of textbooks on spelling, handwriting, mathematics, music, etc., published for use in elementary or secondary education. Each book in one of these groups has the same title — perhaps *Discovering Mathematics* or *Hearing and Making Music* — and, obviously, treats the same general topic. However, each covers only that portion of the topic suitable for a specific grade level — kindergarten, first grade, second grade, etc. Should a library which receives *Hearing and Making Music,* grades K-6, consider these seven books members of a series or parts of a set? (You can, in a sense, do both through analytic entries, covered in AACR2R88, Chapter 13, which we shall discuss further on.) The answer may depend on whether the books are actually going to be used in teaching the various grades or in the training of potential new teachers. It may also have to depend on practical considerations; should the library take the time to catalog each item separately?

Placing items in a series together

Because of the ambiguities discussed above, and for other practical, political, or even aesthetic reasons, a library may elect to place all items in a series together on the shelves. To accomplish this, the library must assign each item in the series the same classification number, usually one denoting a broad topic such as "industrial management" or "elementary education." The call number label affixed to each item will contain the volume number as well as the classification number. If a library is willing to forgo having all items in a series stand together, each can be assigned a more specific classification number.

(We shall further discuss the subject of broad versus narrow classification number at various points throughout chapters 6–11. We shall deal further with additions to classification numbers, such as series volume numbers, in Chapter 14.)

There is one type of series which probably should be classified as a unit, and whose members should stand together. This is the television series the individual episodes of which are available on videotape. Many libraries have such series and many others are likely to obtain them. Whether patrons are seeking one of the documentaries in the *Nova* or *Nature* series, or an episode of *Star Trek*, they are most likely to search under the series title. The problem of allowing access to individual episodes will be discussed at a later point in this chapter.

One example of a true television *serial* is the bread-winning television serial drama, commonly referred to as the "soap opera," which is designed to be open-ended and continue indefinitely. Many of these programs have in fact been on-going for two generations. For a detailed discussion of this form of television, see M. Downing (1975). At the time of this writing, the only such television serial available on videotape of which we are aware is the original *Dark Shadows*. A bibliographic record for this program exists in the OCLC database, OCLC #22638447.

The nature of series

The AACR2R88 treats series as the last area in the body of the descriptive cataloging record, following the physical description, under rules 1.6, 2.6, 3.6, etc. Series are identified by ISSNs (International Standard Serial Numbers), rather than ISBNs (International Standard Book Numbers). Be careful not to confuse the ISSN with the numbering of the series itself. The latter places an individual item within the series, the former places the series within all existing series in the world of published materials.

True series are of two types: the "publisher's" series, and those for which an added entry, a *tracing,* would provide, in the words of AACR2R88, Rule 21.30L1, a "useful collocation" for the patron. The most significant characteristic of a publisher's series is that it has nothing to do with a book's content or authorship. It designates items which a publisher groups together because of identical *details of manufacture,* such as a book's being hard or soft cover. These series usually have what sound like brand names or other proper names — e.g., Modern Library, A Borzoi Book, Everyman's. For a discussion of the contrasts between series which should and should not be traced, see LC (1988).

The "useful collocation" series possesses a unity of subject matter or authorship, contains a relatively limited number of individual items, and has a collective title which clearly designates the unifying subject matter — e.g., Information Science Series, New Directions for Community Colleges.

In both types of series the individual members may stand alone and be cataloged separately. We recommend cataloging and classifying each item separately unless there is a pressing reason for placing all items in a series together.

Constructing the series statement

When cataloging an item in a series, record the title of the series following the last item in the physical description. Separate these two areas of the bibliographic record with a period-space-dash-space (. --). Enclose the series title in parentheses.

If you include a statement of responsibility relating to the series title, separate it from the title with a space-slash-space, as with the main title and statement of responsibility. In line with AACR2R88 Rule 1.6E1, record such a statement of responsibility only when you must do so in order to properly identify the item. One example is a multivolume work written entirely by one author, but treated as a series, such as *The Second World War,* by Sir Winston Spencer Churchill, having, as its first volume, *The Gathering Storm.* The series statement for this book appears below, with several other examples.

If the item has a number within the series, record this last, separated from the rest of the series statement by a space-semicolon-space. Record terms such as "volume," which appear on the item, using the proper abbreviations. Do not supply any such terms that do not appear on the item.

If you must supply the entire series statement from a source other than the item you are cataloging, enclose it in brackets *within* parentheses. The brackets do *not* replace the parentheses.

Following are several examples of series statements, each shown in relation to the physical description. These examples are shown as they would appear on a catalog card or an online public catalog display designed to simulate one.

> 123 p. ; 23 cm. -- (Research in library use ; 4)
> 425 p. : ill. ; 40 cm. -- ([Women today])
> 302 p. ; 28 cm. -- (Annual lecture series / Fels Academy)
> 400 p. ; 25 cm. -- (The Second World War / by Sir Winston Spencer Churchill ; v. 1)

For further discussion of series statements, see AACR2R88 sections 1.6, 2.6, 3.6 ... 12.6.

Series added entries

If a library makes added entries for series, it should do so only for those in the "useful collocation" category. In deciding whether or not to make a series added entry, assuming your library makes them at all, ask yourself these two questions: Will the patron ask for "all the books/ items in the X-Y-Z series" in order to find one particular item in it? and are patrons likely to make a request for "everything in the X-Y-Z series"? Overall, how likely is the patron to use the series title as an entry point? In the case of videorecordings, as we said earlier, the series title may be the only heading the patron is aware of. Remember that AACR2R88 Rule 21.30L states, "In case of doubt, make a series added entry."

The guidelines for making series added entries in the *Library of Congress Cataloging Service Bulletin No. 41* (summer 1988) are as follows:

Trace all series in the following categories:
   a) those published before the 20th century, including contemporary reprints of the same, without regard to the type of publisher;

b) those entered under a personal author whether these are serials, or multipart items, without regard to the type of publisher;

c) those published by any corporate body that is not a commercial publisher. (For this purpose, treat a university press as a non-commercial publisher);

d) those published by small or "alternative" presses, i.e., small printing or publishing firms that, although commercial, are devoted to special causes or to branches of literature usually without a mass audience.

Series statements in MARC records

In a MARC record, most series that you will encounter are placed in either the 440 or 490 field. The 440 field contains series which are traced exactly as they appear therein. The 490 field contains series which are not traced, or are traced differently, that is, the series added entry is not the same as the series title in the 490 field. The alternate form of a series traced differently is given in the appropriate 8xx field.

If you are using an online cataloging system, determine whether it automatically supplies parentheses, as does OCLC. If so, do not include them in the series statement. Be careful not to then end the statement with a period. The display appearing on either a screen or a printout will lack final punctuation, so you may be tempted to add some.

Items in several series

Remember the overarching principle of AACR2 cataloging is to describe the work in hand. If an item belongs to two or more series, give separate series statements, enclosing each in its own set of parentheses. In a MARC record, each series statement receives its own 440 or 490 field. In some cases, the relationship between the several series is not clear. In describing facsimiles, for example, give the data relating to the facsimile in all parts of the description except the note area, where data relating to the original work can be recorded. (See AACR2R88 rules 1.11C and 1.7B12.) Use notes to clarify confusing series information.

Notes

In cataloging various books and other items, you will often feel a need to include details which do not properly belong to the body of the entry, yet are important in the identification and differentiation of the item in question. The AACR2R88 permits you, as did all earlier cataloging rules, to include such information in *notes,* statements whose form and content are less rigidly prescribed than other elements of the bibliographic record. In a MARC record, these notes appear in fields 500–599.

Information in notes

Information you may wish to place into notes includes but is not limited to:

(1) The whole or partial contents of a work which is a collection.

(2) The fact that a work has a bibliography, and the inclusive pages of same.

(3) Additional details of the edition.

(4) Details of the original publication from which the work in hand was translated, reprinted, etc.

(5) Additional details of the physical description.

Statements containing these pieces of information are often too lengthy to be included in the various areas of the bibliographic description we have discussed up to this point. Furthermore, AACR2R88 simply does not permit the inclusion therein of some of this information. Notes may also be needed to justify an added entry. You must derive all added entries from data appearing in the description. If such data are not part of one of the other elements of the description, you must supply the information in a note. We shall provide illustrative examples of the above principles in the balance of this discussion.

An important restriction on notes

While notes allow you to include almost any piece of information about an item in its bibliographic description, they do *not* allow you to make purely subjective statements about that item. You may say that a book is "Printed in red ink in 72-point type." You may *not* say that the book is "Printed in garish and wasteful fashion, using red ink and 72-point type." You may wish to keep in mind, however, that you can tacitly convey opinions by the facts you choose to provide. Consider, for example, a note naming the director and screenwriter of a film, then saying that, "both men removed their names from association with the film before its release." This is both a tool you can use and a trap you can fall into; the cataloger responsible for the preceding note may or may not have intended to make a value judgment.

Recording of notes

Notes follow the series area, or, if there is no series area, the physical description. The most commonly used method of laying out notes is to present each in its own paragraph. The AACR2R88 also allows you to place all notes in a single paragraph, separating them with a period-space-dash-space. Take data for notes from any suitable source (AACR2R88 1.7A2). When each note in a record elaborates on some area of the bibliographic description, place the notes in the same order as the corresponding elements of the description (AACR2R88 1.7A3). If the note is a quotation from the work you are cataloging, use quotation marks. Do not abbreviate words within a quote unless they are actually abbreviated in the work. Notes must be expressed succinctly, using as few words as possible. Here are some examples:

> Translation of: Les misérables / V. Hugo.
> Attributed to: Christopher Marlowe.
> Maps on lining papers.
> Libretto only.
> "A textbook for junior high school students"--Pref.
> Popularly known as: The white album.

The last is an example of a note needed to justify an added entry. The work in question is the Beatles album commonly known as *The White Album* because of its jacket design. Since the only title appearing on the album is *The Beatles*, this is the title you would have to use in the body of the description. If you wanted to make a title added entry for *The White Album*, you would have to include the above note in your description.

Types of notes

The AACR2R88 lists 22 possible notes, and provides a prescribed order in which to give them. However, as directed by AACR2R88, place first any note which is of overriding importance. For instructions of notes, see AACR2R88 sections 1.7, 2.7, 3.7 . . . 12.7.

We have already listed some of the purposes notes serve. Here is a more complete list:

(1) To distinguish the particular edition of the work being cataloged

(2) To clarify authorship

(3) To note errata or imperfections

(4) To indicate when separate works are bound together

(5) To describe supplements

(6) To list contents

(7) To give Romanized titles of titles in a non–Roman script

(8) To supplement the physical description

(9) To indicate something of the nature and scope of the work

(10) To show the language of the work if the language of the text is not obvious

(11) To give a bibliographic history of the work

(12) In the case of facsimiles, to provide data about the original work.

While most of the examples of notes given in AACR2R88 are self-explanatory, we call your attention to several that may require further explanation of the example. Notice that rules 1.7B3, 1.7B4, and 1.7B5 all deal with problems concerning titles. Rule 1.7B3 concerns titles which you must take from a source other than the chief source of information; rules 1.7B4 and 1.7B5 concern titles other than the title proper appearing in the work. These rules contain various explanatory phrases which will help you explain the contradiction between the title proper and other titles which a patron is likely to see on the item. Do not confuse these examples with the "At head of title" note cited in Rule 2.7B6. The latter does not contain information about the source of the title. Rather, they usually contain phrases which may or may not be series statements, and, because their status is doubtful, should not appear in the series area.

We also call your attention to AACR2R88 rules 1.7B10 and 1.7B11. These notes allow you to include significant details which you may not place in the physical description area. For example, you can state, in the physical description area, that a book's illustrative matter includes 23 folded maps. However, you must state in a note that these maps are in a pocket. Also, you can say in a sound recording's physical description that it contains two 12-inch discs, but you must state in a note that they are made of white vinyl.

Rule 1.7B12 provides for commentary on series which cannot be included in the series area. This includes reference to earlier series related to the present one.

You may also make various local notes, some of which are exemplified in AACR2R88 Rule 1.7B20. A local note is one applying only to your library's copy of the item you are cataloging. In a MARC record, these are entered in either field 590 or field 599. One common type of local note states that the library's copy is imperfect in some way—e.g., missing pages. A local note can also indicate where, in the library, accompanying material is kept.

Not all 22 notes are pertinent to all media. You will note that in all chapters of AACR2R88 from Chapter 2 on, numbers are omitted from the sequence of rules describing possible notes. Rules in these chapters are also reworded to reflect the specific medium in question.

Title and notes for items containing several works

Items often appear which consist of several works. Such items may take several forms.

Items with a collective title

First, a group of works may have a collective title, a list of the works contained and continuous paging from first to last. Here, the collective title—which usually takes a form such as *Three Plays by Josephine Tey*—will serve as the title proper. The separate titles will be listed in a *contents note*, provided for in AACR2R88 Rule 1.7B18. The paging given in the physical description will then reflect the last page of the whole work. Here is what such a contents note would look like:

> Contents: Doubt and certainty / Sara Warner -- The truth of ambiguity / Herndon Sinclair -- Questions and answers / S.E. Trescott.

Note that the statement of responsibility *follows* the title and that there are no periods after each work listed.

In a MARC record, the contents note appears in field 505. If you are using OCLC, omit the initial "Contents:" since OCLC's print program supplies this.

Items lacking a collective title

Not all items containing several bibliographically independent works have a collective title. The title page, or analogy to it in the various nonbook media, may list only the titles of the individual works in question. You must follow a different procedure when cataloging such an item. The rules under AACR2R88 Rule 1.1G make a distinction between items of this type in which one work predominates and those in which no one work predominates. If one work predominates, use its title as the title proper and enter the other works in a note as shown above. If no one work predominates, record, as instructed in 1.1G3, all of the titles in the title area. Transcribe them in the order in which they appear on the title page and separate them with a space-semicolon-space, even if they are linked with connecting words. Here are some examples:

> A lodging for the night ; The Sire de Maletroit's daughter ; Dr. Jekyll and Mr. Hyde / Robert Louis Stevenson.
> Essays of Elia ; and, The life of Charles and Mary Lamb.
> Endless night ; A murder is announced ; What Mrs. McGinty saw.

You will find examples of contents notes in rules 1.7B18, 2.7B18, etc. By examining these, you can get a feeling for the type of contents note applicable to the various media.

The AACR2R88 provides another option for certain nonbook items lacking a collective title. In the case of cartographic materials (3.1G1), sound recordings (6.1G1), motion pictures and videorecordings (7.1G1), computer files (9.1G1), and microforms (11.1G1), you may make a separate description for each titled work. You must then connect these descriptions using *"With" notes*, covered in Rule x.7B21 of each chapter. While AACR2R88 Rule 2.7B21 allows the use of "With" notes in descriptions of books, the *Library of Congress Rule Interpretations* (1982–) direct you to use this option only with books that were issued as separate volumes and subsequently bound together.

The standard number and terms of availability area

The final element in an item's bibliographic description is the *standard number and terms of availability area*. This contains the International Standard Book Number (ISBN) which is recorded following the last item in the notes area. The number is recorded as it appears in the publication, preceded by "ISBN:".

Origins of the ISBN number, and of AACR2 punctuation

At the International Meeting of Cataloging Experts at Copenhagen in 1969, the following resolution was adopted:

> Efforts should be directed toward creating a system for the international exchange of information by which the standard bibliographic description of each publication would be established and distributed by a national agency in the country of origin. . . . The effectiveness of the system would depend upon the maximum standardization of the form and content of the bibliographic description [I.F.L.A., *I.S.B.D.(M), 1974*].

Accordingly, in 1974, the International Federation of Library Associations published two monographs, *I.S.B.D.(M)* and *I.S.B.D.(S)*, the *International Standard Bibliographic Description*s for monographs and serials respectively. Each of these attempts to "provide internationally accepted framework for the representation of descriptive information in bibliographic records" (*I.S.B.D.(M)* 1974, Foreword, page vii). The 1974 and 1975 revisions of the *Anglo-American Cataloging Rules* reflect ISBD form and practice, resulting in a complete change in the appearance of the catalog record, largely because of the strange-looking punctuation. Here is the explanation for these changes:

> It was necessary to find a way by which the different elements making up a description could be recognized, by the eye or by a machine, without the need to understand their content. The means adopted is a prescribed system of punctuation. Within any one of the main areas of the description, each prescribed punctuation mark is a signal showing the nature of the element which follows it. . . . For this reason, the I.S.B.D.(M) punctuation sometimes presents an unfamiliar appearance [*I.S.B.D.(M)*, Foreword, page vii].

In 1977, the International Federation of Library Associations and Institutions Working Group on the General International Standard Bibliographic Description published the *I.S.B.D.(G)* or *General International Standard Bibliographic Description: Annotated Text*. Page xxiv of AACR2R88 explains that Part I of AACR2 is closely related to *I.S.B.D.(G)*.

Recording the ISBN number

A typical ISBN number consists of four segments — the country segment, publisher segment, work segment, and check digit — each separated by a hyphen. Here is an example:

ISBN: 0-7131-1646-3

Publishers began using ISBN numbers about 1968, so that earlier works will not have such numbers. (Use of the ISSN — International Standard *Serial* Number — followed a year or so later.) Because inclusion of the ISBN number is voluntary, not every work will include one. In MARC records, the ISBN number is placed in field 020. The OCLC supplies the hyphens and "ISBN:" so that you do not enter these when working with that system.

If the book you are cataloging has an ISBN number, you will find it on the verso of the title page, and often on the back cover. As we noted above, you are to record the number following the last item in the notes area. Examples of ISBN numbers appear in Appendix I. The ISSN number, discussed earlier, performs the same function for serials as the ISBN number does for books.

Rules 1.8B1–1.8B4 of AACR2R88 describe the recording of the ISBN number, including examples of multiple or incorrect numbers. If an item contains identification numbers other than internationally agreed upon standard numbers, give these in a note.

Optionally (Rule 1.8D1), you may give the terms on which the item is available — e.g., price, rental instructions, etc. Since such terms may change, exercise discretion in the use of this option.

Analytics

In reading the foregoing discussion of serials, series, multipart items, and works contained within one physical unit, you have probably deduced that you cannot describe certain items by means of a single bibliographic record without losing considerable information. A record for *Collected Works of Edgar Allan Poe* will not help the high school student who has been assigned to read "The Casque of Amontillado" unless it has the title of that story as an access point. Special issues of serials — for example, monographic supplements dealing with special subjects — may stand unused because the patron has no convenient way of finding out that such issues exist. Many sound recordings exist that consist of several pieces by different composers. See the *Music of Our Time* examples in Chapter 12, on nonbook materials.

The MARC records and online catalogs now make it possible to provide sufficient added entries to solve many of these problems. However, even MARC records have their limits, and the inclusion of numerous added entries can be cumbersome. Furthermore, an added entry cannot provide information such as the running time of a piece of music, or the physical description of a special issue of a serial.

Therefore, *analytics*, the preparation of a bibliographic description for a part of a larger item, may be advisable. There are two possible ways to effect analysis of a separate part: by augmenting the description of the larger item, or by creating a separate bibliographic record for the part.

Augmenting the bibliographic description

This first method has the drawback of providing a limited amount of information about the part, but would probably be sufficient for an item such as the *Collected Works of Edgar Allan Poe* mentioned above. In this case, you would make an *analytical added entry* for each story. You would also have to make a contents note to justify each such entry; remember that any added entry must be derived from data in the description.

According to AACR2R88 rules 13.2A and 21.30M, the basis of an analytical added entry must be the element that would have been the main entry for the part had it been cataloged separately. If "The Casque of Amontillado" had been cataloged separately, it would have been entered under the official form of Poe's name. (We have previously discussed the official form of an author's name in our chapter on personal name authority control.) Therefore, you must make a *name–title* added entry, as follows:

> Poe, Edgar Allan, 1809–1849. The casque of Amontillado.

In a MARC record, such an entry is placed in field 700, the same field as for an author added entry. The title is placed in ‡t. The MARC version of the above added entry would be as follows:

> Poe, Edgar Allan, ‡d 1809–1849. ‡t The casque of Amontillado.

Creating a separate description

The second method, that of preparing a separate description for the part, is known as an *"In" analytic*, and is described in AACR2R88

Section 13.5. The description of the part is entered under the same main entry it would be if it were a complete unit. If the part is the work of one author, it is entered under the official form of that author's name. The body of an analytic entry's description must contain the following elements, here quoted from AACR2R88, Rule 13.5A:

> title proper, other title information, statements of responsibility
> edition
> numeric or other designation (in the case of a serial)
> publication, distribution, etc., details
> extent and specific material designation (when appropriate, in terms of its physical position within the whole item)
> other physical details
> dimensions
> notes

Citation of the whole item, following the description of the part analyzed, begins with *In* (italicized or underlined) and contains, according to AACR2R88 Rule 13.5A:

> name and/or uniform title heading (see Part II) of the whole item, if appropriate
> title proper
> statement(s) of responsibility when necessary for identification
> edition statement
> numeric or other designation (of a serial) or publication details (of a monographic item)

The examples of *"In"* analytics given in AACR2R88 Rule 13.5A and elsewhere give the basic structure of the body of an analytical entry' description but do not exemplify the *entry* for the part being analyzed. Remember that the heading for an *"In"* analytic must be the same official form of an author's name used for any other bibliographic record. (See AACR2R88 Rule 21.30M1.)

While we will be discussing nonbook materials in detail in a later chapter, we want to encourage you at this point to perform analytics on such items as the sound recordings in the *Music of Our Time* series. Otherwise, the individual selections may remain unavailable.

At this point, we have covered all of the essentials of bibliographic description. Having done so, we wish to discuss briefly an issue, regarding the topic of description, which you are likely to encounter when using an online cataloging system.

Use of pre-AACR2 online records in their original form

An online shared cataloging system which was in existence before 1978 will contain many pre-AACR2 records. In fact, there is a MARC field — appearing as "Desc:" in the fixed field portion of an OCLC display — which specifies the rules under which the cataloging was done. It is currently an accepted practice to maintain the descriptive portions of these pre-AACR2 records in the older form, updating only the access points to AACR2.

The OCLC manuals for various record formats acknowledge this practice with discussions of pre-AACR2 formatting. For example, the discussion of the 490 field includes the statement that, in a pre-AACR2 record, ‡x will follow, rather than the precede, ‡v. There are also discussions of the different print constants the OCLC system will supply for AACR2 and pre-ACCR2 records.

The main argument made in favor in this practice is that the time and effort involved in upgrading all of the older records to AACR2 would be prohibitive. It is further argued that library patrons are not overly concerned about what marks of punctuation appear at a given point in a bibliographic description.

We wish to offer two counterarguments. First, the consistent use of punctuation across all records in a catalog *is* important to patrons because, as stated in the above quote from *I.S.B.D.(M)*, it enables them to recognize all parts of a record even if the information therein is somehow confusing. Consider the following:

New York : St. Martin's Press, 1988.
Berlin ; New York : Springer-Verlag, 1978.
London : Whitefield, 1948.
Moylan : Cornerville, 1990.

Anyone familiar with AACR2 punctuation can tell instantly that, in the third example, Whitefield is the name of a publisher rather than a place, because it is preceded by ":" rather than ";". In the fourth example, the AACR2 punctuation lets you know immediately that Moylan — a small suburb of Philadelphia — is a place, while Cornerville is a publisher. Furthermore, if the entire imprint of a bibliographic record is in Yiddish or Chinese, it is still obvious which words denote the place of publication and which denote the publisher.

But there is another argument which concerns the time a library supposedly saves by not upgrading these records to AACR2. To evaluate and edit pre–AACR2 records properly, a cataloger must be familiar with the rules used to create them. This means that a cataloger required to work with older records in their original form must learn the original 1967 rules and the interim 1974 rules in addition to the current ones. The time needed to learn and apply all three sets of rules — and to deal with the resulting negative reinforcement — would seem to far exceed that needed to upgrade the older records, since much of the editing involved would require little thought, consisting mainly of the systematic replacement of one item with another.

Furthermore, there are some cataloging problems whose solutions are not as clear-cut under the old rules. A record having any of these problems could probably be processed more quickly and with less chance of errors if it could be upgraded to AACR2.

Up to this point, we have been dealing with the *distinction between* all items in a library's collection. The next seven chapters of this book, dealing with subject analysis and the Dewey and Library of Congress classification schemes, will deal with the *relationships among* these items.

Review questions for Chapter 4

1. Find an example of a series you consider to be a "useful colloca-tion" series. Why do you think this series should be traced?

2. Why do the bibliographic details appearing in notes not appear in the body of the entry?

3. In what way is the ISBN number useful as an element of the bib-liographic description?

4. How does ISBD punctuation clarify the descriptive content of a bibliographic description?

5. What is the function of an analytical entry?

Sources cited and suggestions for further reading or study

Anglo-American Cataloguing Rules, 2nd ed., 1988 revision, edited by Michael Gorman and Paul W. Winkler. Ottawa: Canadian Library Association; Chicago: American Library Association, 1988.
Downing, Mildred Harlow. *The World of Daytime Television Serial Drama.* Disserta-tion, Ph.D. Philadelphia: University of Pennsylvania, 1974.

International Federation of Library Associations. *ISBD(G): International Standard Bibliographic Description,* annotated text prepared by the Working Group on the General International Standard Bibliographic Description set up by the IFLA Committee on Cataloguing. London: IFLA International Office for UBC, 1977.

_____. *ISBD(M): International Standard Bibliographic Description for Monographic Publications,* 1st standard ed. London: IFLA Committee on Cataloguing, 1974.

Library of Congress. *Cataloging Service Bulletin,* Robert M. Hiatt, ed. 41 (Summer 1988).

Library of Congress Rule Interpretations for AACR2: A Cumulation from Cataloging Service Bulletin Numbers 11–, compiled by Lois Lindberg, Alan Boyd, and Elaine Druesedow. Oberlin, Ohio: Oberlin College Library, 1982–.

OCLC. *Books Format,* 3rd ed. Dublin, Ohio: OCLC, 1986–.

5

Subject Analysis and the Use of a Controlled Vocabulary

Previous chapters have dealt with the *identification* of a work — i.e., how to describe an item so that it can be differentiated from others with which it might be confused. We have discussed the reasons for and methods of selecting key elements such as author, title, date, physical description, identifying numbers, that will enable the patron or user to find the *individual* work desired. The object of providing access points to a standardized bibliographic description is to single out one particular item from the rest of the collection, no matter how it is (reasonably) sought.

Frequently however, the patron or user wants not a particular work but all works dealing with a particular *subject*. Going to the card or online catalog, the user hopes to retrieve a group of items collocated with respect to their common subject content. This grouping of works together on the basis of some shared likeness involves *categorization*, which may be thought of as complementary to identification.

You may accomplish categorization by two distinct operations — subject analysis and classification. The latter involves attaching to each item in the collection a symbol, termed a "call number," designed to best represent the subject of the item as a whole. This call number will designate a specific location in a formal representational scheme. We shall discuss the two formal American classification schemes in common usage, the Dewey Decimal and Library of Congress classification systems, in the several chapters following.

This chapter will deal with the general problem of subject analysis and categorization and with the more pragmatic task of expressing a work's subject content verbally, in words or phrases chosen from a standard list of subject terms.

Subject analysis, categorization and classification

Determination of a work's subject content will be one of your most difficult tasks as a cataloger. A shared online cataloging system, such as OCLC, can assist you but does not eliminate the need for subject analysis; although a record online may include subject terms, you must determine whether these are in fact the most appropriate choices for the work in question.

Whether you must assign subject terms or evaluate those already attached to a record, you will face four problems: (1) Your limited acquaintance with the whole of human knowledge. (2) The difficulty of determining the author's intent. (3) The fact that a work may have several subjects. (4) The impossibility of determining from what point of view the *user* may approach the work.

You should also take care to distinguish between the description of a work's *content* and its *form* — between what the work is *about* and what the work *is*. Past practice required that subject terms designate only content; the classifier was instructed to assign *no* subject headings to works which could be described only in terms of form — which could not be said to be about something. For example, assigning the heading "String quartets" to *Bartok's String Quartet no. 4* was prohibited, as this work was not *about* string quartets. Likewise, a collection of short stories could not receive the heading "Short stories," and *Gone with the Wind* could not receive the heading:

United States — History — Civil War, 1861–1865 — Fiction.

("United States — History — Civil War, 1861–1865" alone would also be incorrect because it fails to distinguish the novel from nonficton works on the Civil War.)

However, the Library of Congress now does assign these form headings, thus sanctioning their use by other libraries. A score for a Mozart violin-and-piano sonata which includes the violin part may now receive the heading:

Sonatas (Violin and piano) — Scores and parts.

Prime Evil: New Stories by the Masters of Modern Horror — OCLC #17260145 — is assigned the subject headings:

> Horror tales, American.
> Horror tales, English.

A Wodehouse Bestiary, a collection of animal-related short stories by P.G. Wodehouse, may receive the heading:

> Animals — Fiction.

Finally, *Gone with the Wind* may now receive the heading:

> United States — History — Civil War, 1861–1865 — Fiction.

These form headings appear in the same MARC fields and in the same position on catalog cards as true subject headings.

We agree that form headings are useful because they provide additional search possibilities. For example, a music student studying the evolution of the piano sonata can retrieve all musical works in that genre regardless of composer. Someone interested in stories about a certain topic can search under:

> [Topic] — Fiction.

There is, however a problem with form headings as they now exist — which is also the reason that form headings were once illegal. If you search under "Horror tales, American," you will find collections of horror tales interfiled with books about the American horror story. It is, at present, impossible to perform a search in which this heading designates *either* a work's form, *or* its content.

We would like to suggest a solution. Perhaps form headings could receive their own fields in MARC records, and appear in a separate list on catalog cards. If form headings were given their own category, patrons could enjoy the benefits they provide without the problem which they now present.

Although form headings are no longer incorrect, you should locate some type of Library of Congress sanction for any you wish to use. Such a sanction might be of use in establishing the same type of heading in a similar situation, or instructions in one of the Library of Congress publications we shall discuss.

This chapter will focus on true subject headings — those which designate a work's *content*. We shall deal with:

(1) The methods of determining the subject of a book.

(2) The problem of deciding among several possible pertinent subjects.

(3) The correct use of a controlled vocabulary, usually termed a "subject heading list," or "thesaurus."

While our discussion will emphasize general principles, we shall include examples from a specific subject heading list when these serve to illustrate a point. Since the Library of Congress is generally regarded as the final authority on cataloging and classification practices, we shall use the most recent print version of its list, the 14th edition (1991).

Attempts to classify human thought, as noted in Chapter 1, are as old as thought itself (Richardson 1964, 1930). Subject analysis is a discipline which can be approached from several points of view, ranging from purely theoretical, as represented by Aristotle and other philosophers, through the hundreds of formal classification schemes developed over the centuries (Richardson 1964, 1930), down to the computer-oriented endeavors of those such as Foskett (1982) and Harris (1970), and many others.

There are certain pragmatic problems to solve, or tasks to perform, in undertaking the analysis and description of the subject content of any work. The first of these tasks is the actual determination of the work's subject — without actually reading the entire book, watching the entire film, etc., which you will not have time to do for every item you handle. While you may not be able entirely to determine a work's content without reading or watching or listening to all of it, you can approximate this content using certain careful procedures. The second task is the assignment of descriptive subject headings so the work can be retrieved by a subject search either online or through an alphabetical arrangement of subject terms.

Classification through a formal scheme, such as the Dewey Decimal or Library of Congress system, serves a purpose reciprocal to the assignment of subject terms. The formal scheme provides the collection with a systematic arrangement of items according to subject and form but, in American libraries, relegates the individual work to a fixed position in the collection, since each item can have only one call number. Subject headings are needed to make the work accessible from several points of view. Also, since subject headings consist of words, they can be interfiled alphabetically with other elements of bibliographic description. The syndetic structure of a subject headings list allows for cross references, so that the user may be directed to various aspects of the same subject.

The following instructions and comments are intended to aid you in the completion of practical everyday tasks, rather than to provide a consideration of the organization of knowledge itself. If you want to further explore the latter topic, consult the wealth of literature dealing with the determination of subject matter in the several information-handling professions. A provocative beginning might be Bliss' *Organizations of Knowledge and the System of the Sciences* (1929).

Determining subject content from a selective examination of the item

Ideally, a document will have an informative title, such as *The History of Nuclear Physics*, which will immediately suggest to you possible subject headings. Some type of ascription to the author, such as "Chairman, Department of Parapsychology," will also suggest subject areas. Specifically, you should examine the following portions of a book for indications of subject content:

(1) The dust jacket, if the work is new. Here the publisher, in order to sell the work, may give biographical information about the author, some history of the background of a work's development, a listing of other works in the same area or informative quotations from reviews. However, in evaluating the accuracy of information from the dust jacket, keep it in mind that much of its purpose is to make the book attractive to a potential purchaser.

(2) Any page preceding the title page containing a series title and works subsumed thereunder. For example, a series entitled *Computer Applications in Library and Information Science* will contain works in an area of content of which the book being cataloged represents one particular facet.

(3) The title page. (a) At the head of the title may be either a series statement or some other identifying phrase that will assist you in circumscribing the book's content. (b) The publisher. Certain publishers are identified with, for example, medicine, art, bibliography, etc. (c) The title itself, which, as stated above, will ideally be definitive. (d) The author's name, which may be notable in his or her field, or the list of titles and honors which follow the name, indicating the author's profession or area of expertise. (e) Coauthors, editors, compilers, corporate authors — all persons other than the chief author whose names may suggest to you areas of subject specialization.

(4) The verso of the title page, which may list former editions or contain other pertinent information. Also, most new books will have Library of Congress *Cataloging-in-Publication* (CIP) data here. This takes the form of a skeleton catalog record which lacks some descriptive data, but always includes a call number and subject headings.

(5) The table of contents. The list of issues named therein may suggest subject content to you.

(6) Preliminary portions of the work, such as preface, foreword or the like, in which the author usually states the purpose and scope of the work.

(7) The introductory chapter, in which the author may outline all of the materials to be covered in succeeding portions of the book.

(8) The final chapter, or "Summary," in which some authors present in condensed form all of the ideas developed in the text as a whole.

(9) Appendices, indexes, and other supplementary material, the details of which may allow you to grasp the compass of the material covered.

(10) Any single chapter whose content may be familiar to you, from which you may infer some idea as to the subject matter of the rest of the text.

For more detailed discussion of what has been called "Reading a book technically," you read a standard text such as that of Mann (1943).

We advise you to seek expert help when none of the above-listed sources of information clearly indicate the subject content of the work you are cataloging. For many works, when the specialist is not available or cannot place the book within the existing classification scheme, you must search external sources, such as reviews, bibliographies, encyclopedias, etc. If even these provide no information, you may be forced to accept the subject headings contained in whatever online bibliographic record exists for the item.

Works with more than one subject: choice of
topic for a call number, order of subject headings

Many works exist which discuss two, several, or many subjects. In American libraries, it is the standard practice to employ either the Dewey Decimal or Library of Congress Classification, both of which schemes require that the book be assigned a location symbol, or call number, representing one position on the shelf only. Therefore, you should assign a call number to the work that will allow the greatest number of users access to the material, assuming they "read" the shelves for information.

We shall discuss the actual mechanics of building Dewey Decimal and Library of Congress call numbers in the chapters following. Our discussion there will assume that you have chosen the topic which the call number must represent. However, the procedure for making that choice is best discussed here, since it involves judgments about an item's content, and is independent of any specific classification system. Here are some guidelines for making this choice:

(1) Classify a work covering two or more interrelated subjects with the one receiving the most emphasis. Often, you can determine emphasis from the amount of space given to each subject. However, there are many cases in which the author's purpose decides the question of emphasis. Merrill (1954) suggests that a work treating of two factors be classed "under the subject influenced or acted upon." For example, a work discussing factory workers' decreased efficiency due to depression would receive a call number denoting factory workers. A work on the use of psychotherapy to treat depression would be classed under depression.

(2) Classify a work dealing with two or more unrelated subjects with that which predominates.

(3) If, in a work falling into Category 2, no one subject predominates, class the work with the subject which comes first in the schedules—i.e., which comes first in the sequence of number and or letters which makes up the classification system. You will more fully understand the meaning of this statement after reading the chapters, following this one, on the Dewey Decimal and the Library of Congress classification systems. This point is also discussed in the *Dewey Decimal Classification*, 20th edition (v. 1, p. xxxi).

(4) A book on three or more subjects, all of which are subdivisions of a broader subject, should be classed with the broader subject.

(5) Many works, consisting chiefly of *belles lettres* or works of art, have no real subject content. In this case, classification is by literary or artistic form. We shall discuss this point further in relation to the Dewey Decimal and Library of Congress classification systems, and the cataloging of nonbook materials.

You must then add words or phrases describing the work's content, *subject headings* in other words, to the catalog record. You must include enough of these to allow access from all possible points of view.

From the above discussion, it should be apparent that not all subject headings included will name topics or aspects of topics denoted by the call number. The subject headings must be placed in a sequence which will properly reflect the work's emphasis or purpose. This order, given the above criteria for choosing a call number, involves beginning the list of headings with one corresponding most closely to the call number. If several headings are needed to encompass the call number's meaning, place these headings first in the sequence.

The above paragraph leads to the issue of how and where you obtain valid subject headings. That is the focus of the next section.

Use of a controlled vocabulary

You may not simply create subject headings at will, using whatever words or phrases you feel best describe the content of the item in question. Such a practice would make any catalog inefficient, if not useless, since there does not exist a one-to-one correspondence between words or phrases and objects or concepts. An establishment which offers hair styling, manicures, etc., may be called a beauty *shop*, beauty *parlor*, or beauty *salon*. The word "soda" can refer to carbonated beverages, sodium bicarbonate or any of several other items, depending on what part of the United States you come from. Words such as "composition" and "keyboards" have multiple meanings having nothing to do with regional dialects.

To avoid problems such as are suggested above, you must make use of a list of valid and invalid subject headings—a list which library patrons are directed to use when performing subject searches. The list itself is usually termed a *subject heading list* or *thesaurus*. The term *controlled vocabulary* refers to the requirement that classifiers and patrons use such a list.

A controlled vocabulary assures that subject headings will be assigned in a consistent manner, so that all works treating the same subject will be found at one place in the catalog, and that usable terms will have a uniform structure. The best subject heading lists provide references among terms by means of syndetic structure (see Chapter 3 for a definition of this term). The act of instituting and maintaining a controlled vocabulary constitutes *subject authority control* analogous to the personal name authority control discussed in Chapter 3.

Added entry tracings on catalog cards—and screen displays designed to simulate them—precede those for author, title, etc., and are numbered with Arabic numerals. Cards intended to provide subject access in a manual catalog have the subject heading printed at the top in all upper-case letters. (When cards were typed by hand, these headings sometimes appeared in red ink.) In a MARC record, the topical subject headings we are discussing in this chapter are tagged 650—as are the form headings we discussed at the beginnings of this chapter. Various types of proper names and titles used as subject headings receive other 6xx tags.

The term "thesaurus" usually refers to a controlled vocabulary within a circumscribed subject field and is most often used with nonconventional systems of organizing materials or information. These thesauri are syndetic structures that attempt to perform for the field in question the same function that conventional subject heading lists serve for the whole body of recorded knowledge. You should become familiar with thesauri and thesaurus building and are referred for more information to such a source as Soergel (1974).

The two most commonly used subject heading lists in American libraries today are Sears (1991) and Library of Congress (1991). For reasons given earlier, we shall use the latter, hereafter referred to as LCSH, to illustrate the organization and features of a subject heading list. We shall present our discussion of the components of an authoritative subject headings list in outline form. We are doing this to give you an accurate representation of the manner in which some of these components are subsumed under others. To aid you in following our discussion, we shall first present the entire outline without any elaboration.

    I. Alphabetic list of all valid and invalid subject headings.
      a. Valid headings in boldface type.
        1. Scope notes.
        2. Parenthetic qualifiers.
        3. Subdivisions.
          (A) Valid under specific heading only.—(B) Valid under specific category of headings only.—(C) Free-floating.
            a.) Historical.
            b.) Geographical.
            c.) Topical.
            d.) Form.
      b. Invalid headings in lightface type.
        1. Parenthetic qualifiers.
        2. Subdivisions.

II. A set of possible relationships among all terms included in I above, together with a symbol representing each.

    a. USE.

    b. UF — "Use for."

    c. BT — "Broader term."

    d. NT — "Narrower term."

    e. RT — "Related term."

    f. SA — "See also."

III. Exhaustive introduction.

    a. General discussion of allowable practices.

    b. List of categories of terms which constitute valid headings even if not listed in LCSH.

    c. List of free-floating subdivisions.

    d. Lists of subdivisions which the classifier may attach only to designated categories of valid headings.

    e. List of categories of headings whose valid subdivisions appear under a representative heading in the subject heading list.

    f. List of categories of terms which constitute valid subdivisions even if not given as such.

Here is the outline once again, with a discussion of each topic and subtopic included.

I. Alphabetic list of all valid and invalid subject headings

The LCSH interfiles usable and nonusable headings in one alphabetic list. This is because anyone who needs to consult the list must begin with conjecture. The existing arrangement eliminates any need to search through two lists. The Library of Congress attempts to anticipate all suppositions as to what the correct term for an object or concept might be; it therefore incorporates an extensive list of invalid headings into LCSH.

Ia. Valid headings in boldface type

All terms appearing in LCSH in boldface type are valid headings. Since all invalid terms include references to usable ones, there is little need to learn the rationale behind LC's choice of valid headings. Furthermore, you will find numerous exceptions to any rules we might provide. However, the ability to deduce the correct heading in at least some cases can save both time and frustration. Therefore, we offer the following *guidelines*:

• Select the most formal term which is still lay English. Use

> Frankfurters.

rather than

> Hot dogs.

but use

> Orchids.

rather than

> Orchidaceae.

• Prefer a neutral or complimentary term to a pejorative one. Use

> Developing countries.

rather than

> Underdeveloped countries.

and use

> Alcoholics.

rather than

> Drunkards.

• If a specific term for the topic in question exists, prefer it over a modified broader term. Use:

> Afro-Americans.

rather than

> Blacks — United States.

and use

> Microcomputers.

instead of

> Personal computers.

• Prefer the plural of a term denoting a tangible object or entity. Such terms given in the singular — e.g. "Man," "Woman," "Planet," "University" — tend to denote abstractions or suggest the *study of* the named object or entity. The names of musical instruments constitute an exception;

these appear in the singular, since they frequently denote the discipline of playing the instrument.

• When attempting to locate an adjective-noun phrase, search first under the direct order unless the qualifying adjective is a nationality. Use

> Complex compounds.

rather than

> Compounds, Complex.

but use

> Horror tales, American.

rather than

> American horror tales.

Be prepared, however, to discover that the term you wish to locate is an exception.

The LCSH uses three auxiliary devices to further clarify or specify the meaning of many valid terms. These are:

Ia1. Scope notes — verbal descriptions of the type of works to be classed under the heading in question. Most of these serve to create boundaries among sets of similar headings; you are instructed to use:

> Drama.

for works dealing with drama as a literary form, to use:

> Theater.

for the performance of drama on the stage, and:

> Theaters.

for the subject of actual performance facilities. Scope notes are also used purely to define a heading the meaning of which may not be readily apparent. Under:

> Compound offenses.

is a description of the particular aspect of continental European law this heading denotes.

Ia2. Parenthetic qualifiers — words or phrases appearing in parentheses following the heading. Like scope notes, these are used to clarify both ambiguous terms:

> Composition (Language arts)
> Composition (Law)
> Composition (Music)
> Composition (Photography)
> Composition (Roman law)

and esoteric or specialized terms:

> CP/M (Computer operating system)
> Houdans (Poultry)

Ia3. Subdivisions—words or phrases appended to a subject heading in order to restrict its meaning. A string of two or more subdivisions may be added to any heading. On catalog cards, subdivisions are separated from headings and each other by dashes without intervening spaces:

> Music—United States—History—20th century—Study and teaching.

In a MARC record, each subdivision is placed in its own subfield, indicated by the "‡" symbol followed by a lowercase letter. The proper MARC format for the above heading is:

> Music ‡z United States ‡x History ‡y 20th century ‡x Study and teaching.

Since each subdivision is understood to modify what immediately precedes it, you must take care to place subdivisions in the correct order. The above heading refers to the study and teaching of the portion of American music history running from 1900 to the present. The heading:

> Music—United States—Study and teaching—History—20th century.

refers to the history, from 1900 to the present, of the teaching of all aspects of American music—without regard to where the teaching is done.

A subdivision may be valid (A) under a specific heading only, (B) under a specific category of headings only, or (C) under any heading, provided the combination makes logical sense. Headings in Group C are termed *free-floating*. A subdivision falling into any of the three preceding categories can be any of the following types, each of which is given with its MARC subfield code:

(Ia3a) Historical — ‡y.

Subdivisions in this category name a period of time. They can designate a century, a range of years, or a named historical period, such as a war or monarch's reign. Subdivisions denoting a named historical period are usually valid only with a specific heading. Historical subdivisions are frequently, but not always, used in conjunction with the subdivision "History."

(Ia3b) Geographical — ‡z.

Many headings in LCSH are designated "(May Subd Geog)," an abbreviation for "May subdivide geographically." You may append names of countries, states, cities, and other geographical or political regions to such headings as subdivisions. With some important exceptions, such as the states of the United States, all political divisions which are portions of a country must be preceded by that country's name — for instance

> Librarians — Florida.

but

> Librarians — Mexico — Mexico City.

When a place name is one of several subdivisions, it must come first unless one of the other subdivisions may be further subdivided by place. A list of these subdivisions appears in the *Subject Cataloging Manual* discussed below.

(Ia3c) Topical — ‡x.

These subdivisions further define a subject heading's topic — for example

> Music — Theory.
> Orchestral music — Analysis, appreciation.

(Ia3d) Form — ‡x.

This category lacks its own subfield code because we, not the Library of Congress, created it. It includes subdivisions such as "Bibliography," when they denote the nature of an item rather than its content. Under current practice, these may be used to indicate the form of the item being cataloged. For example, LC's cataloging of *Horror Literature*, an annotated bibliography published by R.R. Bowker — OCLC #7552224 — includes the heading:

> Horror tales, American — Bibliography.

As we stated earlier, the Library of Congress also assigns headings of the type:

> [Topic] — Fiction.

to certain works of fiction. Be advised, however, that there are some subdivisions which may only be used topically. For example:

> [Topic] — Textbooks.

may be used only for works *about textbooks on* the subject denoted by "[Topic]."

Ib. Invalid headings in lightface type.

These are always accompanied by a reference to one or more valid headings. Invalid headings also make use of two of the auxiliary devices we discussed under valid headings.

Ib1. Parenthetic qualifiers. After encountering parenthetic qualifiers, you will likely begin including them in conjectural headings. In anticipation of this, the Library of Congress includes in its list many invalid uses of qualifiers. For example, LCSH refers a user from

> Twisters (Textile machinery)

to

> Twisting machines (Textile machinery)

and from

> Twisters (Tornadoes)

to

> Tornadoes.

Ib2. Subdivisions. The rationale for these is the same as for parenthetic qualifiers. By way of example here, the user is referred from

> Blacks — United States.

to

> Afro-Americans.

and from

> Alcoholism — Patients.

to

> Alcoholics.

II. A set of possible relationships among all terms included in I above, together with a symbol representing each

These allow the user to move from invalid to valid terms, or from one valid term to another which might be more appropriate or provide additional information. The 12th edition of LCSH was the first print version to use the symbols discussed below.

IIa. USE

This symbol refers the user from an invalid to a valid heading.

>Homilies
>>USE Sermons
>
>Orchidaceae
>>USE Orchids

IIb. UF

Meaning "Use for," this symbol precedes the list of invalid headings from which the user is referred to the valid heading in question.

>Homing pigeons
>>UF Carrier pigeons
>>>Homers (Birds)
>>>Racing pigeons
>
>Orchids
>>UF Orchidaceae

IIc. BT

Meaning "Broader term," this symbol refers the user from a valid heading denoting a tangible or intangible item to a valid heading naming a category into which that item falls.

>Gilles de la Tourette's syndrome
>>BT Syndromes
>
>Orchestral music
>>BT Instrumental music
>>>Orchestra

IId. NT

Meaning "Narrower term," this symbol refers the user from a valid heading naming a category to a valid heading naming a tangible or intangible item falling into that category.

> Orchestral music
>   NT String-orchestra music
> Hounds
>   NT Basset hound
>   [Another exception to the "plurals" rule]

IIe. RT

Meaning "Related term," this symbol refers the user from a valid heading to an equally specific valid heading having a close relationship to it.

> Homonyms
>   RT Puns and punning
> Hours of labor
>   RT Weekly rest-day

IIf. SA

Meaning "See also," this term refers the user from a valid heading to a category of valid headings.

> Homonyms
>   SA subdivision Homonyms under names of languages
> Orchestral music
>   SA [Solo instrument(s)] with orchestra

(Most of the subject headings used in the above examples actually appear in LCSH with extensive lists of broader or narrower terms. We have selected the ones which we feel best illustrate the point in question.)

III. Exhaustive introduction

The most complete and most recent introduction published as an actual part of LCSH appeared with the eighth edition (1975). This introduction was subsequently published separately, rather than being included in each new edition of LCSH. The Library of Congress now publishes a *Subject Cataloging Manual*, a collection of its printed instructions to its subject catalogers. The manual and the material found at the beginning of the 14th edition constitute the most current introduction available.

IIIa. General discussion of allowable practices

This includes the points we have discussed — punctuation, order of headings, order of subdivisions, etc. — along with others which are beyond the scope of this introductory textbook.

IIIb. List of categories of terms which constitute valid headings even if not listed in LCSH

Allowing a user to create any heading not explicitly authorized by the list might seem to undermine the basic goal of a controlled vocabulary. There is little danger, however, if the terms in question already have a prescribed form. Furthermore, there are certain categories of terms which must be used as headings but would fill volumes by themselves. Both statements above apply to proper names — of persons, geographical locations, etc. — which form the major portion of allowable headings not printed in LCSH. When using a proper name as a subject heading, you must give it in its official form, which you determine by performing authority work.

IIIc. List of free-floating subdivisions

The most current list of these appears in the *Subject Cataloging Manual*. The manual also lists restrictions applying to certain subdivisions.

IIId. Lists of subdivisions which the classifier may attach only to designated categories of valid headings

A list of this type applies to a certain category of headings, such as literary authors. The list appears both in the manual, under the name of the category, and in LCSH itself, under a heading within that category — William Shakespeare, in this case. Since the subdivisions on these lists apply to a category of headings, some of them may not be appropriate for the particular representative heading under which they appear in LCSH. For example, some of the subdivisions listed under Shakespeare may not be applicable to Shakespeare. Rather, they are generally applicable to literary authors, and are listed under Shakespeare because that is where all subdivisions applying to literary authors are listed.

IIIe. List of categories of headings whose valid subdivisions appear under a representative heading in the subject heading list

This consists essentially of that portion of the manual's table of contents covering the lists discussed above. The title for each of these lists in the manual is the name of the category, so that the table of contents lists these categories.

IIIf. List of categories of terms which constitute valid subdivisions even if not given as such.

The most important category here is that of place names — both geographical and political units. Other subdivisions of this type are discussed in the manual or appear in certain "SA" references. (See "Homonyms" under IIf above.)

To employ a subject heading list properly, you should become thoroughly familiar with its contents and instructions. Begin by studying the usable and nonusable headings until you can clearly distinguish between the two. Practice following through on all of the various types of cross-references — see II pages 83–84 — in order to get a feel for the syndetic structure of the list as a whole.

You should then study in detail the general introductory material. In the case of LCSH, read the entire introduction to the 14th edition and the earlier, more general portions of the *Subject Cataloging Manual* before proceeding. Consult those portions of the manual dealing extensively with specific issues as the need arises. The importance of a careful study of the explanatory introduction cannot be overemphasized.

Common subject cataloging errors

We must now caution you against some common mistakes. To begin with, subject lists are designed not to match exactly but to *supplement* classification schemes. Here are five often-occurring errors.

(1) Attempting to fit a classification number — i.e., a Dewey or LC call number — into a subject heading framework, rather than the other way around. Assign the call number first, then choose subject headings to match it.

(2) Assigning too many subject headings. Past a point, choose two or three broader headings which cover all of the narrower topics. It is important to avoid conveying the impression that a work deals *extensively* with several topics which it in fact only touches on.

(3) Assigning form headings where they are not allowed. Although the Library of Congress now uses form headings, assigning them to items such as musical and literary works, you should only use them where an instruction or precedent justifies them.

(4) Assigning too few subject headings, denying access to a topic that does not constitute the major portion of the work but is still of significance and potential interest to the user.

(5) Assigning headings which are too broad, frequently in addition to specific headings which describe the work exactly.

This last is a very common mistake. No heading should be broader than the topic of the book, as this gives a false impression of the book's content. If a book on cats receives the subject heading:

Mammals

this implies that the book either covers all mammals — dogs, wolves, bats, etc. — or discusses the general characteristics of mammals — being warm-blooded, suckling their young, etc. In fact, the book discusses cats and only cats.

The rationale often given for this mistake is that it makes the book accessible to the patron who searches under the broad term. Granted, it is desirable, if not essential, to lead such patrons to works that focus on some portion of the broad topic in question. However, this is the job of the "NT" reference discussed above, *not* of any individual catalog record.

Remember also that the online catalog will facilitate user's moving from one term to a broader or narrower one. Assigning a broad term where it is not appropriate will only make that term less effective as a searching tool in the online environment by causing it to retrieve more "false drops."

This chapter has attempted to serve as a brief introduction to the problem of subject analysis and the use of controlled vocabularies. It is in actual practice that you will gain a feel for proper procedure.

In the preceding discussion, we have made several references to the relationship between subject headings and classification schemes. In the following chapters, we shall discuss the two most commonly used schemes, the Dewey Decimal Classification and the Library of Congress classification.

Review questions for Chapter 5

1. What possible clues exist in the work being cataloged as to its subject content?
2. What might you do when required to catalog a work about whose subject content you know nothing?
3. What are the three alternatives for choice of classification number for a book with two subjects?
4. How should you classify a work having three or more subjects?
5. Discuss the advantages and disadvantages of form headings.
6. What are two purposes of a subject heading list or thesaurus?
7. What comes first in a bibliographic record, subject tracings or added entries? How are the two distinguished?
8. What is the difference between "USE" and "SA"?

Sources cited and suggestions for further reading or study

Bliss, Henry Evelyn. *The Organization of Knowledge and the System of the Sciences.* New York: Holt, 1929.
_____. *The Organization of Knowledge in Libraries and the Subjects Appropriate to Books.* New York: H.W. Wilson, 1933.
Chan, Lois Mai. *Library of Congress Subject Headings: Principles and Applications,* 2nd ed. Littleton, Colo.: Libraries Unlimited, 1986.
_____. *Library of Congress Subject Headings: Principles of Structure and Policies for Application.* Washington, D.C. Cataloging Distribution Service, Library of Congress; 1990 [i.e. 1991].
Dahlberg, Ingetraut. *Classification Systems and Thesauri, 1950–1982.* Frankfurt: Indeks — Verlag, 1982.
Dewey, Melvil. *Dewey Decimal Classification and Relative Index,* 20th ed. Devised by Melvil Dewey; John P. Comaromi, Julianne Beall, Winton E. Mathews, Jr., Gregory R. New, eds. Albany, N.Y.: Forest Press, a division of OCLC Online Computer Library Center, 1989.
Foskett, A.C. *The Subject Approach to Information,* 4th ed. London: C. Bingly: Hamden, Conn.: Linnet Books, 1982.
Harris, Jessica L. *Subject Analysis: Computer Implications of Rigorous Definition.* Metuchen, N.J.: Scarecrow Press, 1970.
Library of Congress. Cataloging Distribution Service. *Library of Congress Subject*

Headings, 14th ed. Washington, D.C.: Cataloging Distribution Service, Library of Congress, 1991.

———. Subject Cataloging Division. *Library of Congress Subject Headings,* 8th ed. Washington, D.C.: Cataloging Distribution Service, Library of Congress, 1975.

———. Subject Cataloging Division. *Subject Cataloging Manual: Subject Headings.* Washington, D.C.: Cataloging Distribution Service, Library of Congress, 1988–.

Mann, Margaret. *Introduction to Cataloging and the Classification of Books*, 2nd ed. Chicago: American Library Association, 1943.

Merrill, William S. *Code for Classifiers*. Chicago: American Library Association, 1954.

Richardson, Ernest Cushing. *Classification, Theoretical and Practical*. Hamden, Conn.: Shoe String Press, 1964 (c1930).

Sears List of Subject Headings, 14th ed. New York: Wilson, 1991.

Soergel, Dagobert. *Indexing Languages and Thesaurus Construction and Maintenance.* Los Angeles: Melville, 1974.

———. *Organizing Information: Principles of Data Base and Retrieval Systems.* Orlando, Fla.: Academic Press, 1985.

6

The Dewey Decimal
Classification: An Overview

In the last chapter, we explained that you may assign any number of subject headings to an item you are cataloging. We also stated that every item can only occupy one position within a library or information center's collection. Therefore, in addition to assigning subject headings, you must find some way of characterizing *as a whole* each item you catalog, and denoting that characterization with *a single symbol* which may be attached to the item. You will do this by using a *classification scheme*, two of which are in common use in the United States. We shall discuss the first of these, the Dewey Decimal Classification, in this and the two chapters following.

Attributes of the perfect classification scheme

A perfect classification scheme for library and information center materials must satisfy the following three conditions:

1. It must provide the ideal arrangement of all recorded knowledge.

2. Its notation must be easy for classifiers to work with.

3. Its principles and notation must be easy for end users to understand.

You may feel that the notion of an "ideal arrangement" is largely subjective. In fact, the subjectivity of this concept is one reason why a perfect classification scheme is almost impossible to develop.

It is not, however, the main reason. The true hindrance to the development of a perfect classification scheme is that the three conditions it must satisfy are, past a point, mutually exclusive. We can demonstrate this by examining the attributes a scheme must have in order to satisfy all three conditions in today's library or information center. These are:

(1) A principle of classifying that places like materials together.

(2) Provision for classification by several approaches—e.g., subject matter, form, function, time.

(3) A set of main classes that are mutually exclusive.

(4) Infinite expandability and capacity for modification.

(5) Coherence, order, and comprehensiveness.

(6) A system of notation that: (a) is simple, definitive, and flexible, and (b) can readily be accommodated by computer programs which produce printed products.

(7) Usefulness as a searching and retrieval tool in an online catalog.

Various pairs of attributes from the above list are mutually contradictory, each being intended to satisfy a different one of the three mutually exclusive conditions with which we began. Therefore, no classification scheme ever devised has had all of these attributes. For example, the *Universal Decimal Classification* (1961) and Ranganathan's colon classification (see Neelamegham "Colon Classification," 1971) both permit classification by several principles and have definitive systems, but both systems are difficult to learn and require complicated notation. Simpler schemes (e.g., abridged editions of *Dewey Decimal Classification*) are inadequate for large collections and lack flexibility.

Since no one can devise a classification scheme which completely satisfies all three basic conditions, the inventor(s) of a scheme must do the next best thing, in two ways: Satisfy all three conditions insofar as it *is* possible (remember that they are only mutually exclusive *past a point*). And choose *one* of the three conditions to satisfy completely.

Although Melvil Dewey himself stated that a classification scheme must be practical (Dewey 1876, 1976), he seems ultimately to have chosen the first condition—the ideal arrangement of all recorded knowledge. However, despite a few practical problems, DDC does not ignore the other two conditions. The fact that it has been continually published and revised for over 115 years, is used in more than 135 countries, and has been translated into over 30 languages (DDC, 20th edition, 1989, p. xxvi) indicates that it is a workable, practical means of organizing materials. In the United States, 95 percent of all public and school libraries, 25 percent of all college and university libraries, and 20 percent of all special libraries use DDC (Ibid., p. xxvi).

History of the Dewey Decimal Classification

Melvil Dewey, while an Amherst undergraduate library assistant in 1873, stated that the idea of using "arabic numerals as decimals, with the ordinary significance of nought, to number a classification of all human knowledge in print" (Dunkin 1969, p. 98) came to him while listening to a sermon during chapel service. Dewey published the first edition of DDC in 1876 and listed, in 12 pages, 10 main classes, each subdivided decimally to make a total of 1000 classes, 000–999. Over the next 113 years, 19 more versions of DDC appeared, each expanding and revising the scheme and its method of presentation in new ways. The 20th edition appeared in 1989 with the basic decimal plan unaltered, but in four volumes:

> Volume 1: Tables
> Volume 2: Schedules 000–599
> Volume 3: Schedules 600–999
> Volume 4: Index and Manual

A testimony to the soundness and integrity of DDC is the presence in the 20th edition of numbers listed by Dewey in his original 1876 publication—albeit, in a few cases, with slightly different nomenclature. Several of these are:

> 342: Constitutional and administrative law
> 462: Spanish etymology
> 536: Heat (Physics)
> 677: Textiles [originally]; Textile fabrics [in 20th ed.]
> 752: Color (Painting)

Melvil Dewey was an ingenious man who, in addition to publishing the first edition of DDC, attempted spelling reform, established the *Library Journal,* and was chiefly responsible for the foundation of the American Library Association. He died in 1931. For further details of Dewey's life and work, consult Rider (1944).

In 1924, Dewey established the Lake Placid Club Education Foundation, a nonprofit organization intended to carry on Dewey's various philanthropies. Dewey conveyed to the Foundation all copyrights to DDC, with the stipulation that profits from the sales of DDC should be used for its future editions and revisions. In 1933, the trustees of the Lake Placid Education Foundation incorporated Forest Press as a wholly owned subsidiary for publishing and marketing DDC and related publications, and in 1961, transferred all copyrights in DDC to Forest Press. On July 29, 1988, Forest Press and DDC became part of the OCLC Online Computer Library Center, which we discussed in Chapter 2 (DDC, edition 20, 1989, p. xi). Actual editing of schedules, tables, index, and manual is done by the Decimal Classification Division within the Processing Services Department of the Library of Congress.

Purpose and scope of DDC

As we said earlier, DDC's primary intention is to provide the ideal arrangement of all recorded knowledge. To achieve this purpose, the scheme attempts to denote all topics, from the most general to the most specific, which make up the whole of human knowledge, and to accurately depict the relationship among these topics.

The DDC does not entirely succeed in this purpose because of its emphasis on American and Western European thought in general, and the Christian religion in particular. This emphasis results partly from Dewey's world view and partly from the prevailing attitudes of Dewey's time. The American/Western/Christian emphasis is still evident, despite attempts to remove it. The most obvious example is the 200 class, "Religion," which devotes all of the numbers in the range 220–289 to aspects of the Christian religion while squeezing all other religions and comparative religion into the range 290–299. The 400 and 800 classes allocate numbers to languages and national literatures in a similarly uneven fashion. We shall discuss these two classes in more detail in Chapter 8.

Each successive edition has modified this Western and American emphasis. (The 20th edition even provides a method for removing the Christian bias from the 200 class, but it amounts to discarding the existing system altogether.) Certain classes—the pure sciences, technology, and "Generalities"—suffer only the restrictions and limitations inherent in any scheme that attempts to cover all knowledge. No one can precisely forecast the extent and direction of future human endeavor.

Basics of structure and notation

With the exception of the 000 "Generalities" class, DDC classifies material by subject content. It is divided and subdivided on the decimal principle, using the digits "0" through "9" to represent topics and their subdivisions. There are ten main classes as follows:

000: Generalities
100: Philosophy, parapsychology and occultism, psychology
200: Religion
300: Social sciences
400: Language
500: Natural sciences and mathematics
600: Technology (Applied sciences)
700: The arts. Fine and decorative arts.
800: Literature
900: General geography and history and their auxiliary disciplines

For reasons explained in the introduction to DDC, these ten classes reflect the categories into which most learning institutions divide the subjects they teach.

Each main class has nine subdivisions, represented by the digits "1" through "9." The digit "0" never represents a distinct subdivision of a topic. The subdivision of the 000 and 600 classes are as follows:

010: Bibliography
020: Library and information sciences
030: General encyclopedic works
040: [Not presently in use]
050: General serial publications and their indexes
060: General organizations and museology
070: Documentary media, educational media, news media; journalism; publishing
080: General collections
090: Manuscripts and rare books, other rare printed materials

610: Medical sciences
620: Engineering and applied operations
630: Agriculture and related technologies
640: Home economics and family living
650: Management and auxiliary services
660: Chemical engineering
670: Manufacturing

680: Manufacture for specific use
690: Buildings

The set of subdivisions of a main class is known as the "Second Summary" of that class. There then follows a "Third Summary" of each subdivision, in which the digits "1" through "9" divide the topic in question into nine still narrower subtopics. For example:

026: Libraries for special subjects — one of the nine subdivisions of 020 above.
616: Diseases — one of the nine subdivisions of "610" above
641: Food sciences — one of the nine subdivisions of "640" above.

Each "Third Summary" topic may be subdivided once again by the digits "1" through "9," the result may be likewise subdivided, and so on in a potentially infinite process.

The DDC is, therefore, a hierarchical classification in which each subdivision is subordinate to the more general class of which it is a part. To restate this principle in terms of notation, each digit, "1" through "9," appearing at a given point in a number, represents a subdivision of the topic which the number up to that point represents.

However, the nine subdivisions at a given hierarchical level represent nine topics *at the same level of specificity.* For example, under:

745.5: Handicrafts

appears a list headed:

745.51–745.58: In specific materials

This list includes woods, metals, furs, etc., all of which represent media of handicraft and none of which is subordinate to any other. The DDC Schedules flag many such lists with the symbol " >." Lists so designated are called *centered entries.*

Exceptions to the general rules

If you have examined DDC, you may have noticed one prominent exception to the rule in the above paragraph — the numbers 220–229, designating the Bible and its various parts. If 220 represents the whole Bible, then, according to the rule, the third digit should represent either the Old or New Testament, and the fourth digit should represent some portion of either. In fact, two of the digits do represent the Old and New Testaments, "1" and "5" respectively. However, you are to represent portions of the Old and New Testaments with the remaining digits in the third position, *not* by adding digits to 221 or 225. Thus:

221: Old Testament
222–224: Parts of Old Testament
225: New Testament
226–228: Parts of New Testament

In this case, DDC has bent its rules slightly in the name of common sense; going strictly by the rules would have involved wasting seven of the nine digits in the third position. The only other alternative would have been to provide no numbers designating the entire Old and New Testaments — which would have been even less desirable.

There are other points at which the schedules bend the rules in line with particular needs. Note, for example, that:

680: Manufacture for specific use

could be thought of as subordinate to:

670: Manufacturing.

Also, note the following:

553.8: Gems
553.82–553.86: Specific precious stones
553.87: *All* semi-precious stones

You should expect to find other examples as you work with DDC.

The process of number building

As you may have seen from our examples, a Dewey number is made up entirely of arabic numerals. If a number exceeds three digits, a decimal point separates the third and fourth. There is no upper limit to the amount of digits a number may have, but it must have at least three. Therefore, numbers denoting broad, general topics will have one or two zeroes following the significant digit(s), as follows:

*2*00: Religion
*61*0: Medicine

The decimal notation carries out DDC's hierarchical principle; you are to read a Dewey number from left to right, with the understanding that longer numbers denote more specific topics than shorter ones, thus:

General		Specific
200: Religion →	220: Bible →	221: Old Testament
600: Technology →	610: Medicine →	616: Diseases
000: Generalities →	020: Lib. sci. →	026: Libraries

After the third digit comes a decimal point, after which the process of subdivision continues. For example:

221.9505: Old Testament Bible stories retold

Here is an example of the progression from a number at the most general level to a very specific one.

General   Specific
_____

300: Social sciences →
→   310: Economics →
→   331: Labor economics →
→   331.1: Labor force and market →
→   331.11: Labor force →
→   331.118: Labor productivity

Figure 9 illustrates the manner in which you must make a series of choices among nine alternatives to build this, or any, number.

Whenever you choose a specific number from within the schedules — or especially from the index — *always* consult the broader heading under which the number appears. To understand the importance of doing this, consider a hypothetical book entitled *Stress, Sexism, and the Working Woman*, which deal with the added job stress women suffer because of their male coworkers' sexist attitudes. You might decide that:

331.4: Women workers

is the proper choice for this book.

However, you must realize that this is a part of:

331: Labor economics

which is part of

330: Economics

This number might be suitable for a book on a subject such as women workers' potential to increase a company's productivity. However, 331.4 would be totally unsuitable for *Stress, Sexism, and the Working*

Figure 9. *Graphic Representation of Number Building Process*

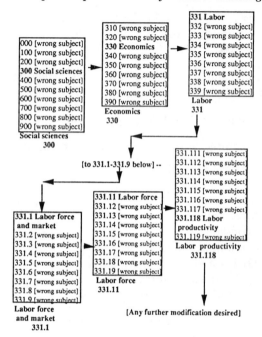

Woman, which discusses women workers from a *psychological* point of view and deals to some extent with ethical issues. A number from somewhere else in the 300s might be applicable, although the most appropriate place for this book is probably in the 100s — most likely in the 150s.

The "Manual on Use of Dewey Decimal Classification," a new feature included in the 20th edition of DDC, deals with problems such as this one in the section headed "Notes on schedule numbers" (pp. 791–958). We shall discuss and evaluate the manual later in this chapter.

Auxiliary tables for number expansion

Once you have built a Dewey number using the schedules, you may, in most cases, further modify it by means of the tables. You may use the tables *only* to expand a number from the schedules; under no circumstances may you use numbers from the tables by themselves. Furthermore, you must use the tables with discretion, and strictly in accordance with DDC's instructions; you may not simply add any subdivision they provide to any call number. While you may add the numbers from Table 1, "Standard Subdivisions," and Table 2, "Areas," to almost any Dewey number — again, according to very precise rules of application — you may only use tables 3 through 7 when the schedules explicitly instruct you to. Following are the names of the auxiliary tables, together with a short description of their use:

Table 1 — Standard subdivisions (point of view, form, etc.) — may be used as required with any number from the schedules in accordance with uniformly applied instructions.

Table 2 — Areas — Geographical subdivision, to be used as required with any number from the schedules, either directly when so noted or by the interposition of "09."

Specific directives — to add area codes directly — will supersede the general instruction — to interpose the "tag" "09."

Table 3 — Subdivisions for Individual Literatures (the literary forms poetry, drama, fiction, etc.) — to be used as directed with the base numbers of individual literatures in the 800 class.

Table 4 — Subdivisions of Individual Languages (Alphabets, spelling, grammar, etymology, etc.) — may be used as required with base numbers for individual languages in the 400 class.

Table 5 — Racial, ethnic, national groups — to be used only as directed in the main schedules.

Table 6 — Languages — to be used only as directed in the main schedules.

Table 7 — Groups of Persons — to be used as directed in the main schedules.

Tables 1 and 2 are those most often used in actual practice. Tables 3 and 4 *must* be used when building language and literature numbers. We shall explain the use of these and other auxiliary tables in the chapters following, which we devote to illustrating their applicability. The DDC contains precise instructions for the use of all numbers from the above-listed tables.

The relative index

One of the most exemplary features of DDC is the "Relative Index." This index, comprising the first portion of Volume 4 of the 20th edition, brings together under one heading all aspects of any given subject. The index provides various numbers for any given subject, each denoting an approach from a different point of view. You may then choose the number which best represents the point of view of the item you are cataloging. We already touched on the problem of denoting the proper point of view in our discussion of 331.4 above. As another example, dogs may be thought of as mammals, pets, guides for the blind, or experimental animals for science. Each facet is as much a part of the concept *dogs* as any of the others. The entries under *Marriage* in the 20th edition of DDC illustrate the integrative function of the relative index:

Marriage	306.81
citizenship issues	323.636
customs	392.5
ethics	173
religion	291.563
Buddhism	294.356 3
Christianity	241.63
Hinduism	294.548 63
Islam	297.5
Judaism	296.385 63
folklore	398.27
sociology	398.354
law	345.016
literature	808.803 54
history and criticism	809.933 54
specific literatures	T3B—080 354
history and criticism	T3B—093 54
music	781.587
personal religion	291.44
Buddhism	294.344 4
Christianity	248.4
Hinduism	294.544
Islam	297.44
Judaism	296.74
public worship	291.38
Christianity	265.5
Judaism	296.444
see also Public worship	
religious doctrine	291.22
Buddhism	294.342 2
Christianity	234.165
Hinduism	294.522
Islam	297.22
Judaism	296.32
social theology	291.178 358 1
Christianity	261.835 81

At the same time, the "Relative Index" in the 20th edition of DDC contains far fewer hierarchical and subordinated headings than in previous editions, using instead direct and specific entries. An interesting example as found at "Ice," which, in the 19th edition of DDC, was a long hierarchical display of 36 subordinate terms. The 20th edition's index instead uses terms such as "ice cream," "ice hockey," and "ice storms," all of which had been formerly subsumed under the broad heading "Ice." The 20th edition's index also reflects social changes that have occurred over the last 10 years. For example, headings such as "AIDS (Disease)" (having eight subheadings), "Househusbands," "Cocaine abuse," and "Insider trading in securities," did not appear in previous editions. The 20th edition's index contains 730 pages, as contrasted with the 1,217 pages of the 19th edition's index. This is largely due to the elimination of "see" references, although "see also" instructions remain.

The manual

The second section of Volume 4 contains a wholly new feature, a "Manual for the Use of the Dewey Decimal Classification." While it "is intended to serve practicing classifiers and students," it will probably be more useful to the former, since it assumes that its user understands the principles of classification outlined in the introduction (Vol. 1, pp. xxv–1). If you examine the manual, you will see that many instructions are very succinct and give limited supporting background detail.

The manual moves sequentially through first the tables, then the schedules, beginning with Table 1, "Standard Subdivisions," and ending with 970.004, "[General history of North American] racial, ethnic, national groups." Of particular interest are the maps on pages 763–770. These maps accompany Table 2, "Geographic areas, historical periods, persons," and actually superimpose the "Areas Notations" from that table onto the geographic regions they represent. You will more fully understand this after reading about Table 2 in the next chapter.

Following all instructions on the use of the tables is a section entitled, "Notes on Schedule Numbers" (p. 791). This section consists chiefly of comparisons between different classification numbers that appear to have the same meaning. The manual cannot, of course, list every possible comparison. Those chosen are not only well developed, but illustrate the need to understand the connotative meaning of the classes compared. An effective example, found on page 150, discusses the difference between 152 and 612.8:

152 vs.   [Psychology of] Sensory perception,
612.8   movement, emotions, physiological
           drives vs. [Physiology of] Nervous
           functions   Sensory functions
               Class in 152 works that emphasize awareness, sensa-
               tion, intentions, meanings, and actions as experienced
               by the individual or observed and described without
               reference to the physics or chemistry of the nervous
               system, e.g., seeing colors, feeling anger. Class in
               chemical 612.8 works that emphasize the physical
               and chemical mechanisms and pathways of sensa-
               tions, emotions, movements, e.g., studies using elec-
               trodes to determine what parts of the brain process
               different kinds of stimuli. Class comprehensive
               works in 152. If in doubt, prefer 612.8.

Unfortunately, you cannot always be certain under which of the
two numbers in question you will find the comparison you desire. Many
of the comparisons are found under the number coming earlier in the
schedules, but a significant number are not. For example:

643.1 vs.   Housing [in home economics] vs.
363.5   Housing [in social services]
621 vs.   Applied physics vs.
530   Physics

The second of the above examples suggests that the manual places
comparisons under the more specific number, but the first example does
not support this theory. A set of guidelines for locating a comparison
might improve the manual.
       The manual's discussion of:

780: Music

is particularly helpful, since the 780 section of DDC, 20th edition, has
been completely revised and enlarged. The manual describes the overall
structure of the 780 class, gives the correct citation order, discusses both
vocal and instrumental music, and lists examples of classification
numbers for both scores and works about music.

Faceting in the Dewey Decimal Classification

At many points throughout the scheme, DDC instructs you to extend a number by adding to it a digit or string of digits from elsewhere

in the schedules, or from the tables. This number building method is known as *faceting*. We will discuss faceting with respect to the tables in more detail in the chapters following.

The DDC's 20th edition provides for faceting by means of "Add" instructions (in former editions, often called "Divide-like" directives). There are three forms of these:

(1) "Add to base number [number you have built up to that point] notation [digit or range of digits] from [a specified point in the Tables or elsewhere in the Schedules]."

133.129: Specific haunted places
"Add to base number 133.129 notation from Table 2, e.g., the Tower of London 133.1294215".

The instruction is telling you to find the string of digits from Table 2 which denotes the place your number is to represent and add those digits to 133.129.

221.1-.8: Old Testament. Generalities
"Add to base number 221 the numbers following 220 in 220.1–220.8, e.g., Targums 221.42, commentaries 221.7"

Here, DDC is telling you to look up the numbers used to denote various aspects of the entire Bible and use those *same* number to denote those *same* aspects of the Old Testament.

341.22: Relations of League of Nations with other countries
"Add to base number 341.22 the numbers following 341.23 in 341.231–341.239," e.g., relations of the League of Nations with France, 341.2244.

The instruction here is similar to the one for the Bible. You are directed to denote relations of the League of Nations with other countries by means of the same numbers you would use to denote relations between the United Nations and other countries.

(2) "Add [further modifying digits] as instructed under [a specified number from elsewhere in the Schedules]."

546.381: Lithium*
*[Footnote] "Add as instructed under 546."

At 546, "Inorganic chemistry," there appears what looks like a mini-table. There are many such tables throughout DDC. They demonstrate, for a whole class of numbers, how to modify each specific number within that class. These tables are used when modifications of a broad topic are also applicable, to all components of that topic. In this case, "546: Inorganic chemistry," is the broad topic of which "546.381: Lithium," an alkali metal, is one of the components.

> 616.8647: Cocaine‡
> ‡[Footnote] "Add as instructed under 616.1–616.9."

This refers back to "616.1–616.9 — Specific diseaes," which displays a long, two-paged, detailed exhibit of directions for the modification of printed numbers for all of the diseases which follow. Included in this long set of faceting numbers are such concepts as "medical emergencies," "rehabilitation," "preventive measures," "therapy," and "case histories."

You may find these long, auxiliary-table-like sets of instructions formidable. In fact, you are somewhat justified because you must carry out various additive mental processes to transport numbers from these tables to point throughout the schedules. Consider, however, that without such summaries, individual instructions would have to be included at *every number printed in the schedules*, resulting not only in unnecessary repetition, but an impossibly long classification scheme. These mini-tables are really only telling you to do the same thing each time with all of the numbers in a certain range.

> (3) "Add to base number [the number you have built up to this point] notation 001–999 [i.e. any complete number from the scheme]."
>
> 026: Libraries.
> 220.8: Non-religious subjects treated in the Bible."

In both cases, DDC instructs you to add 001–999 to specify a topic, as illustrated below.

> 610: Medicine
> 026.61 Medical libraries
> 220.861: Biblical discussions of medicine.
>
> 616: Diseases
> 026.616: Libraries devoted to material on diseases.
> 220.8616: Biblical discussions of diseases.
>
> 780: Music
> 026.78: Music libraries
> 220.878: Biblical discussions of music
>
> 792.8: Dancing
> 026.7928: Libraries devoted to literature on dancing
> 220.87928: Biblical discussions of dancing

The Dewey Decimal Classification's use of mnemonics

The faceting we have just illustrated constitutes one of DDC's more systematic uses of mnemonics — the same digits to represent the same subject matter throughout the scheme. You will find other such examples of planning on the part of DDC's developers — which do not automatically result from certain number-building instructions. Here are some examples:

> 460: *Spanish* language
> 860: *Spanish* literature
> 946: *Spain*
>
> 030: General *encyclopedias*
> 403: Language *dictionaries*
> 803: Belles-lettres *dictionaries, concordances*

There is no table or set of instructions in DDC providing a directive that you shall always use *6* to represent things Spanish or *3* to represent dictionaries and encyclopedic works. Rather, DDC's developers have agreed to use these digits in the above manner whenever possible.

(As we shall demonstrate in a later chapter, there is a systematic use of mnemonics *within* both the 400 and 800 classes, but the mechanisms used in these classes do not extend through the whole of DDC.)

The Dewey Decimal Classification as an online search tool

The DDC is a potentially powerful search tool for users of online catalogs because of its hierarchical structure and use of mnemonics. It is also relatively easy to use as a search tool because it employs only 11 distinct symbols — the 10 Arabic digits plus the decimal point.

The extent to which users of an online catalog will benefit from the ability to search by Dewey number depends on the types of *truncation* the system will allow. To truncate when performing an online search is to enter only a portion of a search term in conjunction with some type of "wild card" symbol. Ideally, an online search system should incorporate two wild card symbols, one to indicate that any *single character* in the specified position is a match, the other to indicate that any *sequence of characters* at the specified point is a match. The purpose of truncation is to retrieve a set of items falling within a set of parameters as narrow or as broad as desired.

In the illustration following, we shall use "@" as a single-character wild card symbol and "#" as one to represent any number of characters.

Many online catalogs at present allow only *right truncation*. This means you may only *end* your query with the wild card character, and thus in this case search for call numbers beginning with the digits you specified. Here are some right truncated searches using the symbols:

> 61#: All material dealing with medicine.
> 616#: All material dealing with diseases.
> 616.86#: All material dealing with addictions.
> 61@: All material dealing with medicine at the next definable level of specificity.
>
> Note the contrast between "61#" and "61@." The former will retrieve any number beginning with "61," while the latter will retrieve only the numbers 610, 611, 612 . . . 619.
>
> 78#: All music and material dealing with music.
> 78@: All music and material dealing with music at the next definable level of specificity.
> 81#: All American literature.
> 813#: All American fiction.
> 81@: All American literature at the next definable level of specificity. This would include only items which comprised or dealt with the definable *categories* of American literature— poetry, fiction, drama, etc.; this search key would retrieve only the number 810, 811, 812 . . . 819.

(In fact, right truncation of the multiple character-variety is automatic, requiring no wild card symbol, in many online catalogs.)

In a system which allowed *internal truncation*, placing the wild card symbol within the query, the following searches would be possible. (Since these involve various tables we have yet to discuss, you may want to return to them after studying the next two chapters):

> 8@3#: All fiction of any nationality.
> 61#092#: All biographies of individuals in any area of the medical profession.
> 616.86#092#: All biographies of individuals known for their work in the treatment of alcoholism or drug addiction.
> 2#0973: Any aspect of religion in the United States as a whole.
> 2#0973#: Any aspect of religion in the United States or any region within the United States.

In a system that included *left truncation*, the following searches would be possible. (Note again, these tables have not been discussed. Note also that the instruction to perform a left-truncated search is analogous to the dash preceding each standard subdivision in Table 1.)

#0973: A treatment of any topic limited to the United States.
#07: Research, study, teaching, etc., of any subject.

You would probably be ill-advised to combine right and left truncation in a query such as:

#0973#: A treatment of any topic limited to the United States or any region within the United States.

This would retrieve any number in which the digits "0973" occurred at any point. When you allow this much latitude, you run a great risk of retrieving irrelevant information. (However, the use of the initial "0" would significantly minimize the risk in this case, for reasons we shall discuss in the next chapter.)

Because of the possibilities they would open up, we hope that systems permitting left and internal truncation, along with right truncation, will become available in the near future.

Problems with the use of the Dewey Decimal Classification

We have already mentioned the DDC's bias toward the Christian religion and Western thought. In Class 200, Christianity takes up the range 210–289 while all other religions are crammed into the 290s. For example:

297: Islam
299.932: Gnosticism [originally a form of Christianity]

In classes 400 and 800 each of the following languages and literatures, English, French, German, Italian, Spanish, Greek, and Latin, receives its own digit in the second position while all other languages/literatures are squeezed into the 490s and 890s, as with:

495.1: Chinese language
895.1: Chinese literature

You could argue that the bias is artificial; since any Dewey number is infinitely expandable, the meanings of the numbers in the 290s, 490s, and 890s can be modified to the same extent possible with all other numbers. This is a valid argument only if you examine DDC from a purely conceptual viewpoint. From a practical standpoint, numbers in these classes are more difficult to work with because they must be so much longer to achieve the same level of specificity. For the same reason, libraries which have a policy of taking every Dewey number out only to a set number of digits will not be able to define as sharply topics falling within these classes.

Because of the bias in the 400 and 800 classes, numbers in the 490s and 890s do not have the same physical pattern as those in the remainder of these two classes. In the case of all the languages or literatures listed above, that part of the number denoting linguistic or literary form begins with the third digit. The third digit of a number in the 490s or 890s is still working to specify nationality. At present, this is not a serious problem, but it will create difficulties with online searches. For example, one of our proposed queries from the previous section, "8@3#: All fiction of any nationality," will fail in the case of the 890s. It will retrieve any number beginning with 893 — all types of literature of several nationalities.

The DDC's hierarchical structure, while elegant and logical, is somewhat inflexible. It is often difficult to expand any section of the scheme to accommodate new subjects. A particularly important new subject is the development and use of computers. In the 19th edition of DDC (1979), "001.6 — Data processing" occupied hardly more than a page for classification number assignment. Now, in the 20th edition, all numbers in the range 004–006 are devoted to aspects of computer science and technology. This was only possible because the numbers so cited were previously unassigned; classes 004 and 005 had never been assigned any content. New classes cannot be assigned arbitrarily by changing the meaning of former classes. If this were allowed, the scheme would quickly lose its integrity. Where unassigned numbers are unavailable, new topics must be accommodated through the extension of existing numbers.

One important exception is the new "Music" schedule of DDC found at 780. While the meaning of the "78" has remained unchanged, the rest of the older schedule has been more or less discarded and replaced with a whole set of new numbers. The number 783, which formerly denoted sacred music now has the meaning, "Music for single voice." Both the introduction and the manual of the 20th edition explain the new schedule, with the introduction providing a conversion table from old to new numbers for many topics. Here, the developers of DDC solved the problem of inflexibility, but at the cost of some of the scheme's integrity.

The various strengths and weaknesses of DDC which we have discussed thus far combine to create what many catalogers and patrons consider DDC's main drawback — that of excessively long numbers, such as:

338.436292097123: The price of automobiles in Alberta, Canada.
338.45613621109771334: Production efficiency of those employed
in hospital services in Lake County, Ohio.

Numbers this long will not easily fit on the spine of a book or the
allotted space on a catalog card. This is true even if you place that portion of the number beginning with the decimal point on a new line. A
library could break such numbers into several lines of three or four
digits each. However, if this were done according to strict rules, the line
breaks would not always correspond to logical units within the numbers. Here is the first number above with the logical units indicated by
spaces:

338.43 6292 09 7123

Here is how the number appears if broken into three- or four-digit lines,
with the decimal point counted into the allotment per line:

338	338
.43	.436
629	2920
209	9712
712	3
3	

Another possible solution is to allow a *maximum* of three or four
characters per line, placing line breaks between logical units, even if
that results in only one or two digits per line, thus:

338	338
.43	.43
629	6292
2	09
09	7123
712	
3	

In this example, the version with a maximum of four characters per
line is more attractive, but that might not always be the case. The formatting rules should provide for a choice between whichever maximum
length results in the fewest single-character lines.

For a computer to handle the task described above, it would need
to have the logical units denoted somehow. In fact, they are in many
MARC records, either by spaces or slashes. (They are also denoted in CIP
data — see Chapter 5 — by apostrophes.) In a MARC record a Dewey

number appears either in field 082, if assigned by the Library of Congress, or in field 092, if assigned by another cataloging institution.

In any case, numbers broken up into separate lines would be difficult to interpret, given the hierarchical nature of DDC. The problems involved are similar to those you might encounter when reading any decimal number broken into lines. The number 2,523.25 would be difficult to read if written as:

> 2,52
> 3.25

In this chapter, we have tried to give you an understanding of the purpose, content, structure, and scope of the Dewey Decimal Classification, with particular reference to the 20th edition. The next two chapters of this textbook will deal with the standard subdivisions, the 900 history and geography class, the 400 language class, and the 800 literature class. Only by actual use and number building in DDC, or any classification scheme, can you obtain a feel for the whole system.

Review questions for Chapter 6

1. Why is it impossible to develop a perfect classification scheme?

2. How old is the Dewey Decimal Classification?

3. What is meant by a "hierarchical classification"? Why is DDC an example of such an approach?

4. What are the advantages of decimal notation? What are the disadvantages?

5. Which of the auxiliary tables have applicability throughout DDC? What restriction is placed on those tables which do not have general applicability?

6. Select one concept from the "Relative Index" capable of being approached from multiple points of view. Examine the schedules to see how differently each of the facets of the concept is coded. Jot down six of these differing classification numbers and write out an explanation of each number's full meaning.

7. Examine the material in the 20th edition's "Manual" under "780: Music," pages 926-938. How much knowledge of both cataloging and music do the instructions and explanations therein assume?

8. You are classifying the books in a church library, and have elected to use DDC for the purpose because of its detailed breakdown of the Christian religion. Not surprisingly, every book in the library

could take a number from the 200s. However, there are many which could be classed either in the 200s or in other areas, such as 151, "Applied psychology" or 170, "Ethics." Why, in this situation, might you want to use the number which is in a class other than the 200s?

Sources cited and suggestions for further reading or study

British Standard Institute. *Universal Decimal Classification,* English abridged ed. London, 1961.

Comaromi, John P. "Use of the Dewey Decimal Classification in the United States and Canada." *Library Resources & Technical Services* 22 (Fall 1978): 402–408.

Dewey, Melvil. *A Classification and Subject Index for Cataloging and Arranging the Books and Pamphlets of a Library.* Originally published: Amherst, Mass., 1876. Reprinted as: *Dewey Decimal Classification Centennial, 1876–1976.* Forest Press Division, Lake Placid Education Foundation. Printed and bound by Kingsport Press, Kingsport, Tennessee, 1976.

_____. *Dewey Decimal Classification and Relative Index,* 19th ed. Albany, N.Y.: Lake Placid Education Foundation, Forest Press, 1979.

_____. *Dewey Decimal Classification and Relative Index,* 20th ed. Devised by Melvil Dewey; John P. Comaromi, Julianne Beall, Winton E. Mathews, Jr., Gregory R. New, eds. Albany, N.Y.: Forest Press, a division of OCLC Online Computer Library Center, 1989.

Dunkin, Paul S. *Cataloging U.S.A.* Chicago: American Library Association, 1969.

Neelamegham, A. "Colon Classification." In *Encyclopedia of Library and Information Science,* vol. 5, pp. 316–340. New York: Marcel Dekker, 1971.

Rider, Fremont. *Melvil Dewey.* Chicago: American Library Association, 1944.

7

Dewey Decimal Classification: Standard Subdivisions, Area Codes, and the 900 Class

In the preceding chapter, we described the several auxiliary tables by which numbers in the schedules may — and in some cases must — be modified. We pointed out that Table 1, "Standard Subdivisions," and Table 2, "Geographic Areas," may be used — according to very precise rules of application — with almost any number in the schedules. It is the purpose of this chapter to explain the use of tables 1 and 2 and to demonstrate their wide applicability. We shall extend our discussion to the correspondence between number modifications using Standard Subdivision 09 and base numbers in the 900 class.

The Dewey Decimal Classification is based primarily on subdivision by subject content, rather than form. However, it is often necessary to specify a work's form, point of view, or geographic limitations. This is accomplished by adding one of Table 1's standard subdivisions to a classification number. These standard subdivisions are constant in meaning and may be used throughout the schedules (except in circumstances hereinafter to be described).

The full expansion of Table 1 for the 20th edition is found in volume 1. To master DDC, you must become familiar with the meaning and function of these subdivisions and understand the number building processes involved in their use.

How standard subdivisions modify numbers

Following is an illustration of how each of the standard subdivisions is applied to the broad topic "Pure Sciences":

		500:	Pure science
01:	Philosophy and theory	501:	Philosophy and theories of pure science
02:	Miscellany	502:	Techniques, apparatus, equipment, materials (i.e. miscellaneous aspects of pure science)
03:	Dictionaries, encyclopedias, concordances	503:	Dictionaries, encyclopedias, etc. of pure science
04:	[Unassigned]		
05:	Serial publications	505:	Serial publications in the area of pure science
06:	Organizations and management	506:	Scientific organizations
07:	Education, research, special topics	507:	Research; use of apparatus and equipment in study and teaching of science (*not for textbooks*)
08:	Natural history	508:	Descriptions and surveys of phenomena in nature
09:	Historical, geographical, biographical treatment	509:	Historical and geographical treatment of science

Observe that in every sample above, the *subject* which the number denotes is pure or general science; the addition of the standard subdivision shows either the *form* in which the work being classified is presented or the *point of view* from which that work treats the subject of pure or general science.

General instructions for adding standard subdivisions

It is important to remember that specific directives from the DDC schedules *always* supersede general instructions. If, however, no specific directive is printed in the schedule with the subject number used,

the standard subdivision, *always preceded by at least one zero*, is added
to the base number that expresses the desired subject. For example:

> 399: Customs of war and diplomacy →
> →   03: Dictionaries, encyclopedias,
> concordances →
> →   399.03: An encyclopedia of the customs of
> war and diplomacy

The zero before the standard subdivision is a signal that what follows *is* a standard subdivision rather than a further modification of the
subject — a signal which is almost always necessary. Observe, for example:

> 364: Criminology

If you wanted to create a number meaning "An encyclopedia of criminology," you would add the standard subdivision 03 to produce:

> 364.03: Encyclopedia of criminology

If you were to omit the zero, you would have:

> 364.3: Offenders

For a further illustration of this point, go back to the hypothetical
online Dewey number searches we presented in the last chapter. If,
assuming you could actually perform these searches, you omitted the
zero from the queries using internal and left truncation, you would retrieve a great deal of irrelevant material.

However, you must not add *unneeded* zeroes. You are most likely
to make this error when modifying a number broad enough to have one
or two trailing zeroes. Such a number is:

> 150: Psychology

You may add the standard subdivision:

> 09: Historical, geographical, or biographical treatment

to denote the history of psychology. However, the correct form of the
number is *not*:

> 150.09: History of psychology

Instead, read the trailing zero of the base number as the necessary initial
zero of the standard subdivision. When you do this, you will see that
the correct form for the number in this case is:

150.9: History of psychology

Another illustration of this principle is the set of "Pure science" numbers with which we began. The first of the two trailing zeroes in the number 500 became the initial zero of each standard subdivision. The resulting numbers were 501–509, *not* 500.01–500.09. In situations such as this, keep the following rule in mind:

When adding a standard subdivision to a number broad enough to have one or two trailing zeroes, *unless directed otherwise*, use the first trailing zero as the initial zero of the standard subdivision.

In some parts of the schedules, some of the standard subdivisions are spelled out, so that you may see the proper form. For example, at 610, there is an instruction to "use 610.1–610.9 for standard subdivisions," along with two examples:

610.6   Organizations, management, professions of medical science

610.7   Education, research, teaching, nursing related technologies of medical science

Use of multiple zeroes in standard subdivisions

Note that we qualified the above rule regarding trailing zeroes rather strongly. This is because you must apply it with caution. The procedure for building many numbers is not quite so simple as in the above examples. For instance, the number that would result from adding one of the standard subdivisions 01–09 to a certain base number may be *assigned another specific meaning*, as with:

617: Surgery →
→   617.07: Surgical pathology

Therefore, if you want to add the standard subdivision 07 to denote education and research in surgery, you must insert an additional zero to avoid confusion with the number for surgical pathology, thus;

617.007: Education and research in surgery

To maintain its consistency and integrity, DDC requires you to place all standard subdivisions at the same hierarchical level; if you must insert an extra zero before one standard subdivision, you must do so before all of them. In fact, the following directive appears in the schedules at 617:

617.001–617.008: Standard subdivisions of surgery

The need for an additional zero can explicitly negate our "trailing zeroes" rule, as in:

380: Commerce, communication, transportation →
→   380.1: Commerce (Trade)

Here, you must use 380.01–380.09 for standard subdivisions, *retaining the trailing zero* which is part of the class number 380. Again, all standard subdivisions must occur at the same hierarchical level.

A similar example occurs at:

320: Political science

where you will find:

320.6: Policy formation

meaning that you must use 320.01–320.09 for standard subdivisions.

The 20th edition provides an extensive set of instructions regarding the number of zeroes used with standard subdivisions in the manual, volume 4, page 740.

When standard subdivisions may not be added

There are certain instances in which you may *not* modify a number by any of the standard subdivisions. You must remember these, because you will not always find specific prohibitions printed in the schedules. In fact, in the first instance we will discuss, it would not be possible to provide such prohibitions; whether or not the condition exists on a given occasion depends on the nature of the item you are cataloging on that specific occasion.

1. Numbers more general than the item being classified

The first restriction occurs when no number exists for the specific topic you are attempting to represent, forcing you to use a number that is more general than the subject of the item you are classifying. The editor's introduction to the 20th edition states (volume 1, page xl, paragraph 8.4):

> The most important caveat with respect to standard subdivisions
> is that in most cases they are added only for works that cover or

approximate the whole of the subject of the number. For example, a work on the black widow spiders of California should be classed in the number for spiders, 595.44 (not 595.4409794, the number for spiders in California). The classifier should not attempt to specify California because black widow spiders do not approximate the whole universe of spiders in California. Further instructions on using Table 1 are found at the beginning of Table 1 and in the Table 1 section of the Manual.

Another example may be found at 677.617. Here is the breakdown of that number:

> 600: Technology (Applied sciences) →
> → 670: Manufacturing →
> → 677: Manufacturing of textiles →
> → 677.6 Manufacturing of special-process fabrics, regardless of composition →
> → 677.61: Manufacturing of fancy-weave fabrics →
> → 677.617: Manufacturing of fancy-weave fabrics in pile weave.

You will see that the examples listed in the schedule under 677.617 include velvet as a pile weave fabric. Therefore, a book on the manufacture of velvet would have the number 677.617. A documentary film on the *history* of the manufacture of velvet would have the same number — *not* 677.61709; since the number available is not as specific as the subject, it cannot be further modified by a standard subdivision.

The reasoning behind this restriction is that it may become possible, in a future edition of DDC, to further modify the number in question; a future edition of DDC may provide digits which you may add to 677.617 to specify velvet. If you wish at that point to change the number for that documentary film, you can easily add the digit onto the end of the existing number. If the existing number had an "09" attached, you would have to insert the digits. This would present no problem in the case of a field in a MARC record, but would create difficulties with regard to call number labels and other printed records of the number.

2. Redundant standard subdivisions

The second restriction concerns numbers which contain within them the concept denoted by a standard subdivision, so that adding that standard subdivision would be redundant. For example:

678.722: Techniques, procedures, apparatus, equipment,
materials for synthetic rubber.

→   028: Techniques, apparatus, equipment
and materials.

The number that would result from the above operation, 678.722028, would mean, "the techniques, apparatus, equipment and materials of the techniques, apparatus, equipment and materials for synthetic rubber," which makes little sense.

3. Adding one standard subdivision to another

A third restriction is that, unless specifically directed to do so, you should not add one standard subdivision to another. In general, avoid overuse of standard subdivisions.

4. Numbers in the 800 class

Finally, observe the cautions throughout the schedules, indicating points at which further subdivision is irregular or limited. Several such prohibitions occur throughout the 800, "Literature," class, in conjunction with the use of tables 3A, 3B, and 3C, "Subdivisions of Individual Literatures," volume 1, page 389. We shall explain this restriction further in the next chapter.

To summarize, you may *not* add standard subdivisions in these four instances: (1) When the number chosen for a work is more general than the subject of the work. (2) When the number already contains within itself the concept described by a standard subdivision. (3) When the result would be the addition of one standard subdivision to another. (4) When modifying certain numbers in the 800 class.

Use of standard subdivision 09 in conjunction with area codes from Table 2

Consider what the following works have in common:

1. A discussion of crime in New York City.
2. A collection of rock music from Great Britain.
3. A guide to restaurants in Philadelphia.
4. A history of coal mining in Pennsylvania.

Each work above addresses its topic only with respect to a specific geographic location.

Works also exist which discuss a topic with respect to a specific time period. Examples of such works are:

5. A history of music in the Middle Ages.
6. A survey of working conditions throughout the world in the nineteenth century.
7. A discussion of diseases that were considered incurable in the eighteenth century.

In most cases, you are to denote historical or geographic treatment of a subject by adding the subdivision 09 to the base number. If, as with examples 5–7 above, a work treats the history of a subject without limiting its coverage to any specific location, denote this with one of the extensions of the 09 subdivision, 0901–0905, listed in Table 1. If the work limits its coverage to a specific location, add to 09 the appropriate area code from Table 2. Use the "09 + area code" combination for any work limiting its coverage to a specific location, even if the work also limits itself to a particular time period. You may add a time period specification to the area code, following the instructions appearing in Table 1 at 093–099.

We suggest that, when trying to find a location in Table 2, you look it up in the "Relative Index," where you can find it in an alphabetical, rather than a classified arrangement. You may also look it up, if you have sufficient knowledge of geography, in the maps which are part of the manual.

Following is an example of the application of standard subdivision 09 to a book entitled *The History of Stunt Flying in New Jersey*:

797.54: Stunt flying →
→   797.5409: Historical or geographical treatment of stunt flying →   (This number by itself would be used for a general history of stunt flying.)
→   797.54097: Stunt flying in North America, and/or history of same →
→   797.540974: Stunt flying in Northeastern United States and/or history of same →
→   797.5409749: Stunt flying in New Jersey and/or history of same

You may give almost any subject a geographic limitation by add 09 + area code 3–9 from Table 2 to the base number. You will find the general directive to do this in Table 1 at 093–099, "Treatment by specific continents, countries . . .":

> Add to base number "09" notation 3-9 from Table 2, e.g., the subject in the United States: 0973; in Brazil: 0981; in North America: 097. Thus, military organizations in Japan: 322.50952; in the United States: 322.50973.

Note that you are to use the subdivision 09, either alone or in conjunction with any of the modifications listed above, only to denote the history *of a subject, discipline, etc.* Do not attempt to apply it to the class of works commonly called "history books." These, which deal with the history of *political entities*, belong in Class 900. We shall discuss this class after making one additional point about area codes.

Use of area codes from Table 2 without standard subdivision 09

At many points throughout the schedules, you will find specific directives to affix an area code from Table 2 directly, without the interposition of the standard subdivision 09. You would encounter the following such directive in classifying a book entitled *The Anglican Church in the United States*:

> 283: Anglican church →
>   →   .4-.9: Treatment by continent, country, locality.
>   "Add to base number 283 notations 4-9 from Table 2."
>   (There is an explicit instruction not to use 09.)
>   →   283.7: Anglican Church in North America
>   →   283.73: Anglican Church in the United States.

The above example is typical of geographic limitation applied *directly* to a base number. Numbers so modified denote purely geographic limitations; they do not designate historical treatment as well.

The 900 class—geography, history and auxiliary disciplines

The 900 class of the *Dewey Decimal Classification* includes "geography, history and auxiliary disciplines." We shall first discuss that portion of the 900 class which warrants its inclusion in this chapter.

Classes 930-990 and subdivisions 093-099

One significant example of systematic mnemonics in DDC is the correspondence between the standard subdivisions 093-099 and the class numbers 930-990. Compare the instructions appearing in the Schedules at 930—

> 930-990: History of ancient world; of specific continents, countries, localities; of extraterrestrial worlds.
>
> Add to base number 9 notations 3-9 from Table 2, e.g., general history of Europe: 940; of England: 942; of Norfolk England: 942.61.

—to the instructions found in Table 1 for the standard subdivisions 093-099:

> Add to base number "09" notation 3-9 from Table 2, e.g., the subject in the United States: 0973; in Brazil: 0981; in North America: 097. Thus, military organizations in Japan: 322.50952; in the United States: 322.50973.

In each case, you are instructed to add an area code from Table 2 to the digit 9. Therefore, any 09 standard subdivision denoting a place, if you remove the base number and initial zero from it, will become a class number denoting the history of that place. We can best illustrate this point with the following table:

Area Code	*Use in Std. Subdiv.* 093-099	*Use in Class #* 930-990
73 United States	322.50973 Military organizations in the United States	973 History of the United States
749 New Jersey	797.5409749 Stunt flying in New Jersey	974.9 History of New Jersey
42 England	780.942 History of music in England	942 History of England
4261 Norfolk, England	792.8094261 History of dance in Norfolk, England	942.61 History of Norfolk, England

Again, you may apply this principle to any Dewey number having a standard subdivision in the range 093-099.

It is also worth noting that DDC uses some area codes from Table 2 in numbers from classes other than 900. For example:

942: History of *England*
823: *English* fiction

946: History of *Spain*
863: *Spanish* fiction

870: *Latin* literature
937.6: History of ancient world — *Rome*

883: *Classical Greek* epics and fiction
938: History of *Ancient Greece*

Many of the history numbers which result from adding an area code to the digit 9 are actually printed in the 900 Schedule. In many cases, this is to provide some further modification of the number. For example, you will find, under the number 942, denoting the history of England and Wales (volume 3, page 740), a set of chronological subdivisions.

Classes 913–919 — Geography

The instructions for denoting the geography of a place are almost exactly the same as those for denoting its history. The only difference is that you are to add the area code from Table 2 to 91 instead of 9. This means that any history number can be converted to a geography number for the same place by inserting a 1 immediately before the area code. Thus:

942.61: History of Norfolk, England
914.261: Geography of Norfolk England

973: History of the United States
917.3: Geography of the United States

When you first begin to study classification, you may have trouble distinguishing between works on geography and those on history. Read carefully the specific directions under "910," "913–919," and "930–990." Also, it is sometimes helpful to think of geography as a cross-sectional description of a locality at a specific time period while history represents a longitudinal treatment. Thus:

Philadelphia Celebrates the Bicentennial, a work that describes Philadelphia as it was during a specific time period, the year 1976: 917.4811043 but:

> *Philadelphia, 1776-1976,* a work that chronicles the city's develop-
> ment over 200 years: 974.811

Note that while *Philadelphia Celebrates the Bicentennial* spans an entire year, it is intended to describe Philadelphia in *a fixed or steady state*—as it was during the Bicentennial. On the other hand, the purpose of *Philadelphia, 1776-1976* is to record the *changes* that took place in the city over those 200 years. In trying to decide between a history or a geography number, ask yourself whether the work you are classifying describes a place in a fixed state, or describes changes in that place over time.

Another point of possible confusion is that materials are classed in "geography" which may appear to you to belong in sociology—i.e., all those works having to do with "social life and customs" of *specific places.* We suggest that you review the comments in Chapter 5 on determining subject content when a conflict appears to exist: "Classify a work having two or more subjects with the one receiving the most emphasis." Also, you should class a work treating two subjects under the subject influenced or acted upon. For further discussion of this, see the 20th edition's "Introduction," page xxxi, paragraph 5.6. In dealing with "social life and customs" of a particular *place*, it is the *place* which is of interest. Consider the journal *National Geographic* which, under the rubric of geography, discusses many aspects other than terrain and climate and the like in a specific locality.

Classes 920-929—Biography

The classes in the range 920-929 are as follows:

    920: Biography, genealogy, insignia
   *921: Philosophers and psychologists
   *922: Religious leaders, thinkers, workers
   *923: Persons in social sciences
   *924: Philologists and lexicographers
   *925: Scientists
   *926: Persons in technology
   *927: Persons in arts and recreation
   *928: Persons in literature
    929: Genealogy, names, insignia

Use of the classes marked "*" is, in the 20th edition of DDC, optional. You are told to prefer a class number denoting the discipline with the subdivision 092 added to indicate biographical treatment.

There is a direct correspondence between Class 920 and the above-mentioned subdivision 092. However, the main mnemonic device employed here is a correspondence between the third digit of each class number and the digits which represent each of the main classes.

From the above, you can see the DDC provides two possible methods of classifying biographies. You can place them in one of the classes listed above, or give them a number for the subject area with which the biographies is associated, followed by the subdivision 092, as in:

355.224092: Biographies of conscientious objectors

Some libraries use a third method, which is to class all biographies at 920, and then arrange them on the shelves alphabetically according to the biographee. The advisability of this method depends largely on the nature of the collection in question and the needs of the patrons who will use it. In deciding whether to employ this method for a particular work, you may wish to consider whether the work provides only a general discussion of the biographee's life and times or emphasizes details of that person's life which relate to a specific subject area.

Standard subdivisions of Class 900

Since we began by discussing the standard subdivisions, we shall conclude by listing the standard subdivisions of Class 900. These are:

    901: Philosophy and theory of history
    902: Miscellany of history
    903: Dictionaries, encyclopedias, concordances of history
    904: Collected accounts of events
    905: Serial publications of history
    906: Organizations and management of history
    907: Education, research, related topics of history
    908: History with respect to kinds of persons
    909: World history

Again, notice that the first trailing zero in the number 900 serves as the initial zero of each standard subdivision.

Note also that the meanings of two of the above numbers, 904 and 908, do not correspond exactly to the meanings of their respective standard subdivisions. Standard subdivision 04 has no meaning assigned to it in the 20th edition, and a specific meaning, "Collected accounts of events," is provided for *this particular number*. Standard subdivision 08 denotes natural history, yet the number 908 denotes history with respect to kinds of persons. It would, of course, make little sense for a number to denote the natural history of history. These two examples are further proof that you must always search for specific directives in the schedules which override general instructions.

In this chapter, we have attempted to familiarize you with Table 1's standard subdivisions, Table 2's area codes, the 900 class, and the close relationship among the three. In the next chapter, we shall describe the 400 and 800 classes, which include another significant use of systematic mnemonics.

Review questions for Chapter 7

1. What is the purpose of the standard subdivisions listed in Table 1?

2.a. What is the purpose of the initial zero in a standard subdivision?

b. Examine the simulated online Dewey number searches in Chapter 6. In those searches which involve standard subdivisions, what would happen if you omitted the initial zero from your query? Why?

3. Give the correct Dewey number for:

a. A history of medical science

b. A history of wind instruments and their music

c. A history of the psaltery (a plectral musical instrument)

d. A history of heating

e. A history of central heating

f. The current state of computer technology in the United States

g. A history of computer technology in the United States

4. What is meant by a mnemonic feature? Give some example from those parts of DDC that we have discussed so far.

5. What is the difference between a classification number consisting of 9 plus an area code from Table 2, and one consisting of 91 plus an area code from Table 2? Which type of number would be appropriate for a work on daily life in ancient Egypt? For a work on Rome covering the period of Julius and Augustus Caesar?

6. The digit 4 is used throughout DDC to denote Europe. Why is the number 909.094 incorrect as a code for the history of Europe? What does 909.094 mean?

7. What is the correct number for the geography of ancient India — 913.34 or 913.4? What is the reason for your choice? What would the number be for the geography of ancient Palestine?

8. How would you classify a book dealing with the influence of China on the history of Japan? Why?

9. How would you classify a work dealing with the life and customs of Brazil?

10. You are classifying a short film which describes the passage of a tornado through a certain city. The entire film covers only a period of fifteen minutes, but chronicles the destruction which the tornado caused during that time.

a. Would you give this film the number 9 + [Area code of the city] or 91 + [Area code of the city]?

b. Why should you give the film a number for the city, rather than one for tornadoes?

Sources cited

Dewey, Melvil. *Dewey Decimal Classification and Relative Index,* 20th ed. Devised by Melvil Dewey; John P. Comaromi, Julianne Beall, Winton E. Mathews, Jr., Gregory R. New, eds. Albany, N.Y.: Forest Press, a division of OCLC Online Computer Library Center, 1989.

8

Dewey Decimal Classification: Number Building in the 400 and 800 Classes Language and Literature

Throughout the last two chapters, we demonstrated the various types of faceting which the Dewey Decimal Classification uses. In the course of studying these two chapters, along with the actual schedules and tables, it has probably become apparent to you that DDC does not take faceting to the point where a given digit or group of digits *always* represents the same concept. The digit 7 appearing first in a number represents the fine arts, while in the number 617, it denotes surgery. Even a digit appearing in the *same position* in two different numbers is likely to have a different meaning in each case. The digit 2 in 320 denotes "Politics and government," while in 520, it denotes "Astronomy and allied sciences."

(Two classification schemes which do take faceting to the point where a given digit or group of digits always represents the same concept are the Universal Decimal Classification and Ranganathan's colon classification. However, as we said in Chapter 6, these two schemes, especially the colon classification, are much more difficult to use than DDC.)

Faceting methods used in both the 400 and 800 classes

The 400 and 800 classes, Language and Literature, use a much more refined method of faceting than the rest of DDC. We are discussing both of these classes in a single chapter because they both use the number building mechanisms we wish to illustrate herein.

In fact, *both* classes 400 and 800 use essentially the same set of digits in the same position to convey the same meaning. The following diagram illustrates the common ground between the two classes.

Figure 10. *Number Building in the 400 and 800 Classes*

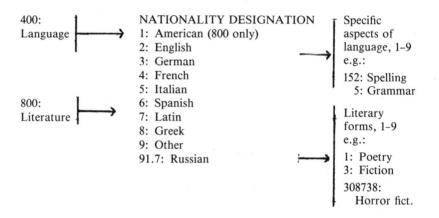

As the diagram shows, the digits 2–8 appearing in the second position in any 400 or 800 number always represent the nationalities indicated. The digit in the third position, or group of digits starting in that position, then represent either some aspects of the language associated with that nationality, or some form of literature written in that language. Although numbers for "other" languages and literatures sacrifice most of the positional significance of the digits — i.e., since the nationality designation requires more than one digit — they retain the general configuration of (4/8) + (Nationality) + (Aspect of language/ literary form).

Be advised, however, that the nationality designations which the 400 and 800 classes use are *not completely identical.* In fact, there are warnings to that effect in several places throughout the 20th edition. For example, as shown in the above diagram, the designation:

> 1: American

applies only to Class 800. Also, the "other" nationalities do not match exactly. Therefore, when building numbers in either of these two classes, adhere precisely to the instructions for that class; do not attempt to carry a nationality designation from one class to the other.

Class 400: Language

The 400 class of DDC deals with the display and study of languages in themselves—that is, with the expression, transmission, and comprehension of *all* ideas, concepts, designations and definitions of tangible objects, etc. through systematic symbolism. The language of a particular discipline is classed with the discipline; for instance:

> 610.14: Language of medicine

To understand why this is so, consider that the discipline is being acted upon by its language; the language represents the discipline to those who wish to understand and work within it.

The numbers 400–419 refer to the *concept* "language," and not to any specific language. The series 401–409, the standard subdivisions of the concept "language," treat that concept in the broadest sense:

> 401: Philosophy and theory
> 402: Miscellany
> 403: Dictionaries, encyclopedias, concordances
> 404: Special topics of general applicability
> → 404.2: Bilingualism
> 405: Serial publications
> 406: Organizations and management
> 407: Education, research, related topics
> 408: Treatment of language with respect to kinds of persons
> 409: Geographical and persons treatment

Like the numbers 901–909, listed in the previous chapter, the meanings of certain of these numbers do not correspond exactly with the meaning of the standard subdivisions in Table 1.

Linguistics

The next series, 410–419, represents linguistics, defined as, "science and structure of spoken and written language." Most of the digits 1–9, appearing in the third position of these numbers have the same significance as in classes 420–480 and the various "other languages" numbers beginning with 49. Notice that most of the concepts in the following list can apply to a specific language as well as to languages in general:

> 410: Linguistics
> 411: Writing systems (Alphabets, syllabaries, ideographs, braille)
> 412: Etymology
> 413: Dictionaries
> 414: Phonology
> 415: Structural systems (Grammar)
> 416: [Unassigned]
> 417: Dialectology and historical
> (Diachronic) linguistics
> 418: Standard usage. Applied linguistics.
> 419: Structured verbal language other than spoken or written
> [e.g., the manual alphabet of the deaf]

The above numbers are used only when describing the concept "language" as a whole. Classes 410–419 cover such aspects of language as the science and structure of spoken and written language, paleography, polyglot dictionaries, morphology and syntax, and multilingual phrase books.

Specific languages

The numbers 420–490 cover topics similar to those listed above as they apply to specific languages. The numbers 2–8 in the second positions of these numbers represent the various languages. The 490 "other languages" class, including such numbers as

> 491.7: Russian language
> 495.1: Chinese language

demonstrates DDC's Western bias in the uneven allocation of content among subclasses. See Chapter 6 for further discussion of this bias.

You may modify most, but not all, of the numbers 420–490 by the "Subdivisions of Individual Languages" found in Table 4. The numbers which may be so modified are indicated with one of three symbols; an asterisk (*), a single dagger (†), or a double dagger (‡). The "*" seems to denote instances in which only the base number appears in the schedules. The "†," and "‡" each seem to indicate cases in which some application of Table 4 is displayed in the schedules. We shall discuss this distinction more fully in a later section. The manual, volume 4, page

881, does not mention the "*," "†," and "‡" symbols, but states very clearly:

420–490 Specific languages
   The citation order of 420–490 is straightforward and without exception: Language + language subdivision from Table 4 + standard subdivision from Table 1.
   1. Grammar of the Hungarian language:
      494.511 + T4−5 = 494.5115
   2. History of the Korean language:
      495.7 + T1−09 = 495.709
   3. Dictionary of foreign words in the English language:
      42 + T4−24 + T1−03 = 422.403

The notations from Table 4 are never used alone, but are added to the base number for the individual language in question. Examples of numbers so built are:

English spelling and pronunciation: 42*1.52*
French spelling and pronunciation: 44*1.52*
Spanish spelling and pronunciation: 46*1.52*
Welsh spelling and pronunciation: 491.66*152*
Polish spelling and pronunciation: 491.85*152*

English, Etymology: 42*2*
French, Etymology: 44*2*
Spanish, Etymology: 46*2*
Welsh, Etymology: 491.66*2*
Polish, Etymology: 491.85*2*

Note that there are some languages and groups of languages which you may *not* subdivide by Table 4, such as:

439.9: East Germanic languages
492.1: East Semitic (Akkadian) languages

You must examine carefully the instructions appearing in conjunction with each language to determine how—and *if*—you must apply Table 4 in any specific case.

Dictionaries

The subdivision 3, "Dictionaries," warrants additional explanation. The numbers denoting dictionaries for a single language *intended for native speakers* of that language are straightforward:

German dictionary: 433
Classical Latin dictionary: 473
Czech dictionary: 491.863

However, *bilingual* dictionaries, those which match words in one language with equivalent words in another, may require a bit more thought. The basic formula for a number denoting a bilingual dictionary is:

(Proper designation, 42–48, 49 →   , for first language) + 3 + (Proper designation, 2–9 from Table 6, for second language)

This formula, however, begs the question, which of the two languages should you consider the "first language"? You must base your decision on the native language of those who will use the dictionary in question, and on the assumption that people will (a) use the dictionary to learn more about the language with which they are the least familiar and (b) search for the dictionary under the language they want to learn more about. So when you apply the formula, consider the first language to be the one with which the users of the dictionary will be the least familiar. If one of the two languages is the users' native tongue, that should obviously be the second language. Therefore:

English-to-French dictionaries to be used by those whose native language is:
English: 443.2
French: 423.4

If neither of the two languages in the dictionary is that of its intended users, you must decide which language will be the least familiar — the most foreign — to them; then class the dictionary with that language — i.e., use that as the "first language" in the above formula:

Chinese-French dictionaries to be used by those whose native language is:
English: 495.134
Japanese: 443.956

(We are asking you to concede that English speakers will consider Chinese more foreign than French, while Japanese speakers will consider Chinese more familiar than French.)

Here is a detailed breakdown of a bilingual dictionary number. In this case, the number is for a Chinese-Czech dictionary to be used by *Czech-speaking* individuals.

General	Specific

400: Languages →
  → 490: "Other" languages →
    → 495: Languages of East and Southeast Asia →
      → 495.1: Chinese language
        → Go to Table 4:
        "Subdivisions of Individual Languages" →
          → 495.13: Dictionaries of the Chinese
          language →
            → Go to Table 6 →
              → 9186: Czech language →
                → 495.139186: Chinese-Czech Dictionary
                for Czech-speaking individuals

If, in your judgment, both of the dictionary's languages are equally familiar or unfamiliar to its intended users, class it with the language coming *later* in the sequence 420–490:

A French-German dictionary for use by Korean-speaking people: 443.31.

Polyglot dictionaries — those containing three or more languages — are assigned to 413.

Before leaving the subject of dictionaries, we offer a warning: When classifying dictionaries, be sure to use the "Dictionaries" subdivision from Table 4, *not* subdivision 03 from Table 1. However, when classifying a dictionary of a specific discipline — music, mathematics, psychology, etc. — use the number for that discipline with the standard subdivision 03.

A source of possible confusion

Encountering the 400 schedules for the first time, you may be confused by the apparent redundancy between the numbers printed therein at 420–490 and those found in Table 4. As we said before, the various languages in the 400 schedules are flagged with one of three symbols, "*," "†," or "‡," which refer you to the instruction to add notations from Table 4. But if you must *add* these notations, why do you find in the schedules sets of numbers such as:

421: Writing system and phonology of standard English
422: Etymology of standard English

    423: Dictionaries of standard English
    424: [Unassigned]
    425: Structural system (Grammar) of standard English

in which they appear to have *already* been added? These lists are designed to aid you in carrying out the instruction by showing you what should result when you do so; when you add the numbers 1–5 from Table 4 to the base number 42 for English, you should end up with the numbers listed above.

    Be advised that these demonstrations appear only for the classes 420–480. From 490 on, the schedules list *only the base number for the language.* For example:

    491.62: Irish Gaelic

represents *only* Irish Gaelic. To represent the etymology of Irish Gaelic, you must add *another* 2:

    491.622: Etymology of Irish Gaelic

    As we stated earlier, "*" indicates that *only* the base number appears in the schedules, while "†"and "‡" indicate points at which what is printed in the schedules represents an application of Table 4. It appears that DDC uses the two symbols "†" and "‡" to facilitate reference to two different base numbers on a single printed page.

    So far in this chapter, we have described briefly how language numbers may be built, using the DDC base number for the national language and modifying that number by the appropriate suffix in Table 4. We shall now move to Class 800, "Literature (belles-lettres)." The close relationship between classes 400 and 800 should become apparent in the course of the following discussion. The 20th edition's manual discusses this relationship in the section entitled, "400 vs. 800: Language vs. Literature (belles-lettres)", volume 4, page 878.

Number building in Class 800: Literature

Determining what belongs in Class 800

    Literature (belles-lettres) is a difficult variety of recorded thought to classify or even to circumscribe. To begin with, most literary works are not intended primarily to explain a given subject, but are, rather, meant as vehicles of artistic expression. On the other hand, certain works describing various subjects use language in a skillful and artistic enough manner that they may be classed either with the subjects they cover or as *belles-lettres.*

In some cases, an author may deliberately attempt to blur or remove the distinction between artistic expression and explanation. For example, Hilbert (1986) has suggested that Melville's *Moby Dick* could be considered as either a discussion of whaling, using a fictional whale hunt as an illustrative example, or a novel about good and evil, incorporating expository passages on cetology to provide needed background information.

The DDC states, at the beginning of the 800 Schedule, "Option: Class belletristic essays, speeches, letters, satire, humor, quotations, epigrams, anecdotes, diaries, journals, reminiscences on a specific subject with the subject, e.g., essays on architecture: 720."

Works about literature

Another distinction you must keep in mind in classifying literature is the differentiation between works *of* and *about* literature. The subclasses 810–890 represent the literatures of specific languages, and are, for the most part, reserved for works *of* literature. The general classes 801–809, the standard subdivisions of literature as a whole, deal with literature as a subject, as follows:

801: Philosophy and theory of literature
802: Miscellany about literature
803: Dictionaries, encyclopedias, concordances of literature
804: [Unassigned]
805: Serial publications dealing with literature
806: Organizations devoted to literature
807: Education, research, related topics concerning literature
808: Rhetoric and collections of literary texts from more than one literature
809: History, description, critical appraisal of more than one literature

Nationality and form subdivisions of literature

Materials falling into classes 810–890 are classed by the language in which they were *originally* written. In some cases, it is possible for the same DDC number in the range 810–890 to denote works *of* and *about* a given type of literature, e.g., 811 applies to works *about* American poetry as well as works composed solely of American poetry.

Furthermore, any national literature can be written in a variety of literary *forms*, among them poetry, drama, fiction, essays, speeches, letters, satire and humor. *Form* subdivisions takes precedence over chronological or standard subdivisions, a point we shall expand upon in the discussion below.

Works by and about individual authors are classed with the language and literary form in which they principally write (or wrote). The DDC explicitly forbids you to add standard subdivisions to numbers denoting the works of a single author. We shall discuss other aspects of numbers for individual authors after discussing the classification of a national literature as a whole.

In general, you should use the following sequence of precedence to classify works of and about literature: (1) By language in which *originally* written; (2) by literary form; (3) by chronological or standard subdivision.

You have probably deduced, from the above discussion, that considerable number building is necessary in Class 800, especially with reference to the use of Table 3, "Subdivisions of Individual Literatures." We have already noted above the relationship between classes 400 and 800. Here are some further examples of how language numbers may be turned into literature numbers.

420: English language	*820*: English literature
460: Spanish language	*860*: Spanish literature
492.7: Arabic language	*892.7*: Arabic literature
495.91: Thai language	*895.91*: Thai literature

Table 3 has, in the 20th edition, been divided into three sections:

Table 3A: "individual authors"
Table 3B: "Subdivisions for works by or about more than one author."
Table 3C: "Notation to be added where instructed in Table 3B and in 808–809"

National literatures may be subdivided by literary form, according to instructions in Table 3B, as follows:

1: Poetry	5: Speeches
2: Drama	6: Letters
3: Fiction	7: Satire and humor
4: Essays	8: Miscellaneous

Here are some examples of numbers constructed using these form subdivisions:

> English poetry: 82*1*
> Spanish poetry: 86*1*
> Arabic poetry: 892.7*1*
> Thai poetry: 895.91*1*
>
> English fiction: 82*3*
> Spanish fiction: 86*3*
> Arabic fiction: 892.7*3*
> Thai fiction: 895.91*3*

Further subdivision of form

You may further subdivide each of the literary forms in Table 3B according to the various *kinds* or *types* of literature within each form. Under poetry, for example, Table 3B lists:

> 102: Dramatic
> 103: Narrative
> 104: Lyric and balladic
> 105: Didactic
> 106: [Number discontinued]
> 107: Satirical and humorous
> 108: Light and ephemeral verse

Using the above, you may build the following numbers:

> English dramatic poetry: 82*1.02*
> English narrative poetry: 82*1.03*
> English lyric and balladic poetry: 82*1.04*
>
> Arabic dramatic poetry: 892.7*102*
> Arabic narrative poetry: 892.7*103*
> Arabic lyric and balladic poetry: 892.7*104*
>
> Thai dramatic poetry: 895.91*102*
> Thai narrative poetry: 895.91*103*
> Thai lyric and balladic poetry: 895.91*104*

Note that the significant digits for the *specific types* of poetry are preceded by a zero. The type designations for other literary forms are also preceded by a zero, e.g.,

> English horror fiction: 823.*08738*

Chronological subdivisions

The zeroes discussed above serve to distinguish digits specifying types of the various literary forms from digits denoting chronological subdivisions of a form as a whole. Each national literature, 820–890, has its own table of chronological subdivisions, which you may apply either to the national literature as a whole, or to any of the literary forms. When applying them to a literary form as a whole, append them directly to the digit for the form; for instance:

822: English drama →
→   822.3: English drama of the Elizabethan period.

When applying chronological subdivisions to a national literature as a whole, you must use the standard subdivision 09, which Table 3B defines for classes 820–890 as "History, description, and critical appraisal of works in more than one form." Table 3B then instructs you to, "Add to 0900 the notation from the period table for the specific literature, e.g, earliest period: 09001." Following this instruction will give you:

820.9003: English literature of the Elizabethan period

Some tables of chronological subdivisions are also found in Table 3B, e.g., under "11–19: Poetry of specific periods," and "21–29: Drama of specific periods." However, you should use these only when there exists no chronological subdivisions in the schedules to overrule them.

There is one final and very important rule you must follow when subdividing a national literature chronologically: **Never attempt to add chronological subdivisions of one national literature to numbers for another national literature.**

Examples of literature numbers

Class 820: This is a broad, inclusive number, meaning "Literature of English and Anglo-Saxon languages." This number is unlimited by *any* literary form, by *any* chronological period, or by *any* standard subdivision. Only a comprehensive survey of everything literary written in the English language, from Anglo-Saxon origins through contemporary slang would receive this number.

Class 820.8: The subject, English literature; the form, a collection. This number represents works by various English authors, in various literary forms, unlimited by any time period.

Class 823: English fiction. There are two instances in which you would use such a number: (1) As an inclusive, comprehensive number for English fiction, unlimited by either standard or period subdivision. (2) For the works of a single author. Works of an individual author are classed with the *form*—fiction, poetry, essays, etc.—in which that author usually writes.

Class 823.008: Note the use of two zeroes. This shows that 08 represents the standard subdivision for collections, rather than a type of fiction. This number represents a collection of fiction by three or more English writers, unlimited by chronology. You may *not* assign this number to a collection of works by a single author.

Class 823.08738: This number represents English horror fiction. The single zero here shows that 08 has an entirely different meaning than in the previous example.

Class 823.0873808: Collections of English horror fiction.

Class 823.1–823.9: English fiction, *as a whole*, from specific time periods.

Possible confusion between standard subdivisions and form subdivisions

Observe that the final digits of the standard subdivisions 01–08 are the same digits used to specify literary forms. This may cause some confusion. Remember that a form designation appears first if there is one, and that standard subdivisions always appear with an initial zero. Thus:

811: American poetry
810.1: Theory of American literature

813: American fiction
810.3: A dictionary of American literature

817: American satire and humor
810.7: Education and research in American literature

Remember that the standard subdivision 08 means "Collections in more than one form by more than one author." Class a collection by a single author with the rest of that author's works. As we said earlier, work of individual authors are classed under the form in which they usually write. The one exception to this is William Shakespeare, and he receives only a subdivision of 822.3, "Elizabethan drama," his number being 823.33.

Also, distinguish carefully between the 08 "Collections" standard subdivision and such numbers as 808 and 818. The number 808 means "Rhetoric and collections of literary texts from more than one literature." This can include works on the effective use of language (as opposed to the 400 class which deals with the analysis of language itself). Texts taking this number will demonstrate good writing style, as in:

> 808.06665: Style manuals for business writing

or

> 808.241: A collection of one-act plays.

(A single play will, of course, take one of the numbers 822–882, 89 → 2.)

The number 818, on the other hand, denotes American miscellaneous writings. One of the best ways to get a sense of the works often classified under 818 is to examine the shelves of a public library. You will find essays, humor, even works about an individual author, all assembled under 818. You may also find works by an individual author, in cases where the author is not chiefly identified by a single library form. Any single work by such an author, however, should be classed with the form of that work.

Differences in classification of a national literature taken as a whole and of specific forms of a national literature

There are certain differences between the process of number building for a national literature *taken as a whole* and for building numbers within one of the literary *forms*. These are as follows:

1. *Standard subdivisions.* Notice the difference between the following two sets of numbers:

810.9: History, description, critical appraisal of American Literature	811.009: History, etc., of American poetry
	811.0409: History, etc., of American lyric poetry

The standard subdivision 08 is used only for collections by more than one author regardless of time period. Collected works of an individual author are, as noted above, *not* modified with 08. They, like critical appraisals and biography of the individual author, are classed under the form with which he or she is chiefly identified.

2. *Time period.* Similar differences occur with the attempt to modify classification numbers to indicate time period. The following illustrates the different manner of indicating time periods for an entire national literature and for one of its literary forms:

810.90054: History of
20th century
American literature

811.5409: History of
20th century
American poetry

811.04: 20th century
American lyric
poetry

Note that DDC does not allow you to modify a number for a *specific type* of literary form by a time period. The number 811.04 must serve as both a number for American lyric poetry in general and for 20th century American lyric poetry.

You may infer from the above exhibits that, in a sense, you are to handle modification of a classification number by standard subdivision or time period designation in an *opposite* manner for the literature as a whole and for specific literary forms. Note that in

810.90054: History of 20th century American literature

the period designation 54 follows the history designation 09, while in

811.5409: History of 20th century American poetry

the period designation 54 precedes the history designation 09. One probable reason for this is that 811.54 can also be used to describe the works of a single 20th century American poet, in which case the 09 would be prohibited.

(Generally speaking, you should avoid over-refinement of Dewey numbers.)

Procedural sequence to use when building a number in Class 800

In summary, before beginning to assign a classification number to a work of literature, determine the following:

1. The language in which it was originally written.

2. Whether the work deals with the national literature as a whole, or with one of the literary forms—poetry, fiction, etc.

3. Whether the work, if confined to one literary form, represents a further subdivision of that form, e.g., epic poetry, drama for radio and television, short stories.

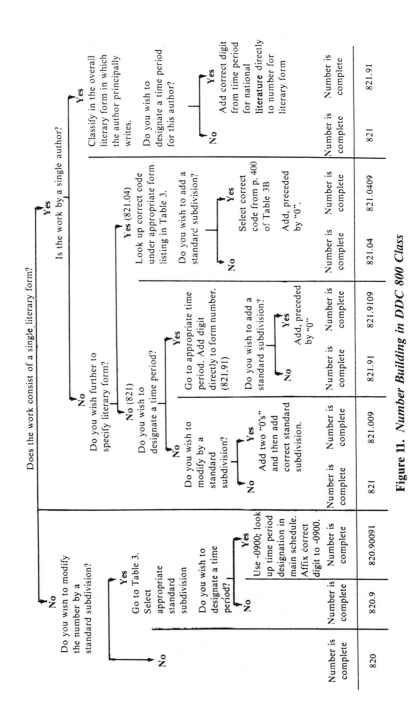

Figure 11. *Number Building in DDC 800 Class*

Assign Base Number According to Language in Which Originally Written (English = 82)

4. Whether the work is confined to a single time period—a time period which you should represent in the classification number.

5. Whether the work is the creation of a single author.

Having analyzed the work, follow the steps suggested in the flow chart shown in Figure 11. See also DDC 20th edition, volume 1, tables 3A and 3B, and the flowcharts in the manual, volume 4, page 775, 780.

In the preceding three chapters, we have examined the most important aspects of the Dewey Decimal Classification. In the three chapters following, we shall examine the other system in widespread use throughout the United States, The Library of Congress Classification.

Review questions for Chapter 8

1. What is the difference between the etymology of a language and the history of that language?

2.a. Which number correctly classifies a Welsh dictionary— 491.663 or 491.6603?

b. Which number correctly classifies a polyglot dictionary—413 or 410.3? Would the other number be valid for a work of a different type? If so, what type?

3. In classifying a Chinese-Russian bilingual dictionary, what number would you assign to it if it were to be placed:

a. In a Chinese library?

b. In a Russian library?

c. In an American library to whose patrons each language was equally unfamiliar?

d. In a library in San Francisco located in the heart of Chinatown?

What are your reasons for the above choices?

4. What is the correct classification number for a work describing the Bulgarian alphabet?

5. The numbers for English drama and German drama are, respectively, 822 and 832. Which number would you assign to an English translation of Goethe's *Egmont*?

6. What is the correct number for "Collections of German drama"?

7. What is the correct number for "Collections of German literature"?

8. What is the correct number for "Collection of the works of Goethe"?

9. What is the correct number for "Thai epic poetry"?

10. What is the correct number for "History of Thai poetry of the 20th century"?

11. What is the correct number for a work describing the art of writing essays in English?

12. What is the correct number for a collection of essays written by an individual British author of the 20th century?

13. Although DDC forbids you to add standard subdivisions to numbers to works by and about single authors, it does not provide an explicit rationale for this prohibition. Why do you think the developers of the scheme have included this rule?

Sources cited and suggestions for further reading or study

Dewey, Melvil. *Dewey Decimal Classification and Relative Index*, 20th ed. Devised by Melvil Dewey; John P. Comaromi, Julianne Beall, Winton E. Mathews, Jr., Gregory R. New, eds. Albany, N.Y.: Forest Press, a division of OCLC Online Computer Library Center, 1989.
Hilbert, Betsy. "The Truth of the Thing: Nonfiction in *Moby Dick*." *College English* 48 (1986): 824–831.

9

Library of Congress
Classification: An Overview

The Library of Congress Classification's priorities differ significantly from those of the Dewey Decimal Classification. Recall that, in Chapter 6, we preceded our overview of the Dewey system with a discussion of the perfect classification scheme. Such a scheme, we concluded, was impossible to create because the conditions it would have to satisfy were, past a point, mutually exclusive.

We then demonstrated that the Dewey Decimal Classification's primary goal is to create the perfect arrangement of all recorded knowledge. While its general principles are easy to understand and apply, it presents practical problems of inflexibility and cumbersome notation. In contrast, the Library of Congress Classification is designed solely for ease of implementation, subordinating or eliminating philosophical considerations whenever necessary.

The Library of Congress Classification's orientation results from its original purpose of organizing a specific collection—that of the Library of the United States Congress. The Library of Congress Classification has found favor with academic libraries—only 25 percent of which presently use DDC—for two reasons. First, as we shall demonstrate in the next three chapters, classification numbers which designate narrow topics are no more cumbersome than general numbers. Second, any library which uses this scheme can take classification numbers directly from Library of Congress catalog records.

The main disadvantage of the Library of Congress Classification is the inconsistent relationship between similarity of content and closeness within a collection. Again, we will provide examples further on. However, this may or may not be bothersome to the students, teachers, and researchers who are the usual patrons of an academic library. The first two groups often want a specific item. If not, they often want groups of items having a narrow enough focus to stand together under the Library of Congress Classification. While researchers are more likely to want all material on a broader topic, their interests will probably be specific enough to require the use of the subject catalog.

History of the Library of Congress Classification

While the Library of Congress Classification is centered around pragmatism rather than philosophy, its ancestry does reflect the thinking of such men as Bacon and D'Alembert, because of their influence upon Benjamin Franklin and Thomas Jefferson.

The Library of Congress was founded in 1800 and consisted at that time of 740 books. These volumes were classified first by size—folios, quartos, octavos and duodecimos—and then subarranged by accession numbers. A subject arrangement based on the scheme of Benjamin Franklin's Library Company of Philadelphia was adopted in 1812. Franklin based his Library Company scheme on the ideas of Francis Bacon (1805) and D'Alembert (1751).

1. Sacred history
2. Ecclesiastical history
3. Civil history, including chronology, biography, antiquities
4. Geography and topography
5. Law
6. Ethics (moral system) theology and mythology
7. Logic, rhetoric and criticism
8. Dictionaries, grammars
9. General and local politics
10. Trade and commerce
11. Military and naval tactics
12. Agriculture
13. Natural history: Natural and experimental philosophy
14. Medicine, surgery, chemistry
15. Poetry, drama, fiction, wit, etc.
16. Arts and science, miscellaneous
17. Gazettes
18. Maps, charts and plans

Under each of the above 18 classes, books were subdivided by size and then arranged alphabetically.

In 1814 the British burned the Library of Congress, destroying the majority of the collection. Congress, in 1815, purchased the library of

Thomas Jefferson for $23,950. Jefferson owned 6,487 books, which he classified into 44 main classes or "chapters," and his scheme, like Franklin's, was based on those of Bacon and D'Alembert. Jefferson subdivided his main classes and used geographic modifications. Librarians at the Library of Congress developed a notation combining the "chapter" number and the book number in a fraction-like arrangement. Revised by librarian Spofford, the denominator became a shelf number, and the notation then denoted a fixed location within the collection.

With modifications, Jefferson's system continued to be used throughout the 19th century. However, by 1890, the collection had grown from 7,000 volumes to one million. In 1897, the library moved to a new building and Herbert Putnam, who supported the idea of an entirely new scheme, became Librarian of Congress.

Hanson, who was then head of the Catalog Division, and Martel, chief classifier, examined three well-known schemes of the time: Melvil Dewey's *Decimal Classification*, fifth edition; the first six expansions of C.A. Cutter's *Expansive Classification*; and Otto Hartwig's *Halle Schema*.

Dewey's classification had many advantages. It was universal in scope; it had a clear, simple principle of notation; it had already been tested in American libraries. However, it required alterations in order to meet the needs of the Library of Congress. This proved to be an insurmountable obstacle, because Melvil Dewey was reluctant to compromise the integrity of his system. Otherwise, DDC would probably have been chosen as the national system of classification.

Hartwig's *Halle Schema* was judged too strongly oriented in traditional German philosophic thought for the purpose of a congressional library. Hanson and Martel, therefore, turned to the *Expansive* system of Charles Ammi Cutter for a scheme on which to base the new Library of Congress classification. Cutter was amenable to changes, such as the elimination of lower case letters as a principle of subdivision and the addition of arabic numerals in an integral, not a decimal, sequence. Hanson had previously worked with Cutter's *Expansive Classification* at the University of Wisconsin Library. Cutter used capital letters — omitting "P"* — to designate major classes, which were:

Cutter, in his 1891–93 Expansive Classification, Part I *comments (p. 23) "Now appears the reason why some of the letters of the alphabet were not used at first, namely, that they were reserved for classes to be inserted later . . . in the classification here set forth . . . the classes chosen are part of a carefully prepared whole, and the notation is such that other classes, which are sure to be needed in a library grown larger, can be intercalated without changing the classes already in use."*

A	General works	M	Natural history
B	Philosophy	N	Botany
BB	Religion	O	Zoology
C	Christianity	Q	Medicine
D	Historical sciences	R	Useful arts. Technology
E	Biography	S	Constructive arts
F	History	T	Fabricative arts
G	Geography and travel	U	Art of war
H	Social sciences	V	Recreative arts, music
I	Demotics, sociology	W	Fine arts
J	Civics	X	Language
K	Legislation	Y	Literature
L	Sciences and art	Z	Book arts

Hanson, working on the new Library of Congress classification, modified the list of major classes, employing the capital letters with the exception of I, O, W, X and Y. The 1904 outline of the Library of Congress classification contained the following major classes:

A	General works, polygraphy		pology
B	Philosophy	H	Social sciences
BL-BX	Religion	J	Political sciences
C	History — Auxiliary sciences	K	Law
		L	Education
D	History and topography (except American)	M	Music
		N	Fine arts
E	American general and U.S. general history	P	Language and literature
		Q	Science
F	U.S. local and American outside U.S. history	R	Medicine
		S	Agriculture
		T	Technology
G	Geography, anthro-	U	Military sciences
		V	Naval sciences
		Z	Bibliography

Development of the 22 classes listed above was not the work of one man. Subject specialists at the Library of Congress worked on each of the schedules individually, so that the separate schedules were completed not only independently of each other but at different times. The first to be published, in 1898, was Class Z, Bibliography, under the direction of Charles Martel, who also prepared the second and third editions of Class Z (in 1910 and 1926 respectively).

Since the Library of Congress schedules were utilitarian in purpose, classifiers worked with the collection as it actually existed, following the principle which Hulme later dubbed "literary warrant"—i.e., classifying in accordance with the specific collection in hand. Individual schedules organized the books contained in the subject area as exigency demanded, resulting in variations from schedule to schedule in content, scope, indexing and use of auxiliary tables. One consequence is an imbalance in certain areas, as in the allocation of two entire classes to American history, a single class for "Military science" and another for "Naval science."

Also, basic principles of organization differ from one class to another. Class P places all literary works by a given author together; a play, poem, short story and novel by James Joyce will all stand next to each other to the shelves. In contrast, Class M groups musical compositions by form; in an LC library, one will find string quartets by Beethoven, Schoenberg and Terry Riley standing together, while finding Beethoven piano sonatas and Beethoven symphonies in separate locations.

You should keep in mind that the Library of Congress Classification's inconsistencies are not the result of bias but of the needs of the Library of Congress. In a sense, the Library of Congress Classification is a scheme originally developed for a huge special library—that of a bicameral legislative body of democratic government.

Overall arrangement of the system

The Library of Congress Classification is a comprehensive practical system for the arrangement of a large collection of books (or other items). It consists of the following schedules:

A	General Works
B–BJ	Philosophy, Psychology
BL, BM, BP, BQ	Religion: Religions, Hinduism, Judaism Islam, Buddhism
BR–BV	Religion: Christianity, Bible
BX	Religion: Christian denominations
C	Auxiliary Sciences of History
D	History: General and Old World (Eastern Hemisphere)
DJK–DK	History of Eastern Europe (General), Soviet Union, Poland

DS	History of Asia
E–F	History, America (Western Hemisphere)
G	Geography, Maps, Anthropology, Recreation
H–HJ	Social Sciences: Economics
HM–HX	Social Sciences: Sociology
J	Political Science
K	Law (General)
KD	Law of the United Kingdom and Ireland
KDZ, KG–KH	Law of the Americas, Latin America and the West Indies
KE	Law of Canada
KF	Law of the United States
KJV–KJW	Law of France
KK–KKC	Law of Germany
L	Education
M	Music
N	Fine Arts
P–PA	General Philology and Linguistics Classical Languages and Literatures
PA Supplement	Byzantine and Modern Greek Literature Medieval and Modern Latin Literature
PB–PH	Modern European Languages
PG	Russian Literature
PJ–PK	Oriental Philology and Literature Indo-Iranian Philology and Literature
PL–PM	Languages of Eastern Asia, Africa, Oceania; Hyperborean, Indian and Artificial Languages
P–PM Supplement	Index to Languages and Dialects
PN, PR, PS, PZ	General Literature, English and American Literature. Fiction in English. Juvenile belles lettres
PQ, Part 1	French Literature
PQ, Part 2	Italian, Spanish, and Portuguese Literature
PT, Part 1	German Literature
PT, Part 2	Dutch and Scandinavian Literatures
P–PZ	Language and Literature Tables
Q	Science
R	Medicine
S	Agriculture

T	Technology
U	Military Science
V	Naval Science
Z	Bibliography, Library science

The Library of Congress publishes each of these schedules as a separate volume. A new edition of a given schedule may appear at any time independently of all others. Although the schedules use a common system of notation, many people created them at different times. The Library of Congress publishes quarterly lists of revisions but reissues an entire schedule only when a significant amount of revisions have accumulated. This function has been taken over by Gale Research, Inc., a publisher of scholarly reference works. It publishes a new version of each schedule incorporating all additions and changes to date. Gale omits a schedule from this series only when the amount of change is very slight or the Library of Congress is about to publish a new edition.

Relationships among main classes

Most schedules contain one or more main classes. Some of these are roughly analogous to the Dewey Decimal Classification's main classes 000–900. Others correspond more closely to the Dewey system's two-digit and three-digit subclasses. In the Library of Congress Classification, a capital letter, or a group of two or three, designates a main class. Since most practicing librarians refer to these simply as "classes," we shall do so from this point on.

Note that the preceding exhibit lists several classes beginning with B, D, H, K and P. In fact, most of the schedules contain several multi-letter classes sharing an initial letter. (The preceding list was of *schedules* — designating each by whatever title the Library of Congress has given it — not classes.) However, a multiple-letter class does not always represent a logical subdivision of the topic which its initial letter alone designates. Classes BL–BX, covering various religions, do not represent logical subdivisions of Class B, which covers general philosophy. Class GV, "Recreation," has nothing to do with Class G, "Geography."

The above example is our first illustration of one of the Library of Congress Classification's most significant attributes. Although hierarchical arrangements appear at many points throughout the scheme, they are not a requirement of it. They appear only when and if they make the system easier to use.

The classes might be grouped into four broad categories: (1) Schedule A: General works, Polygraphy. (2) Schedules B–P: Humanistic disciplines and the social sciences. (3) Schedules Q–V: Natural sciences and technology. (4) Schedule Z: Bibliography and library science. Schedule Z overlaps the others somewhat in that it denotes bibliographies of all subjects. This separation of bibliographies from other works on a subject is one example of the Library of Congress Classification's failure to class similar items together.

Arrangement of individual schedules

With the exceptions noted, each schedule contains:

(1) A prefatory note on its history and scope. Most of these notes are very brief. The Gale editions lack these notes.

(2) A synopsis, listing all classes covered therein. This appears in the majority of schedules, but not all of them.

(3) An outline of the whole schedule.

(4) The schedule itself, which is essentially a list, numbered 1–9999, of topics within each class. Although this list contains groups of topics subordinate to others, there is no consistent representation of hierarchy in the corresponding numbers. Many decimal numbers appear but only some denote subdivisions of the topics which their integer portions alone represent. The Library of Congress Classification incorporates decimal numbers solely to facilitate infinite expansion.

(5) A set of auxiliary tables. This appears only in certain schedules. *All* tables, except one for arranging biographical material, apply *only* to the schedule in which they appear. (Note that one of the separately published volumes is made up entirely of tables to be used with classes P–PZ.) Some tables apply to only a single number in the 1–9999 range, others to a span of numbers. Each table contains a set of instructions which you may apply to many numbers or number spans. We will discuss the purpose and use of specific tables in subsequent chapters.

(6) A detailed index covering only the schedule involved.

Earlier editions of the schedules also contained a list of additions and changes, followed by a index to those. The regular appearance of Gale's revised schedules has made these two sections unnecessary.

The first ten or so numbers in the 1–9999 range for each class denote various aspects of the class as a whole. Like the Dewey Decimal Classification's Standard Subdivisions, they designate either form of publication—periodicals, encyclopedias, etc.—or point of view—theory, methodology, philosophy, etc. Certain number spans designating broad topics *within* some classes also begin with a set of form and point-of-view designations.

Expanding the system

The Library of Congress may add whole new classes to the scheme by means of previously unused combinations of capital letters. In fact, the Library has created several of the double and triple-letter "K" classes very recently, and is now constructing others. These classes, covering the law of various countries, are subordinate to Class K, "Law." However, the Library of Congress could create a three-letter class which bore no such relationship to any other.

Expansion through use of vacant letters is a second possibility, although for two reasons we doubt the Library of Congress will do this. First, some of the letters present inherent problems. "I" and "O" resemble the digits "1" and "0." A library patron may believe "X" represents either the obliteration of an error or an instruction to disregard what precedes or follows. Second, the National Library of Medicine has already claimed one of the vacant letters, "W," so that Library of Congress may be anticipating some other institution's doing the same.

Parts of a Library of Congress call number

Each Library of Congress Classification number, or *call number*, uses a combination of capital Roman letters and Arabic numerals. Most call numbers contain between three and five distinct sections. On catalog cards and spine labels, each section usually appears on a separate line, as in the following example:

ML
200.5
.T36
1987

The Library of Congress has assigned this number to a 1987 book

entitled *A Most Wondrous Babble: American Art Composers* ...
1950–1985, by Nicholas E. Tawa (OCLC #14165763).

A Library of Congress number may also appear on one line:

ML200.5.T36 1987

However, a form such as

ML200.5
.T36 1987

is rarely used.

Because Library of Congress classification numbers are easily separated into short units, they are easy to print on catalog cards and spine
labels, whether a human or a computer is handling the task. For further
discussion of computer printing of LC classification numbers, see OCLC
(1986–).

Following is a diagram of the above number, with each component
labeled. A fuller description of each portion of the number follows this
illustration.

Figure 12. *Component Parts of a Library of Congress Call Number*

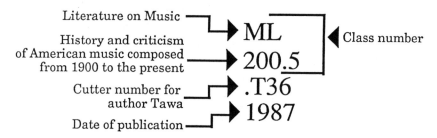

The first element of a number is the letter or group of letters designating the class. In this case, it is "ML," meaning "Literature on
Music." This is not subordinate to Class M, which covers music itself —
actual scores and sound recordings. Therefore, "M" and "ML" are two
subdivisions of the broader topic, "Music and writings about music,"
which does not have its own class.

The decimal number "200.5" represents the history and criticism of
American music composed from 1900 to the present. This number *is*
subordinate to "200," which represents history and criticism of
American music in general.

Together, the above two portions of the call number make up the
class number. These will appear on *any* book classified as history and
criticism of American music from 1900 to the present.

The ".T36" is a *cutter number*, named after its inventor, Charles A. Cutter. The Library of Congress Classification uses cutter numbers for several purposes, one of which is to place all items bearing a given class number in a logical order on the shelves. A cutter number with this function is termed an *item number*, and is a part of every Library of Congress call number.

At this point, we will discuss only what you need to know in order to use cutter numbers as item numbers. We will cover other types of cuttering — the term catalogers use for the process of assigning cutter numbers — as they become relevant to our general discussion.

A cutter number — whether or not it serves as an item number — is a decimal number in the range .1 to .9999..., with a capital Roman letter between the decimal point and first digit. The cutter numbers with which we are concerned at this point stand for some word or phrase, the capital letter being the first letter of same. The digits *loosely* represent the remaining letters of the word or phrase. The Library of Congress uses the following as a guide:

Figure 13. *Cutter Tables*

After initial "S"

a	ch	e	hi	mop	t	u
2	3	4	5	6	7–8	9

After initial "Qu"

a	e	i	o	r	y
3	4	5	6	7	9

After other initial consonants

a	e	i	o	r	u	y
3	4	5	6	7	8	9

After initial vowels

b	d	lm	n	p	r	st	uy
2	3	4	5	6	7	8	9

For third letter

a–d	e–h	i–l	m	n–q	r–t	u–w	x–z
2	3	4	5	6	7	8	9

Most item numbers represent a book's main entry, since that is what libraries generally use to arrange items. Returning to our example, "T" represents the first letter of "Tawa," and "3" represents the following "a."

Applying the preceding tables, you would expect the second digit to be "8," rather than "6." As we stated previously, however, these tables are only a *guide*, a starting point. You must choose digits which will fit the new number into the existing sequence. In this case, the Library of Congress may, when cataloging *Wondrous Babble*, have already had a book by an author named "Tawney," "Tawns," "Taws," etc., at ML200.5.T38. This would have required Library of Congress to use ".T36" in order to place "Tawa" in the proper position.

The above begs the question of why a library need worry about Library of Congress's choice of cutter numbers. In fact, no library *must* use Library of Congress's cutter numbers. An OCLC member library which routinely prefers Library of Congress records, however, often finds it advisable. If such a library rejects one Library of Congress cutter, it may create a sequence into which no others will fit.

The final component of our call number is the date of publication — 1987, in this case. This element is required only on certain call numbers, such as those assigned to any edition of a book other than the first. The date is always permitted, however, and the Library of Congress has adopted a policy of adding to it all call numbers. You are advised to add it whenever there is any possibility it might be needed. For further discussion of dates in call numbers, see LC (1982).

The call number we have just examined is one of the two most common types found in the Library of Congress Classification. The number below illustrates the other. The Library of Congress has assigned this number to *Building for the Arts*, by Catherine R. Brown:

NA
6813
.U5
B7
1984

Unlike our first example, this one has two cutter numbers. Note the absence of a decimal point before the second of these. The only place where a second decimal point may appear is in the numeric component of the class number, as in:

TS
1774.5
.U5
S64
1990

When a call number of the above type is written on a single line, the two cutter numbers are generally written without an intervening space:

>NA6813.U5B7 1984
>TS1774.5 U5S64 1990

In "NA6813.U5B7 1984," the "B7" is an item number, analogous to the previous example's ".T36." The ".U5" is part of the class number, which denotes the construction of arts centers in the United States. "NA" represents the main class "Architecture." The number "6813" denotes arts centers in a specific country. The ".U5" then specifies the country, the United States. (That cutter number in "TS1774.5 U5S64 1990" has the same meaning. You will discover the significance of the entire number in the next section of our discussion.) This is a *geographic cutter*, and is one of several type of cutter numbers which further specify the class number's meaning.

Layout of the schedules

Having examined single call numbers in detail, we now turn to a schedule's listing of class numbers. The following is a section of Class TS, "Manufactures." The physical layout reflects that appearing in the actual schedule. We have inserted the "1-2-3-4" to define a set of "levels" designed to facilitate our discussion.

```
TS
            MANUFACTURES
            Textile industries
            1-2-3-4
                Carpets, rugs, etc.
            1-2-3-4
1772            Periodicals, Societies, etc.
1773            Directories
1774            Exhibitions
                History
            1-2-3-4
      .4            General works
      .5            Special countries/regions, A–Z
            1-2-3-4
1775            General works
      .5            General special
```

```
            1-2-3-4
1776            Catalogs, etc.
1777            Rugs
                    Cf. NK2775 + , Art
1778            Oriental rugs
                    Cf. NK 2808 + , Art
1779            Other floor coverings, A–Z
                    e.g. .G7 Grass rugs
                         .L5 Linoleum
                         .M2 Matting. Straw, etc.
                         .O5 Oil cloth
        .5      Carpet measuring, cutting, laying, etc.
            1-2-3-4
1780            Tapestry
                    Cf. NK2975 + , Art
                    TT849, Hand weaving
1781            Miscellaneous textile articles and products
                    e.g. bagging, shawls, towels, etc.
                    For artificial fur, see TS1070
                    For flags, see TS2301.F6
1782            Lace (Machine made)
                    Cf. HD9933, Trade
                        NK9400–9499, Decorative arts
                        TT800–805, Needlework
        .5      Braid (Machine made)
1783            Embroidery (Machine made)
                    Cf. NK9200–9299, Decorative arts
                        TT800–805, Needlework
```

A degree of hierarchy is present in the list of topics, as illustrated by the "1-2-3-4." (These numbers represent the *first, second, third,* and *fourth* indentions. The LC shows hierarchy by indented positioning.) Carpets, tapestry, lace, braid, embroidery, and "miscellaneous textile articles and products" — at Level 2 — are all textile industries. The subject of textile industries — at Level 1 — is subordinate to that of manufacture, which is itself a subdivision of "Technology," the subject of the entire Schedule T. Furthermore, "Carpets, rugs, etc." is followed by a list of topics — at Level 3 — subordinate to it.

However, most of the corresponding notation fails to reflect this hierarchy. To begin with, the number ranges 1770–1779 and 1880–1889 *do not each represent a second-level topic with nine third-level subdivisions.* The range 1772–1779.5 is devoted to divisions of a single second-level topic, while 1780, 1781 and 1782 *each* denote a topic at that level. Furthermore, 1779 and 1779.5 *both* denote a topic at the third level; 1779.5 *does not* represent a subdivision of 1779. These are the most obvious examples of nonhierarchical notation; you will probably notice others, and may wish to argue that certain topics listed are not actually subordinate to others in the manner suggested by the page's layout.

This example illustrates three other noteworthy points about the Library of Congress Classification:

1. There is no mention of item numbers. You are expected to know it is standard procedure to add these numbers.

2. At 1779 is an example of another type of content-specifying cutter number. The numbers representing "other floor coverings" are called *topical cutters* or *subject cutters*. The brief list provided here essentially gives you *carte blanche* to insert new topics; a book on the manufacture of no-wax floors by John Walker, published in 1989, could be classed at TS1779.N6W34 1989.

3. There are occasional references to other classes, such as those at 1782. However, these are provided for a very small percentage of numbers. This is true throughout the whole of the Library of Congress Classification — and brings us to the next section of our discussion.

Available indexes to the Library of Congress Classification

A major drawback to classification by the use of Library of Congress schedules is the lack of any sort of overall index. Separate indexes appear at the ends of schedules, with only the occasional cross-reference — similar to those in the above example — to another point in the scheme. Furthermore, these indexes are alphabetical listings that make no attempt to draw together the various aspects of a subject into one coherent whole, as does the Dewey Decimal Classification's very useful Relative Index.

Nancy Olson (1975), in a multivolume work published by the U.S. Historical Documents Institute, has attempted to fill this gap by combining the many indexes into a few overall indexes, each organized by a different principle. For example, numbers 1 and 2 of the 15 volumes are titled *Author-Number Index to the Library of Congress Classification Schedules, 1974, in two volumes*. The next enumeration, labeled as "Set II," is titled *Biographical Subject Index to the Library of Congress Classification Schedules, 1974, in three volumes*.

Probably the most useful set of volumes within Olson's *Combined Indexes to the Library of Congress Classification Schedules* are, first, those in which subjects are listed by call number, and second, those volumes which, in contrast, provide an alphabetical list of subjects showing all call numbers assigned to each one. This permits some kind of a subject approach to the LC scheme and does demonstrate the various points in the schedule where the same subject is treated from different aspects. In this respect, several volumes in the combined index may be thought of as a quasithesaurus, although the Olson work cannot be considered, nor was it intended as, a relative index.

Another comparable, albeit smaller work is that of Williams, Manheimer and Daily, *Classified Library of Congress subject headings* (1972). This contains two volumes, one an alphabetical list of subject headings with corresponding call numbers, the other an ordered list of call numbers, or ranges of same, with corresponding subject headings.

The *Library of Congress Subject Headings List* also serves as a partial index to the LC scheme. As of the 14th edition, approximately 36 percent of the headings appear with at least one call number. Many appear with several, denoting approaches to the designated topic from multiple points of view. One such heading is:

> Homing pigeons
>   SF469 (Animal culture)
>   UH90 (Military art and science)

In cases where no call number is given, the "BT" references will help guide you to the proper schedules. (See Chapter 5 for a discussion of the reference structure of *Library of Congress Subject Headings List*.)

You may also use your library's subject catalog as an index to the Library of Congress Classification. An online catalog able to display a list of items under a given subject, each with its call number, will facilitate this operation. A search of the subject catalog will provide a list of possible call numbers and tell you whether any one number predominates as the choice for a given subject. However, anyone using this method should always verify the numbers found, since (a) numbers on older records may no longer be valid, (b) a given subject heading may not represent the primary topic of a book listed under it, and (c) the subject headings and call numbers in a given catalog may reflect biases of various past classifiers.

Learning to use the Library of Congress Classification

From the previous discussion, you will have already inferred that there are few instructions generally applicable for use throughout the LC schedules. There is no relative index and there are no form divisions common to all classes. There are a number of points at which one group of numbers serves as an example for subarranging several similar groups, but these apply strictly to the class in which they appear. Only a few general procedures, such as the use of item numbers, apply across all schedules, and there are even exceptions to these.

The best approach, therefore, is to plunge in by tackling several of the individual schedules, one by one. The above discussion of a portion of the TS schedule should give you some notion of what to expect. While facility in one class does not guarantee competence in another, experience with several of the classes should give you a "feel" for the purposes and methods of the scheme as a whole. Learning to use any classification scheme is a little like learning mathematics; by solving one problem after another, the underlying principles become evident. Only by carefully and painstakingly following a coherent set of procedures over and over again will you gain ease in the selection and modification of LC Classification numbers.

The hugeness of the LC scheme can be overwhelming. Keep in mind that the great size of the classification does not reflect complexity; rather, that the scheme was designed to provide numbers for a great many very specific topics. Remember also that the majority of call numbers take one of the two forms we have discussed:

CAPITAL LETTERS	CAPITAL LETTERS
Decimal number 0-9999	Decimal number 0-9999
.Item cutter	.Class cutter
Date	Item cutter
	Date

Keeping these models in mind will allow you to determine whether you are building numbers correctly.

Hints and partial instructions for number buildings are scattered among the schedules and auxiliary tables. For example, each of the auxiliary tables in the Z schedule—book publishing, library science, bibliography—contains the following footnote: "The numbers (1), (2), etc., are not part of the notation. They indicate sequence and are printed to facilitate reference." The footnote is saying that the table applies to a sequence of numbers in the schedule, and that the (1), (2), (3), etc., indicate the first, second, third, etc., number in that sequence. From this, you may infer that sets of numbers, (1), (2), (3), etc., found in auxiliary tables for other schedules may be applied to those schedules in the same way.

Entire books have been written on the use of the LC system. Chan (1990) after a consideration of the general characteristics of the LC classification, discusses special problems of its use and gives examples of the use of the auxiliary tables. Chan then explains each of the individual classes in turn. Another useful work is *The Use of the Library of Congress Classification* (ALA 1968), edited by Schimmelpfeng and Cook, especially the chapters dealing with the special problems found in classes H, J, P, Q–V, and assignment of author numbers. This work, however, requires that you already have some sophistication; it does not serve either as an introductory or a complete manual for the use of LC. You may also wish to examine Grout's *An Explanation of the Tables Used in the Schedules of the Library of Congress Classification* (1940).

Learning to use any or all of the individual schedules will not, of course, solve the problem of selecting the appropriate schedule for the work needing classification. As stated above, you may wish to consult Olson or Williams et al., or *Library of Congress Subject Headings List*, or an existing subject catalog. You should remember that this choice also involves matters of judgment which are not specific to the Library of Congress Classification.

To date, the Library of Congress itself has published neither a detailed instruction manual for the Library of Congress Classification nor an index to the scheme as a whole. However, the materials we have discussed above meet a large portion of the need for these two items; this and the following two chapters of our textbook are intended to fulfill the need for the former.

It is imperative that if you seek a cataloging position in an academic setting, you gain skill and understanding in the use of the Library of Congress Classification. It is highly desirable for you to learn this system in any case, given that the Library of Congress has become, by default, our national library. This and the growing emphasis on centralization in the online environment increase the probability that any given institution will adopt the Library of Congress Classification in the near future.

Review questions for Chapter 9

1. Contrast the priorities of the Library of Congress Classification with those of the Dewey Decimal Classification.

2. Why is a collection arranged by the Library of Congress Classification less suited for browsing than one arranged by the Dewey Decimal Classification?

3. Why is it easier for both computers and human typists to print Library of Congress numbers than Dewey numbers on labels, cards, and other printed products?

4. Contrast the hierarchy present in the Library of Congress Classification with that present in the Dewey Decimal Classification.

5. Why is it easier for the Library of Congress Classification to accommodate new subjects than it is for the Dewey Decimal Classification?

6. Without looking up the numbers, can you make any deductions about the relationship between ML111 and ML111.5 — *other than* that they both denote subdivisions of Class ML? Why or why not?

7. You are cataloging a book for which the main entry is "Rhodes, Lisa." This book will stand on the shelves between two others whose main entries are "Rhoad, John," and "Riley, Timothy," respectively. Describe the relationship among:

a. the letters in the name, "Rhodes"

b. the item number you will have to assign the book by Lisa Rhodes.

c. the letters in "Rhoad" and "Riley."

d. the item numbers already assigned to the books by Rhoad and Riley.

8. If you have encountered the MARC records bearing the symbol UKM, which come to us from the United Kingdom, you may have noticed that the Library of Congress Classification numbers therein never include item numbers. What might be the rationale for this practice?

9. If you do not have access to either the Olson or the Manheimer and Daily indexes to the Library of Congress Classification, what might you use instead?

10. Both the Dewey and Library of Congress Classifications contain more than one number for many topics. What question must you answer before you can evaluate the choices, *regardless* of which scheme you are using?

Sources cited and suggestions for further reading or study

American Library Association. *The Use of the Library of Congress Classification,* edited by Richard H. Schimmelpfeng and C. Donald Cook. Chicago: American Library Association, 1968.

Chan, Lois Mai. *Immroth's Guide to the Library of Congress Classification,* 4th ed. Englewood, Colo.: Libraries Unlimited, 1990.

Crawford, Walt. *MARC for Library Use: Understanding Integrated USMARC,* 2nd ed. Boston: G.K. Hall, 1989.

Cutter, Charles Ammi. *C.A. Cutter's three-figured author table.* Chicopee, Mass.: H.R. Huntting Co., 1969.

_____. *Expansive Classification. Part I. The first six classifications.* Boston: C.A. Cutter, 1891–93.

Grout, Catherine W. *An Explanation of the Tables Used in the Schedules of the Library of Congress Classification.* New York: School of Library Science, Columbia University, 1940; microfilm-xerography facsimile: Ann Arbor, Mich.: University Microfilms, 1969.

Hulme, E.W. *Principles of Book Classification.* Reprinted from the *Library Association Record.* London: Association of Assistant Librarians, 1950.

LaMontagne, Leo E. *American Library Classification with Special Reference to the Library of Congress.* Hamden, Conn.: Shoe String Press, 1961.

Library of Congress. *Cataloging Service Bulletin,* Robert M. Hiatt, ed., 19 (winter 1982): 25–26.

_____. *Cataloging Distribution Service. Library of Congress Subject Headings,* 12th ed. Washington, D.C., 1989.

Library of Congress Classification Schedules Combined with Additions and Changes through 1987: Class T, Technology. Helen Savage, editor; Kathleen Droste and Rita Runchock, associate editors. Detroit: Gale Research, 1988.

Library of Congress Classification Schedules Combined with Additions and Changes through 1988: Class M, Music and Books on Music. Rita Runchock and Kathleen Droste, editors. Detroit: Gale Research, 1989.

Library of Congress Classification Schedules Combined with Additions and Changes through 1988: Class N, Fine Arts. Rita Runchock and Kathleen Droste, editors. Detroit: Gale Research, 1989.

Library of Congress Classification Schedules Combined with Additions and Changes through 1988: Class Z, Bibliography and Library Science. Rita Runchock and Kathleen Droste, editors. Detroit: Gale Research, 1989.

OCLC. *Books Format,* 3rd ed. Dublin, Ohio: OCLC, 1986–.

Olson, Nancy B. *The Combined Indexes to the Library of Congress Classification Schedules, 1974.* Arlington, Va.: Carrollton Press, U.S. Historical Documents Institute, 1975.

Williams, James G., Martha L. Manheimer, and Jay E. Daily. *Classified Library of Congress Subject Headings.* New York: Marcel Dekker, 1972.

10*

Subdivision and the Use of the Tables in the Library of Congress Classification

In this chapter, we shall examine the various methods by which the Library of Congress Classification subdivides a given topic. We shall give particular emphasis to the use of the various tables appearing both within certain schedules and appended to them.

Notation of subject subdivision

As we explained in the previous chapter, the Library of Congress Classification has been developed with little attention to hierarchical notation. What little hierarchy is present exists purely for the sake of convenience, rather than for any philosophical reason. An example of the Library of Congress Classification's lack of hierarchical notation is evident in the following example:

HJ	TAXATION
	Treatises
2300	Early works to 1800
	Modern, recent
2305	English
2307	French

*By J. Paul Bain, as revised and expanded by David H. Downing.

165

2309	German
2311	Italian
2313	Spanish and Portuguese
2315	Other (*not* A–Z [i.e., A treatise on taxation in Hebrew by G. Berg would receive the number HJ2315.B47; there would *not* be a preceding "content" cutter H42 to represent Hebrew.])

Observe that the numbers 2305–2315 do not represent subdivisions of the topic denoted by 2300.

Observe also the omission of 2301–2304, 2306, 2308, 2310, 2312, 2314. Not all numbers within a given range are always used. This is mostly to permit the subsequent insertion of new topics, but can also be the result of deletions. Previous editions of this schedule used 2306 to denote "Minor works."

A decimal number does not necessarily denote a subdivision of the subject assigned to the corresponding whole number. However, a series of consecutive decimals can designate a set of logical divisions of a given topic. In the example below, the division is by time period.

HC	Economic history and conditions—of the U.S., by period.
	1901–1945
106	General works
.2	World War, 1914–1918
.3	Reconstruction, 1919–1939
.4	World War, 1939–1943
.5	Reconstruction, 1945–1961
.6	1961–1971
.7	1971–1981
.8	1981–

Observe that 106.2–106.5 denote subdivisions of the topic at 106—economic history and conditions of the U.S. from 1900 to 1945—while 106.6–106.8 denote later time periods.

Logical division of a topic may also be accomplished with cutter numbers. The following example divides a topic by form and location:

HV676	Prevention of accidents—United States.
.A1	Periodicals, Societies, Serials
.A2	General works
.A3	By state, A–W
.A4–Z	By city

Notice that the cutters A1–A3 do not represent any word or phrase beginning with the letter "A." All cutter numbers discussed so far have been derived from words or phrases — an author's last name, a place name, a subject term, etc. — using the letters of the alphabet to suggest numbers. However, this procedure makes sense only when it helps cutter numbers to achieve their goal — arranging items in a logical order. The most desirable arrangement often involves grouping together items sharing some characteristic. In these cases, you must eschew the representational cutter in favor of one which will place items in their desired position. The use of these "reserved" cutter numbers will be more fully demonstrated further on.

Use and location of tables in LC Classification

The LC schedules themselves could actually be considered a series of tables. For example, many subjects which are to be subdivided geographically by country will have this division enumerated in the main schedule, each country listed with its own number or cutter number. The subject "Statistics" is subdivided in this fashion in Schedule H, at HA175–4020.5.

However, the geographic division of the subject "Real Estate," at HD311–1130.5, is not worked out in the schedule. Instead, there is a reference to Table VII. You will find this table at the end of Schedule H, where it is one of several such tables. These are printed as a row of columns running across several pages — an arrangement which allows the actual list of country names to appear only once. There are many such tables located outside the Library of Congress Classification's various schedules. (In the case of Class P, they are printed as a separate volume.) Each table is used in conjunction with many numbers or number ranges within its corresponding schedule. There are no tables designed for use with the scheme as a whole, although a very few may be used with more than one schedule.

The correct procedure for applying these tables varies from one schedule to the next. Following is a demonstration of several such procedures, using hypothetical numbers.

When using the geographic tables from Schedule H, you are to add the correct number from the table to a base number given in the schedule. If the base number is 200 and the number for the country you must specify is 350, you must add the two, obtaining the result of 550.

When using certain other tables, including those found in Schedule Z — and discussed in the previous chapter — you are to read the table as a list of positions within a given number span. In a table of this type (1), (2) and (3) represent the first, second and third numbers in the span respectively. If the topic you wish to denote has a span of 100–102, and the table you must use assigns the number (2) to the specific subtopic you need to specify, your classification number will be 101, the second number in the span 100–102.

If a table includes cutter numbers, these are appended to a number either given in the schedule or resulting from one of the two operations listed above. If, in Schedule H, you are given a base number 200, then directed to a table which gives you a number 344.D2, your resulting classification number will be 544.D2.

In the chapter following, we shall demonstrate the operations listed above with actual numbers from the schedules.

The types of tables found throughout the Library of Congress Classification, both within and outside of the schedules, correspond, for the most part, to the types of subdivision which the scheme uses. Following is a discussion of these methods of subdivision and the tables used for each.

Types of subdivision in LC Classification

There are five main types of subdivision used in the LC Classification. They appear in the form of both appended tables and tables or enumerative sequences within the body of the schedules. While these subdivisions proceed in a generally logical manner, they do not possess a mathematical basis. For the most part, a given subject is arranged under a main class, then a subclass, then a sub-subclass, etc. The works on the class as a whole appear first in the schedules; then come the works dealing with the special phases or divisions of the subject in question.

1. Form divisions

The first major subdivision to appear under each main class is the logical form division applicable to the class as a whole. In most cases, the form divisions are as follows:

1. Periodicals
2. Yearbooks

3. Societies
4. Congresses
5. Collections
6. Encyclopedias; Dictionaries
7. Theory, method, scope; Relation to other sciences
8. History of the subject
9. Biography
10. General works
11. Study and teaching; Textbooks
12. General special. (This designates works on the subject as a whole treated from a particular point of view, or in a special manner.)

In fact, some of the above subdivisions are not "forms" as such. For the purpose of our discussion, we are using this term to denote both format and approach.

The order of these divisions varies among the classes and subclasses, and they are often further subdivided by time period or geographic location. For example, the history of a subject is often broken down by centuries or other periods. Earlier in this chapter, we illustrated this with the numbers at HC106 + . Although the Library of Congress Classification does not employ a general pattern of "form" subdivisions across all classes and subclasses, it does enumerate these divisions in the schedules, so that they present no special problems for you.

There is one type of "form" subdivision which requires the use of tables outside of a schedule. This occurs in Class P, where literature is arranged by author, then broken down by type of work. This will be illustrated in the following chapter.

2. Geographical divisions

Another very important type of subdivision is the geographical arrangement of a subject. Almost every main class—especially in Schedule H—may be subdivided geographically, usually by country, but often by state or city.

In many cases, a subject is subdivided by country and then by form. Returning to HD311-1130.5, we find along with the reference to Table VII, a table headed "Under each:" printed in the schedule. You must obtain the proper sequence of numbers from Table VII, then "plug" them into the "Under each:" table. The "Under each" tables are of the same type as those from Class Z already discussed in both this and the previous chapter; (1) denotes the first number in the sequence, (2) the second, etc. This operation yields a single number which one adds to the base number HD310 to produce the correct class number.

The above example illustrates a potential source of confusion for the uninitiated classifier. The schedule gives HD*311* as the first number in the range allocated to the geographic subdivision of *Real Estate.* However, the accompanying footnote instructs one to add the appropriate number from Table VII to HD*310*. Although the footnote may appear to contradict the schedule, it in fact does not; you are to *add* the correct number from Table VII *to* HD310, in order to produce a number which *falls within the range* HD311–1130.5. The resulting class number is correct if it has the same final digit as the proper number from Table VII; if the correct table number is 25, the correct class number is HD335, *not* HD336.

3. Chronological divisions

This type of subdivision allows a given subject to be differentiated by date or time period. This type of subdivision usually appears in the form of an enumeration in the main schedule, often headed, "By Period." Again, the numbers listed at HC106+ provide one example of this. Another is at HF5607, where the subject *Accounting* is broken down as follows:

HF5607 Ancient (Egyptian, etc.)
HF5609 Medieval
HG5611 Modern

You are *not* at liberty to create new subdivisions to denote time periods narrower than those provided. Thus, you would have to place a work entitled *Accounting in the 17th Century* at HF5611.

In general, you are not permitted to compose numbers not printed in the schedules. An important exception to this is the practice, discussed in the following section, of creating cutter numbers for subjects.

4. Subject modification (special topics) division

The Library of Congress classification often uses the whole number or decimal number portion of a class number to denote a category. Then follows a list of cutter numbers each representing an item within that category. This type of subdivision may be termed subject modification or special topics subdivision.

In the previous chapter, we discussed the example of TS1779, which denotes the manufacture of floor coverings other than rugs. The whole number 1779 must be followed by a cutter number representing a specific floor covering. In this case, the schedule provides only a brief list of cutter numbers, with the understanding that you may create a cutter number for any floor covering you need to specify.

You will find a slightly different example at HF5716. Again, this number, a subdivision of the topic *Business Mathematics*, denotes a category — "Tables of quantity, weight, etc., of particular commodities." However, the list of cutter numbers given here is quite extensive. What appear below is only an excerpt from that list:

A8: Awnings	M4: Neat
B3: Beets	N4: Netting
B4: Books	O4: Oil
C5: Coffee	S9: Sugar
E3: Eggs	T25: Tea
E4: Electricity	W6: Woolen goods
L8: Lumber	

You are permitted to cutter for items not on the list, so that you could place a *Table of the Cost of Nickel* at HF5716.N5 — between "netting" and "Oil." ("Nickel" does not appear even on the complete list from which we excerpted the above.) However, there are some indications that LC may prefer you to consider the more extensive lists closed. For instance, the revised version of a schedule may have items deleted. The number RC553 denotes a subdivision of psychiatry termed "Specific pathological states." The list which follows formerly contained the cutter "G8" for "Guilt," but this was deleted in subsequent editions.

5. Name division

Class P makes extensive use of this final type of subdivision, lists of proper names. In fact, since LC classifies most literary works under the name of the author, the various P schedules consist largely of lists of names denoted by a range of numbers, a single whole number or cutter number. Several other classes also contain lists of persons who are important figures in a given field. As with subject subdivision, you either locate the desired name on a list, such as that given above for commodities, or insert it by means of cuttering.

Many name tables must be used in conjunction with various form or subject tables, in order to further subdivide works by and about a specific person. We shall discuss this matter more fully in the following chapter, which focuses on the use of the tables in Classes H and P.

Location of subdivision instructions in the Library of Congress Classification

For the most part, the tables and enumerations relating to form, chronology and subject subdivision occur within the main schedule. Geographic subdivision sometimes occurs within the main schedule, as with classes E and F, and sometimes occurs in auxiliary tables, as with Class H. The tables designed to be used at many points within a schedule are usually printed at the end of that schedule, or, in the case of Class P, in a separate volume.

Having discussed the various types of subdivision separately, we must now point out that it is often necessary to consult several tables in order properly to classify a particular work. One table will often provide a range of numbers or cutter numbers which you must "plug into" a second table. The following chapter contains a set of detailed examples.

Use of cutter numbers in LC Classification

Before proceeding to illustrate the use of specific tables, we must discuss the subject of cutter numbers in more detail. They are an integral part of the Library of Congress Classification, so that you must gain a complete understanding of their nature and function to use the Library of Congress Classification.

First, we should clarify several points about terminology. In practice, the term "cutter number" is often shortened to "cutter," usually when referring to a type of cutter number: "subject cutter," "geographic cutter," and so on. Furthermore, "cutter" is often used as a verb, meaning "to assign a cutter number." To "cutter for" a given element is to construct a cutter number representing that element; one usually *cutters for* the main entry of a work. We may also use the phrase, "cutter on" in conjunction with *n*th letter of a word or phrase. This refers to the use of that letter as a starting point in the construction of a cutter number; you usually *cutter on* the first letter of an author's name, but certain portions of Class P require you to *cutter on* the second letter.

Thus far, we have kept our use of these terms to a minimum. Having defined them, we shall use them more freely in the remainder of this textbook. Since they are in common use among practicing librarians, you should become familiar with them.

Dedicated and "reserved" cutter numbers

We have, in fact, already discussed several types of dedicated cutter numbers, such as those used to represent subject terms. A dedicated cutter number is one which *must* be used to denote a specific piece of information, and *only* for that purpose. Returning to the list of commodities under HF5716, the cutter number T25 is used to represent "Tea"; you must use this cutter for a work on the price of tea, and may not use T25 to represent some other commodity.

At this point, we wish to focus on a special type of dedicated cutters which we earlier termed "reserved" cutter numbers. These are usually used to denote form or general approach to a topic. A significant characteristic of these numbers is that their initial letter and following digits are not derived from a specific word or phrase. Reserved cutters are constructed solely on the basis of where they will place a group of items relative to all others having the same class number.

We can best explain the use of reserved cutter numbers by providing an example. The following, which we discussed briefly earlier, divides a topic by form and location:

HV676	Prevention of accidents
	– United States.
.A1	Periodicals, Societies, Serials
.A2	General works
.A3	By state, A–W
.A4–Z	By city

Following is a set of hypothetical works which will illustrate the arrangement resulting from use of these reserved cutters:

HV676.A1A3274	Accident prevention journal

HV676.A1A3277	Accident prevention review
HV676.A1A3278	Accident prevention weekly
HV676.A1S237	Safety review
HV676.A1P82	Public safety
HV676.A1T44	This week in safety
HV676.A2B37	Barlow, Joel Safe work and play in the U.S.A.
HV676.A2G66	Goldman, Thomas A study of accident prevention in the United States
HV676.A2S56	Simmons, Charles Safety in America
HV676.A2W36	Wallace, Stephen Guarding against hazards in the American workplace
HV676.A3A42	Abrams, Roger Dangers of the dark : safe living during the Alaskan dark season
HV676.A3A45	Martin, Gary Fighting hazards of the Alaskan climate
HV676.A3A49	Yarwood, William Alaska stays safe
HV676.A3C24	Emmerson, Larry California safety
HV676.A3C242	Farmer, Jerry Accident prevention in California
HV676.A3C25	Manning, Donna Battling California's hazards
HV676.A3N7688	Wallace, Ronald A study of accident prevention in the state of New York
HV676.A3N77	Wilson, Janet Safe living in New York State
HV676.A3N78	Wolper, Ed New York State safety
HV676.A4S65	Smith, Walter Atlanta accident prevention
HV676.C232C37	Carson, Laura Safety in Chapel Hill
HV676.N5R62	Rockford, Anne Keeping the Big Apple as safe as possible

HV676.P5T56   Thompson, Sylvia
                    Accident prevention in Philadelphia

Because of the reserved cutters .A1–.A3, all periodicals come first, followed by all general works. After these come the works that deal with accident prevention in a single state. At the end of the sequence are works dealing with accident prevention in a single city.

You may feel that the above example gives rise to several questions regarding the practice of cuttering. We shall address several of these in the following sections.

Call numbers without a separate item number

The numbers in the above display beginning with "HV676.A3" lack a separate item number to represent their respective authors. With a few exceptions, it is not standard practice to add more than two cutter numbers to a class number. In this case, you must use both cutters to denote content — "A3" to indicate division by state, plus a geographic cutter for the state. To subarrange the items at HV676.A3 by main entry, you must create a range of cutters to represent each state. You then represent each item's main entry, and its place relative to the main entries of other items at HV676.A3, by means of the appropriate number within the range. In our example, we have used a fixed stem to represent each state, with additional digits to represent main entries:

HV676.A3*C24*   Emmerson, Larry
                    California safety
HV676.A3*C242*   Farmer, Jerry
                    Accident prevention in *California*
HV676.A3*C25*   Manning, Donna
                    Battling *California*'s hazards

In each case, C2 represents California. The digits after the 2 place Emmerson before Farmer, and Farmer before Manning.

Using more than one digit in a cutter number

In our example, we have given each cutter at least two digits. This section will explain why we encourage you to adopt this practice.

The item numbers on the first three serial publications are taken out to four digits and given the common stem "A327." Because of this, they do not usurp a large portion of the range A2–A999... — a range which will likely be needed for titles beginning with "Accidental," "Accidents," "Accident awareness," etc. Although there is only one serial whose title begins with "Safety," its item number has been given three digits in anticipation of future publications with similar titles.

The three books at HV676.A3N7 + —

HV676.A3N7688	Wallace, Ronald
	A study of accident prevention in the
	state of New York
HV676.A3N77	Wilson, Janet
	Safe living in New York State
HV676.A3N78	Wolper, Ed
	New York State safety

— illustrate a problem which can arise when you choose not to extend a cutter number. We are supposing that our hypothetical library received these books in reverse-alphabetical order. The cataloger who handled the Wolper book took the second cutter out to two digits — the "N7" for "New York," plus "8" to represent the "W" of "Wolper."

When the Wilson book was added to the collection, its cutter had to come before "N78." Again, the cataloger only used a single additional digit — the "7." The cutter for the Wallace book, therefore, had to come before "N77" — at a point in the range N7–N7999... which perhaps should have been reserved for authors having names beginning with "M" through "O." Realizing this, the cataloger assigned the cutter "N7688," leaving the range N76–N7687999... for authors in the M–O range.

The cataloger might instead have sacrificed the "N7" stem for "New York," but this would have interfered with numbers for New Mexico, and possibly New Jersey. The problem would have never arisen if the cataloger had cuttered the Wolper book "N786," and the Wilson book "N785."

Again, we wish to stress that none of the cutters used were wrong. They simply created an awkward situation which could easily have been avoided.

Types of cutter numbers — a summary

At this point, we have either described or displayed all types of cutter numbers in general use throughout the Library of Congress

Classification. For reference purposes, we will now list these types with a brief description.

AUTHOR CUTTER NUMBERS: This is the most frequently used type throughout the Library of Congress Classification. In all classes except P, the call number for a work with an author main entry has, as the last element before the date, a cutter representing that main entry. In Class P, the author cutter is used as a special type of subject cutter. This will be discussed in detail in the following chapter.

TITLE CUTTER NUMBERS: Outside of Class P, call numbers for works with a title main entry employ a cutter derived from that title. Anonymous works also are often cuttered for title. This cutter number occupies the same position as the author cutters described above. In Class P, the title cutter becomes an item number to subarrange all works by a given author. A similar practice is frequently used to arrange musical works in Class M, but only at the cataloger's discretion. An example of title cuttering in Class P is:

PR3489:	Oliver Goldsmith
.T72:	*The Traveler*
PR3489.T72:	*The Traveler* by Oliver Goldsmith.

We shall explain further how to build a number such as the one above in the next chapter.

GEOGRAPHIC CUTTER NUMBERS: These represent a geographical location—country, state, city, etc. Unlike the "Areas" numbers from DDC, you are not at liberty to add a geographical cutter to any class number in order to denote treatment of a topic within a specific location. This type of cutter may only be added to whole or decimal numbers denoting geographical treatment of a subject. Examples of geographic cuttering are:

HG6024.9:	Investment, speculation, financial futures.
.C6:	China
HG6024.9.C6	Investment, speculation, financial futures in China.
HG6024.9:	Investment, speculation, financial futures.
.G83:	Greenland
HG6024.9.G83	Investment, speculation, financial futures in Greenland.
HG6024.9:	Investment, speculation, financial futures.
.L4:	Lebanon
HG6024.9.L4	Investment, speculation, financial futures in Lebanon.

We shall explain further how to build a number such as those above in the next chapter.

SUBJECT CUTTER NUMBERS: When a whole or decimal number denotes a category — specific products, ethnic groups, diseases, issues, etc. — it is followed by a cutter which represents a specific item within that category. In some cases, the schedule will provide an extensive list of items, in others it will give only a few. An example of subject cuttering is:

HJ4653:	Income tax in the U.S.
.E75:	Evasion (from a list of special topics in the schedules)
HJ4653.E75:	Income tax evasion in the U.S.

"RESERVED" CUTTER NUMBERS: These are used to group together works having a particular form or using a particular approach. Unlike the other types, they are not mnemonic. Since their purpose is to place a group of items either before or after all other works having the same class number, they usually fall within the range A1–A4, as do those at HV676, or Z5–Z999. Examples of reserved "A" cutter numbers at HV676 appear earlier in this chapter. Examples of "Z" cutter numbers will be found in the discussion of Class P in the following chapter.

Review questions for Chapter 10

1. List the types of subdivision present in the Library of Congress Classification.

2. How do the various tables serve to shorten the schedules in which they appear?

3. What is the relationship between a range of numbers, e.g., 100–102, in a table and the numbers (1), (2), (3) appearing in a schedule in conjunction with the instruction to use that table?

4. List the various types of cutter numbers.

5. Whenever you are free to create your own cutter numbers, why should you take them out at least to two digits?

6. You have given a work a class number which denotes conferences on artificial intelligence. The work is to be entered under its title, *A Conference on Artificial Intelligence: Can a Computer Be Self-Aware?* Therefore, you must derive the work's item number from this

title. Why might you want to take this cutter number out to more than two digits? From what portion of the title would you derive the final digit(s)?

7. Why is it that item cutter numbers are derived from an item's main entry in a clear majority of cases, *even though they do not have to be*? Give an example of an item *other than one that takes a "reserved" cutter number* to which you might want to assign an item number *not* derived from the item's main entry.

Sources cited and suggestions for further reading or study

Chan, Lois Mai. *Immroth's Guide to the Library of Congress Classification*, 4th ed. Englewood, Colo.: Libraries Unlimited, 1990.

Library of Congress Classification, Class B, Subclasses B–BJ. Washington, D.C.: Office for Subject Cataloging Policy, Collections Services, Library of Congress, 1989.

Library of Congress Classification Schedules Combined with Additions and Changes through 1989: Class H, Subclasses H–HJ. Rita Runchock and Kathleen Droste, editors; Victoria A. Coughlin, associate editor. Detroit: Gale Research, 1990.

Library of Congress Classification Schedules Combined with Additions and Changes through 1989: Class H, Subclasses HM–HX. Rita Runchock and Kathleen Droste, editors; Victoria A. Coughlin, associate editor. Detroit: Gale Research, 1990.

Library of Congress Classification Schedules Combined with Additions and Changes through 1987: Class P, Language and Literature, Subclasses PN, PR, PS, PZ. Helen Savage, editor; Kathleen Droste and Rita Runchock, associate editors. Detroit: Gale Research, 1988.

Library of Congress Classification Schedules Combined with Additions and Changes through 1989: Class R, Medicine. Rita Runchock and Kathleen Droste, editors; Victoria A. Coughlin, associate editor. Detroit: Gale Research, 1989.

Library of Congress Classification Schedules Combined with Additions and Changes through 1988: Class Z, Bibliography and Library Science. Rita Runchock and Kathleen Droste, editors. Detroit: Gale Research, 1989.

Material from *Library of Congress Classification Schedules Combined with Additions and Changes*, copyright 1989 by Gale Research Inc., reproduced by permission of the publisher.

11*

The Use of Tables in Library of Congress Schedules H and P

In this chapter, we shall actually "walk through" the process of using various Library of Congress Classification tables to construct a call number. Unfortunately, since we must, in this textbook, give equal coverage to *all* aspects of cataloging and classification, we cannot and should not demonstrate the use of every Library of Congress Classification table. We have chosen to examine schedules H and P for two reasons. First, if you are a novice classifier, you are likely to find these two schedules the most difficult to use. Second, our experience in the field suggests that if it is your job to handle all acquisitions by a general academic library, you will encounter these two schedules more often than the others which make use of tables.

The H schedules

Class H and subclasses HA–HX cover the social sciences. The Gale editions of the Library of Congress Classification place the H schedules into two volumes, H–HJ and HM–HX. The subclasses are as follows:

> H: Social sciences, General
> HA: Statistics
> HB: Economic theory
> HC: Economic history and conditions

By J. Paul Bain, as revised and expanded by David H. Downing.

HD: Economic history and conditions
HE: Transportation and communications
HF: Commerce
HG: Finance
HJ: Public finance
HM: Sociology
HN: Social history and conditions; Social problems; Social reform
HQ: The family. Marriage, Woman
HS: Societies: secret, benevolent, etc.
HT: Communities; Classes; Races
HV: Social pathology; Social and public welfare; Criminology

Many works on some aspect of the social sciences discuss a topic with respect to a specific region, country, state or city. To provide for such works, the various H classes contain number spans devoted to the treatment of a topic "by region or country," or a similar phrase. This designation includes a reference to one of ten tables which appear at the end of the schedule. (The complete set of tables appears at the end of both physical volumes covering the H classes.)

These tables, numbered with the Roman numerals I through X, appear as a set of columns of numbers or number ranges running across several pages. Each successive table fits the various countries and regions of the world into an increasingly larger span of numbers. Since the numbers in Table I run only from 1 to 100, there is only "room" for one number to denote most countries — one important exception being the United States. On the other hand, the highest number in Table X is 996, so that most countries may receive a range of numbers. Mexico, for example, is assigned the range 161–170.

The actual list of country/region *names* is printed only once, in its own column. You are to read down this list to find the desired country, then across to the proper table. You must then take the number or number range back to the schedule, where a "form" table will provide further guidance.

As we mentioned in the previous chapter, the footnote accompanying a "by region or country" designation may confuse you if you are using Schedule H for the first time. This footnote instructs you to add the correct number from the tables to a base number which is *one less than* the span given in the schedule. For example, the topic

Demography of deaths — by country

is assigned the number span

HB133*1*-1530

with a reference to Table II. However, the footnote tells you to add the number from Table II to

HB133*0*

The schedule is instructing you to *add* the correct number *to* HB1330, *in order to produce* a number which *falls within the range* HB1331-1530. Table II begins with the number "1," which denotes "America." You add 1 to HB1330 in order to produce

HB1331: Demography of deaths in America

We will now move through the process of actually building several call numbers using Schedule H.

Procedures for using Schedule H

The first significant use of tables in Schedule H, occurs at

HA175-4020.5: Statistics, by country

Here, rather than sending you to one of the tables, the schedule provides HA numbers for the various countries. Each country is assigned a range of 5, 10 or 20 numbers; you must consult the "form" table at HA175 to determine which of these to use.

Thus, the procedure for building a number denoting a general work on statistics in Spain is as follows:

1. Locate the numbers for Spain in the schedule. Spain is assigned 20 numbers, 1541–1560, inclusive.

2. Return to the "form" table at HA175, and locate the number for general works, which is 14.

3. Using 14 as an ordinal number, determine the 14th number in the range 1541–1560. This turns out to be 1554. (You may obtain the same result by reading 14 as a cardinal number and adding it to 1540, per the above discussion.)

4. Once you have produced the proper class number, HB1554, add the appropriate item number, and date, if desired, to produce the complete call number. For a book written by William Carson published in 1981, the final call number might be

HB1554.C37 1981.

In contrast to the preceding example, the number span

HD311–1130.5: Economic history and conditions, Land use, other countries [i.e. other than the United States]

requires the use of Table VII, one of those at the end of the schedule. To build a number denoting land use in Tokyo, Japan, follow these steps:

1. Obtain, from Table VII, the correct number range for Japan. This is 611–620 — a span of 10 numbers.

2. Return to the form table, headed "Under each," at HD311. Determine which number in the "10-numbers" column corresponds to the designation, "By city, A–Z." Here, it is "(10)," or the 10th number, which is 620.

3. Add this number, 620, to the base number given in the footnote, 300, to produce HD920. In this case, we have a base number which is *eleven* less than the first number in the allocated span. Again, this is not a contradiction. The first number in Table VII is "11," to denote Canada, the spaces corresponding to the United States being blank. Remember that HD311–1130.5 denoted land use in countries other than the United States; specific numbers for the United States are given on the preceding page.

4. Add a geographic cutter for Tokyo. We shall use T6. Thus, the class number for land use in Tokyo is HD920.T6.

5. Add the appropriate item number and date. For a book written by James Wilson and published in 1988, the complete call number would be

HD320.T6W55 1988

(In subsequent examples, we shall omit the final date unless we are discussing a call number which requires one.)

Note that the "form" table does not assign any meaning to the seventh number in the range for a given country. Many such unassigned numbers appear throughout the H schedules, and may be given a meaning in future editions; formerly, the sixth position in this table was also unassigned.

At

HD3441-3570.9: Economic history, Cooperation, Mutuality

we find a more complex form table, which is used in conjunction with Table V. In this case, the correct number from that table is added to

HD3440. Here, we shall illustrate the application of each form designation to both a four-number and a one-number country.

France,
4 nos.:
53–56
(1)

Chile,
1 no.:
36
.A2–39

Periodicals. Societies. Serials.
Papers on Industrial Cooperation in France by Institute de Mutualité Industrielle. HD3493.I68. The cutter is for "Institute de Mutualité Industrielle," the organization responsible for the papers.

Papers on Industrial Cooperation in Chile by the Congresso Industrial: HD3476.A25. In the previous chapter, we illustrated the use of what we called "reserved" cutter numbers, such as A1, A2, A3, etc. You are directed to add cutters of this type to many Library of Congress Classification numbers either before or in place of the usual representational item numbers. The purpose of reserved cutter numbers is to place all items of a certain type on the shelves before all other items having the same class number. ("Z" numbers, which we shall discuss further on, place such items after all others.)

The cutter number .A25 has properties of both a representational and a reserved cutter. In this case, the Library of Congress Classification reserves not one but a *range* of cutters to designate periodicals, societies, and serials. You are to choose a number from this range which best represents the position of the item's main entry within the alphabet. (You must also, of course, take into account cutter numbers of previously-classified items.) Just as "Congresso" is near the beginning of the alphabet, .A25 is near the beginning of the sequence A2(0)–A39. If you were classifying a collection of papers emanating from an organization whose name began with "Y," you might want to assign the cutter .A38.

(2)   .A4, A–Z   General works. History and description.

The History of Industrial Cooperation among Industries in France, by G. Larmerie: HD3493.L37. This call number uses a straightforward class number + item number format.

The History of Industrial Cooperation in Chile, by E. Alvar: HD3476.A4A58. Here, the whole number portion of the class number is followed by the "reserved" cutter .A4, which is then followed by the item number.

(2.5)   .A45, A–Z   Biography, by author.

Jean Blot and the Rise of Industrial Cooperation in France, by Gaston Gruyere: HD3494.5.G78. The class number is the second number in the sequence 53–56 + .5.

Tomasso Camposantos and Modern Industrial Cooperation in Chile, 1890–1935, by Eduardo Beyelan: HD3476.A45B488. (You may feel we should use B49 for "Beyelan." Although this would be correct, we suggest avoiding 9 as a final digit unless it is absolutely necessary. Constructing a cutter number to follow one ending in 9 can be problematic.)

(3)   .A5, A–Z   Public policy

Policies of Industrial Cooperation in Modern France, by Robert Lavater: HD3495.L38.

The Law and Industrial Mutualism in Chile, by R. Runyel: HD3476.A5R86.

(4).A1+   .A6A1+   General cooperative societies.

Report on Industrial Cooperation, by the Labor Assoc. of France: HD3496.A1L3. One should probably *not* expand this final cutter to two digits; other "L-" items at this class number will more likely have to be filed after "Labor Association" than before it.

Report on Industrial Cooperation, by the Labor Assoc. of Chile: HD3476.A6A12.

The + in this case simply means that you may expand the cutter .A1, either by treating it as a range of reserved cutters, .A1–.1A19, or by adding a representational item number.

(4).A3, A–Z	.A6A2–Z	By state, province, etc.

Industrial Cooperation in Somme, by P. Gaston: HD3496.A3S663.

[Not readily applicable to Chile; since you must use one form table for all countries with a number span of a given size, it will sometimes be the case that not all subdivisions are applicable.]

(4).A5–Z4	.A–Z4	By city

Industrial Cooperation in Amiens, by P. Gaston: HD3496.A64G37.

Industrial Cooperation in Santiago, by R. Rodrigues: HD3476.S36R63.

Most of the form tables found in Schedule H use procedures identical or similar to those demonstrated above. However, there are several other special problems you may encounter in working with Schedule H. Following are four examples of numbers which will illustrate these problems.

1. A book on statistics about Paris: HA1229.P3.

HA1211–1230: number span, from the internal table beginning at HA175, devoted to statistics in France.

19: number from the "form" table at HA175 denoting treatment by city. You may either:

(a) Add this to the base number 1210, yielding the result 1229.

(b) Read it as an ordinal number signifying the 19th number in the range 1211–1230: which is 1229

P3: A geographic cutter for Paris. Added to 1229, this produces the complete class number HA1229.P3

2. A book about domicile in India: HB2099.

HB1961–2157: number span denoting *Domicile, by country*.

139: one of the two numbers for India—the correct one in this situation—from Table II. This is added to the base number 1960 to produce HB2099.

3. A book on the national production of France during the 19th century: HC275.

> HC95–695: number span denoting *National production, by country.*
>
> HC271–280: number range, within the above span, devoted to France. Some of these numbers have a more specific meaning than the "form" table at HC95 indicates. For example, "(5)" in that table means "by period: later." However, the 5th number in the above range, HC275, denotes France during the years 1601–1900.
>
> Since the period 1601–1900 includes the 19th century, HC275 is the correct number for the topic in question.

4. Banking reports of the Banque de France in Paris: HG3040.P33B3.

> 2700: The base number: i.e., from the footnote: for *Banking, by country.*
>
> 340: the correct number from Table VIII; this table allots to France the 20-number span 321–340 and the "form" table at 2701 assigns treatment by city to the 20th number in the span.
>
> P3: geographical cutter for Paris.
>
> P33: geographical cutter meaning "Paris, subdivided by bank," which comes from the subdivisions under "(20) – By city." These subdivisions refer to the set of ten cutter numbers produced by adding a second digit to a given city cutter: .P3(0)–.P39 in this case. Again, the numbers in parentheses are ordinal; (4) refers to the 4th number in the sequence .P3(0)–.P39, which is .P33.
>
> B3: cutter for the Banque de France. This is yet another example of a call number which, because both cutter numbers are devoted to defining content, lacks a separate item number.

Schedule P

Class P represents the languages and literature of the world. Our discussion will focus on the schedules, or portions thereof, dealing with literature. Class P's overall plan is to group literature first by the language in which it was originally written, then by time period, then by author. Only within a group of works by a single author does Class P subdivide by literary form. The only exceptions are two sections of subclass PR – *Elizabethan Drama*, and *Medieval Metrical Romance* – in which the broadest subdivision is by form. This arrangement is quite different from that of the Dewey Decimal Classification, in which *all literature written in a given language is classified first by form.*

One of the more noteworthy attributes of Class P is that it places works *about* an author and his or her writings together with works *of* that author. This feature is especially useful to patrons of an academic library; a person who wishes to *study* a given author will be glad to find biographies, appraisals, etc., of an author on the shelves alongside that author's works.

There is not a one-to-one correspondence between two-letter subclasses and languages. Both PQ and PT are divided into two sections, each dealing with a separate language or group of languages. On the other hand, PR and PS both cover English-language literature, the latter being devoted to American authors.

The P schedules allot some space to discussions and collections of the various languages' literatures as a whole. However, each schedule, or portion thereof, devoted to the literature of a given language consists chiefly of alphabetical author lists. An author falls into one of a set of categories, according to how many numbers the schedule gives him or her. At most, an author may have 49 numbers. At the other extreme, many authors have only a cutter attached to a whole number; the whole number signifies all authors whose names appear at a certain point in the alphabet.

As you examine the P schedules, you may wonder why some relatively obscure authors have received more numbers than others who are better known. This is mainly due to each author's being treated in accordance with his or her prominence or the needs of the Library of Congress *at the time the schedules were constructed*. It is also partly because any new author, or newly discovered author from the past, must be fit into the scheme as it now stands, and thus can receive only a cutter number.

Location and types of literature tables

Like Class H, Class P requires you to fit numbers and sequences of numbers into "form" tables. As with Class H, these tables indicate which number in a sequence to use for a given purpose or how it is to be cuttered. However, in Class P, it is the form tables which are external to the schedules. Furthermore, these tables differ from each other enough that Class H's parallel-column arrangement is impractical — although it is used for certain pairs of tables.

The literature tables — which, as we mentioned previously, are found in a separate volume—can be divided into main and auxiliary tables. The main tables subarrange all works by and about authors. There is one table for each category—49-number authors, 9-number authors, etc. The auxiliary tables are those you must go to from the main tables in order to further subarrange some group of material, such as various editions of a single work. (The "language" portion of Class P has a separate set of tables, which we are not going to discuss here.)

Renumbering of the P tables

Before proceeding to demonstrate the use of specific tables, we wish to briefly discuss the renumbering of all P tables from earlier editions of the Library of Congress Classification. Although we shall make no further references to the old system in the remainder of this chapter, you should learn to recognize outdated editions of the P tables, so as not to use them in error. You may also wish to understand why the tables we are going to discuss have the numbers they do.

Originally, the Library of Congress Classification numbered the various language and literature tables in several sequences. Locating or even identifying a table by its number, therefore, proved difficult. Insertion of new tables into a sequence by means of numbers such as XIIa, VIIIb, etc. made the system increasingly cumbersome. The new system uses *one* sequence to number *all* tables, placing the language tables first. Author tables appear last in the sequence.

The new system reflects the consolidation of several tables and the deletion of others. Among the canceled tables was one applied to authors with 98 numbers. Since there were no such authors, this table existed purely to accommodate those who *might* be added later. Authors such as William Shakespeare, who require an extremely detailed breakdown, have their numbers spelled out in the schedule.

Arrangement of works by and about an author

The Library of Congress Classification uses the same general arrangement for every author, and thus in every table. As might be expected, a major portion of each table is devoted to the arrangement of an author's separately published works. However, these do not come first; they make up the second of three major categories. Following is a list of each category and its subdivisions, given in outline form.

   I. Items containing more than one work
     A. "Collected" — i.e., complete — works
     B. Specific groups of works
  II. Separately published works
 III. Biography and criticism
     A. Specific types of material
     B. General biographical/critical material

When classifying works by and about authors with only a single number or cutter number, you arrange these purely by further cuttering. However, in the case of 49-number authors, you use spans of whole numbers, or at least a single whole number, for most of the above categories and subdivisions. The tables for author in the intermediate categories — 19 numbers, 9 numbers, etc. — use various combinations of number spans, single whole numbers and cuttering.

Since space permits us to demonstrate the use of only a few tables, we have chosen those applied to authors having the least and the most possible numbers. Each of these tables illustrates a distinct method of denoting subdivisions; the other tables use these same methods in various combinations.

We shall use authors from classes PR (English [other than American] literature) and PS (American literature), which are typical of all P subclasses. The instructions for the use of tables in these subclasses can be applied to literature of other languages with little difficulty.

We shall begin with authors having the least amount of numbers, then move to those with the largest possible number span. In a few cases, where we were unable to locate existing works to exemplify a point, we have used hypothetical examples.

Authors having only a single number or cutter number — Tables XXXVII, XXXVIII, XXXIX and XL

Following is a list of authors who fall into this category. This list includes 20th century and pre–20th century American — PS — and other than American — PR — English-language authors. To give you some notion of how the Library of Congress arranges authors, we are arranging them in call number order.

Brown, Sir Thomas: PR3327
Mallet, David, 1705–1765: PR3545.M4

Marvell, Andrew, 1621–1678: PR3546
Byron, Henry James (not to be confused with Lord Byron): PR4399.B3
Merival, John Herman: PR5020
Christie, Agatha, 1890–1976: PR6005.H66
Joyce, James: PR6019.09
Lawrence, D.H. (David Herbert): PR6023.A93
Wodehouse, P.G. (Pelham Grenville), 1881–1975: PR6045.O53
Barker, Clive, 1952–: PR6052.A6475
Warren, Mercy Otis, 1728–1814: PS858.W8
Alger, Horatio: PS1029.A3
Bierce, Ambrose: PS1097
Eliot, T.S.: PS3509.L43
King, Stephen, 1947–: PS3561.I483

Remember that any author with a cutter number must "share" his or her whole number with other authors; one will find many authors whose call numbers begin with PR6019 or PS3561. The number PS1097, on the other hand, is found only on works by and about Ambrose Bierce.

The cutter number for a 20th century author is *always* on the *second* letter of the author's name—Clive Barker, T.S. Eliot, James Joyce, Stephen King. The portion of any schedule covering 20th-century authors uses each whole number to represent all authors whose names begin with a specific letter of the alphabet; PR6019 means "all authors who have published the major portion of their work between 1900 and 1960 whose names begin with 'J'." Therefore, to cutter on the first letter of a 20th century author's name would be redundant.

All cutter numbers used in the above list have been assigned by the Library of Congress, appearing in either the schedules, authority file, or bibliographic records. To understand why some of them "look wrong," refer to our earlier discussions of cuttering in chapters 9 and 10.

In examining the schedules, you will see that most authors' names appear without a specific table number. However, portions of some schedules give the instruction, "Table XXXIV or XL unless otherwise specified." Apply this throughout all of Class P, even when not explicitly directed to do so. From this instruction, you may deduce, correctly, that Tables XXXIX and XL are used more often than any others. In fact, Table XL must be used for all new authors and newly-discovered authors.

We shall now demonstrate the use of each subdivision in Tables XXXIX and XL. We will then discuss Tables XXXVII and XXXVIII.

XXXIX — 1 no.	XL — cutter no.
.A1	.x

Collected works. By date.

Complete works of	Complete fiction of
Ambrose Bierce. Pub. 1920	Clive Barker. Pub. 1992
PS1097.A1 1920	PR6052.A6475 1992

Complete works of	Complete novels, stories
John Herman Merival	and plays of Agatha Christie.
pub. 1930.	Pub. 1990.
PR5020.A1 1930	PR6005.H66 1990

Throughout Table XL, "x" simply refers to the cutter number for the author in question.

.A11–13	.xA11–13

Collected works. By editor, if given.

Complete works of	Complete works of
Ambrose Bierce, edited by	T.S. Eliot, edited by
S. Anderson.	P. Wilson.
PS1097.A112	PS3509.L43A128

This is another case of needing to fit a name into a range of "reserved" cutter numbers. Since "Anderson" is near the beginning of the alphabet, we use a cutter near the beginning of the range — albeit one which leaves room for something in front of it. The cutter for "Wilson" is near the end of the range, although not the last possible number.

.A14	.xA14

Collected prose works. By date.

Complete prose works of	The complete fiction and
Sir Thomas Brown	drama of James Joyce.
Pub. 1901	Pub. 1972
PR3327.A14 1901	PR6019.09A14 1972

.A15	.xA15

Collected fiction. By date.

Complete short stories and	Complete novels and short
fables of Ambrose Bierce.	stories of Agatha Christie.
Pub. 1989	Pub. 1987
PS1097.A15 1989	PR6005.H66A15 1987

.A16	.xA16
Collected essays. By date.	
A collection of Bierce's non-fiction works which qualify as essays, Pub. 1956 PS1097.A16 1956	Complete essays of T.S. Eliot. Pub. 1976 PS3509.L43A16 1976

.A17	.xA17
Collected poems. By date.	
Collected poems of Sir Thomas Brown. Pub. 1903 PR3327.A17 1903	Complete poems of T.S. Eliot. Pub. 1980 PS3509.L43A17 1980

.A19	.xA19
Collected plays. By date.	
If there existed a collection of plays by John Herman Merival, it would go at: PR5020.A19	Complete plays of T.S. Eliot Pub. 1979 PS3509.L43A19 1979

.A199	.xA199
Collected translations. Modern versions of early authors in the same language. By date	
A modern version of certain works of Sir Thomas Brown PR3327.A199	A modern version of certain works of Henry James Byron PR4399.B3 A199

.A1995	.xA1995
Collected translations. Polyglot. By date.	
A collection of the short stories of Ambrose Bierce translated into French, German, Spanish, and Italian. Pub. 1960 PS1097.A1995 1960	A collection of the short stories of Stephen King translated into French, German, Spanish, and Italian. Pub. 1993 PS3561.I483 1993

.A2-29	.xA2-29
Collected translations. English. By translator, if given, or date.	

The "Collected English translation" numbers do not apply to any of the authors we are using for this illustration, since all of their works are in English. Therefore, this portion of the tables is simply omitted for these authors. These numbers *would* apply to authors such as Franz Kafka or Jean-Paul Sarte, who originally wrote in German and French, respectively.

.A3–39	.xA3–39
Collected translations. French.	By translator, if given, or date.
A French translation, by	Poemes de T.S. Eliot, trans.
Maurice DuBois, of the short	into French by Adolph Ruse.
stories of Ambrose Bierce.	PS3509.L43A37
PS1097.A33	

"Ruse" and "DuBois" must be fit into the range of cutters A3–39. We use A37 for "Ruse" because it is as near to the end of that range as "R" is to the end of the alphabet. We use A33 for "Dubois" because it is relatively near the beginning of the range, as "DuBois" is relatively near the beginning of the alphabet. This portion of the tables would be omitted for authors whose works were originally in French.

.A4–49	.xA4–49
Collected translations. German.	By translator, if given, or date.
Short stories of	Short stories of
Ambrose Bierce	Stephen King
translated into German by	translated into German by
Karl Buntz	Albert Weiss
PS1097.A422	PS3561.I483A48

The principle for cuttering these is the same as for the French translations shown above. This portion of the tables would be omitted for authors whose works were originally in German.

.A5–59	.xA5–59
Collected translations. Other.	By language
Short stories of	Short stories of
Ambrose Bierce	Stephen King
translated into Arabic	translated into Hebrew
PS1097.A52	PS3561.I483A54

The principle for cuttering these is the same as for the French translations shown above, except that the cutter represents the name of the language, rather than that of the translator.

.A6	.xA6
Selected works. Selections.	By date.
Selected short stories	Six Mary Westmacott novels
of Ambrose Bierce.	by Agatha Christie.
Pub. 1962	Pub. 1986
PS1097.A6 1962	PR6005.H66A6 1986

This number is for any set of works by an author, published as a unit, which is definitely not that author's complete works. For example, the set of Agatha Christie novels shown above consists only of those she wrote under the pseudonym Mary Westmacott. Note that the classification number is the same one used for works Christie wrote under her real name.

.A61–Z48	.xA61–Z458
Separate works. By title.	
Orlando in Roncesvalles	Cast upon the breakers
by John Herman Merival	by Horatio Alger
PR5020.075	PS1029.A3C27
Devil's dictionary	Ulysses, by
by Ambrose Bierce.	James Joyce.
PS1097.D48	PR6019.09U4
Comments on Bierce's Devil's	The original manuscript
dictionary, by S. Winston.	of Joyce's Ulysses.
PS1097.D483W56	PR6019.09U422

It is with this subdivision that the representational cutters begin. Classifying almost any separately published work involves simply adding a title cutter. The only difficulty is with titles near the beginning or end of the alphabet. For example, if an author were to write a book whose title began with "Abbey," or "Academic," it would have to receive a cutter such as A62, since all cutters up to A6 are reserved — including the range A3–39, where you would want to put these titles. Likewise, a book with a title beginning, "Zulu Warriors," would require a cutter such as either Z48 for a one-number author or Z458 for an author with only a cutter number.

A discussion, analysis, etc. of a specific work is also classed here. Some authors, such as Joyce, receive a breakdown in the schedule, while others must be arranged using an addition table, XLIII, as a guide. Following is a summary of this table:

> (1)   Texts.
>   A–Z Translations. By language.
> (2)   Selections. By date.
> (3) A–Z Criticism.

The numbers (1), (2), (3) refer to successive cutter numbers — i.e., D46–48, D48–483, etc. The directions in this table must be rather freely adapted to the requirements of a specific author. For example, in the case of a Table XL author, criticism must be indicated solely by expansion of the title cutter, since triple-cuttering is nonstandard practice.

.Z481–489   .xZ4581–4589
Biography and criticism. Periodicals. Societies. Serials.

A periodical devoted to   A periodical devoted to
Ambrose Bierce's work and   T.S. Eliot, entitled
titled *Bierce* would go at: *Words* would go at:
PS1097.Z482   PS3509.L43Z4588

.Z49   .xZ459
Biography and criticism. Dictionaries, indexes, etc. By date.

Index to the works of Sir   Character index to the plays
Thomas Brown. Pub. 1954   of T.S. Eliot. Pub. 1956
PR3327.Z49 1954   PS3509.L43Z459 1956

.X5A3–39   .xZ46–479
Biography and criticism. Autobiography. Journals. Memoirs. By title.

Memoirs of Sir Thomas   Memoirs of T.S. Eliot.
Brown.   PS3509.L43Z472
PR3327.Z5A35

Z5A4   .xZ48
Biography and criticism. Collected letters. By date.

Letters of Ambrose   The letters of T.S.
Bierce. Pub. 1942   Eliot. Pub. 1982
PS1097.Z5A4 1942   PS3509.L43Z48 1982

.Z5A41–49   .xZ481–499
Biography and criticism. Letters to and from particular
correspondents. Alphabetically by correspondent.

Letters between   Letters between
Sir Thomas Brown   T.S. Eliot
and an individual whose   and an individual whose
last name begins with "B"   last name begins with "W."
PR3327.Z5A42   PS3509.L43Z498

.Z545–Z   .xZ5–999
Biography and criticism. General works.

Ambrose Bierce, by   James Joyce, by
M.E. Grenander.   Richard Ellmann.
PS1097.Z5G72   PR6019.O9Z5332

                               James Joyce, by
                               Bonnie Kime Scott.
                               PR6019.O9Z79444

                               Stephen King, the art of dark-
                               ness, by Douglas E. Winter.
                               PS3561.I483Z95

You may disagree with our placement of several works within the categories .A1–.A19 in the previous display. For example, you may feel that we should have placed our hypothetical *Complete Fiction of Clive Barker* at A15, and our *Complete Stories and Plays of Agatha Christie* at A14. In fact, it is possible that, by strict interpretation of the LCC's instructions, we have "misclassified" these items.

However, we believe that the classification of such items should also reflect the portion of an author's entire output contained within them. Furthermore, we feel that to class a collection under one of the specific forms at A14–19 implies that the author wrote also in another form. Therefore, we recommend that any collection comprising an author's complete works be classed at A1 or A1–13.

A classifier who follows this procedure will rarely use A14, "Collected prose"; this subdivision would only apply to a collection comprising multiple forms of prose by an author who also wrote poetry.

The tables we have just illustrated are used with the majority of authors having a single number or cutter number. However, certain authors in these categories are arranged using Tables XXXVII (one number) and XXXVIII (cutter number). These tables are used for authors who have written either very few works or very few separately published works. For example, Andrew Marvell, who takes Table XXXVII, wrote only poems, which usually appear in collections. Tables XXXVII and XXXVIII include most of the same subdivisions as Tables XXXIV and XL. One difference is the lack of provision for collected works of a specific literary form.

The most significant overall difference is the subdivision assigned to the major portion of the A1–Z999... cutter number range. In Tables XXXVII and XXXVIII, this is "Biography and criticism. General works." *not* "Separate works," which must be fit into the range A61–A78. Consequently, *The Excursion*, by David Mallet, is at PR3545.M4A675, and *Andrew Marvell*, by Robert Wilcher is at PR3546.W56. Do not use these two tables unless specifically instructed to do so in the schedules.

Authors with 49 numbers — Table XXXI

Table XXXI uses essentially the same subdivisions in the same order as the tables for one-number and cutter-number authors. Each subdivision receives a whole number or range of whole numbers, so that it may be further broken down. The table assigns every topic or sub-

topic two numbers or number ranges, one falling between 0 and 48, the
other between 50 and 98. This is because the schedules may assign an
author to either the first or second half of a given 100-number span. The
numbers 0–48 or 50–98 in the table correspond to the schedule numbers
x00–x48 or x50–x98. We shall demonstrate the use of Table XXXI using
two authors, one assigned to each half of a 100-number span.

Percy Bysshe Shelley	William Wordsworth
PR5400–5448	PR5850–5898
0	50

        Collected works.
        Editions and reprints.
        By date, as follows:

To 1500	A00–A99
1500–1599	B00–B99
1600–1699	C00–C99
1700–1799	D00–D99
1800–1899	E00–E99
1900–1999	F00–F99

Complete poems and	Complete works of
Political Essays of	William Wordsworth
Shelley. Pub. 1897	Pub. 1954
PR5400.E97	PR5850.F54
Complete works of Percy	Collected works of
Bysshe Shelley. Pub. 1973	Wordsworth. Pub. 1954
PR5400.F73	PR5850.F54a

Here, "Collected works" does not mean, "Complete works," but rather
"Complete works in a certain form." Subarrangement is by date rather
than form. The date is represented by a cutter in which the initial letter
represents the century and the two digits specify the year. If two or
more items falling into this category are published in the same year, all
after the first receive a cutter number with a lowercase letter appended,
as shown.

1	51

        Collected works. Editions with commentary, etc.
        By editor, A–Z.

Here is the first example of a source of potential confusion within Table
XXXI. While the table itself assigns the above subdivision to 1 and 51,
the schedule gives an alternate meaning to the corresponding numbers
for both Shelley and Wordsworth:

1	51
Facsimiles of manuscript poems. By date.	Collected prose works.
Bodleian Shelley Manuscripts. Pub. 1986 PR5401 1986	Prose works of Wordsworth, edited by Owen. PR5851.09

The schedule often assign a meaning to a number within a span covered by Table XXXI. Some of these contradict the table, others constitute specific examples of a broad category given in the table. In any case, designations in the schedules always supersede those from the table.

2	52
Selected works. By editor.	
Specific meaning for Shelley is "Poems."	
Posthumous Poems of Shelley. Pub. 1969 PR5402 1969	Wordsworth: Poetry and Prose, selected by W.M. Merchant. PR5852.M47

3	53
Selections, anthologies, extracts.	
Selected Poems of Shelley edited by H. Dawson. PR5403.D38	Shorter Poems: 1807–1820, ed. Karl H. Ketchum. PR5853.K48 1989

No specific provision is made for cuttering. The cutter for editor is an example of the way a library might choose to arrange items with this call number.

4	54
Translations. By language, subarranged by translator.	
.F5 French.	
.G5 German.	
.I5 Italian.	
.S5 Spanish.	
.Z5 Other.	
A French translation of Shelley's poems by Debardier. PR5404.F5D42	A Spanish translation of Wordsworth's poems by E. Martinez. PR5854.S5M37
An Italian translation of Shelley's poems by	A German translation of Wordsworth's poems by

Alfredo Morello.
PR5404.I5M67

A Chinese translation of
Shelley's poems by
Hsu Kein.
PR5404.Z5H78

L. Schoen.
PR5854.G5.S34

A Hebrew translation of
Wordsworth's poems by
B. Goldman.
PR5854.Z5G65

5–22
    Separate works.
Prose works at PR5405,
cuttered by title

Prometheus Unbound.
Pub. 1960
PR5416.A1   1960

Prometheus Unbound,
trans. into French by
Clement Briand
PR5416.A42

55–72

Excursion, Pub. 1955
PR5858.A1   1955

Prelude, Pub. 1970
PR5864.A1   1970

Prose works at PR5871,
cuttered by title

The schedule allocates the numbers within this range. Some works receive their own whole number, others only a cutter number. The various editions, versions, translations, etc. of a work are arranged using Table XLI for works with a whole number, and either Table XLII or XLIII for works with a cutter number. In Table XLI, as shown above, A1 denotes the complete text of a work, and the range A4–A9 is assigned to French translations.

23
    Collections of doubtful or spurious works.
A collection of poems
which may or may not
have been written by
Shelley would go at:
PR5423

73

For Wordsworth, this
subdivision has been pushed
back to PR5872. The num-
ber PR5873 denotes works
edited by Wordsworth.

24
    Collections of imitations, adaptations, parodies, etc.
Parodies of various poems
by Shelley would go at:
PR5424

74

Parodies of various poems
by Shelley would go at:
PR5874

Remember that this number is only for collections. Separately published imitations, parodies, etc. of individual works are classed with the work.

25	75
Relation to drama and the stage. Dramatizations.	
Dramatic Adaptations from Shelley's Narrative Poems, by J. Profumo. PR5425.P78	Dramatic Adaptations from Wordsworth's Poems, by J. Wallace. PR5875.W35
26	76
Translations (Comparative studies etc.)	
Comparative studies of Shelley PR5426	Comparative studies of Wordsworth PR5876

In earlier editions of LCC, these numbers denoted illustrations. The schedule now directs you to place illustrations in Class N.

27	77
Not assigned in table; no meaning in schedules for either author.	
28	78
Not assigned in table.	
For Shelley: Societies. By place A–Z Notebook of the Shelley Society, London PR5428.L6 (Cutter for London)	For Wordsworth: no meaning assigned in schedules.

Biography, criticism, etc. –

29	79
Periodicals. Societies. Collections.	
Ariel [Periodical about Shelley and his influence] PR5429.A75 (Per instructions in Schedules, "Societies" is at PR5428)	Wordsworth Circle PR5879.W87
30	80
Dictionaries, indexes, etc.	
The Shelley Cyclopedia, by Thomas Barrow. PR5430.B37	A Concordance to the Poems of William Wordsworth, edited by Lane Cooper PR5880.C66

30.5	80.5
Historical sources and documents of the author's biography.	
Historical sources of biographical information on Shelley: PR5430.5	Historical sources of biographical information on Wordsworth: PR5880.5

31.A2	81.A2
Autobiographical works. Autobiography.	
Shelley's autobiography: PR5431.A2	Wordsworth's autobiography PR5881.A2

31.A3–39	81.A3–39
Autobiographical works. Journals. Memoirs.	
Such a work for Shelley with a title falling near the start of the alphabet might go at: PR5431.A32	Such a work for Wordsworth with a title falling near the end of the alphabet might go at: PR5881.A38

31.A4	81.A4
Autobiographical works. Letters (Collections)	
A collection of Shelley's letters: PR5431.A4	A collection of Wordworth's letters: PR5881.A4

31.A41–49	81.A41–49
Autobiographical works. Letters to and from particular individuals. By correspondent, alphabetically.	
Shelley's Letters to Lord Byron. PR5431.A42	Letters to William and Dorothy Wordsworth PR5881.A48

31.A5–Z	81.A5–Z
General biographical works.	
Percy Bysshe Shelley by Richard Holmes: PR5431.H65	William Wordsworth by Hunter Davies: PR5881.D34

32	82
Early life, education.	
Shelley at Harrow, by J. Yablonski. PR5432.Y32	William Wordsworth of Rydal Mount, by Frederika Beatty. PR5882.B4

33	83
Relation to contemporaries, times, etc.	

Life with Shelley and his
Circle in Italy.
PR5433

Wordsworth and Coleridge:
A Study of Their Literary
Relations in 1801-1802, by
William Heath.
PR5883.H4

34
Homes and haunts. Local associations. Landmarks.

Description of the Places
where Shelley Lived and
Visited in Italy, by
Thomas Gordon.
PR5434.G68

84

Description of the Places
where Wordsworth Lived, by
John Smith, would go at:
PR5884.S65

35
Anniversaries. Celebrations. Memorial addresses. Treatment in
literature. By author or title A-Z89.

A discussion of literary
works that refer to
Shelley, written by
G. Williams would go at:
PR5435.W56

85

A discussion of literary
works that refer to
Wordsworth, written by
B. Jenson would go at:
PR5885.J46

35.Z9
Misc. minor pieces, etc.

A minor piece about
Shelley. Pub. 1930
PR5435.Z9   1930

85.Z9

A minor piece about
Wordsworth. Pub. 1940
PR5885.Z9   1940

36
Authorship—i.e., works on sources, forgeries, forerunners, etc.

A dicussion of poems
falsely attributed to
Shelley, by A. Rose
Would go at:
PR5436.R67

86

A discussion of poems
falsely attributed to
Wordsworth, by T. Mills
Would go at:
PR5886.M56

37
Chronology of works.

A List of the works of
Shelley in the Order of
their Appearance, by
J. Jordan.
PR5437.J68

87

A List of the works of
Wordsworth in the Order of
their Appearance, by
F. Wilson.
PR5887.W56

Criticism and interpretation—

37.3	87.3

History, general.

A work dealing with the history of criticism of Shelley's works, by G. Bartlet would go at: PR5437.3.B37

A work dealing with the history of criticism of Wordsworth's works, by B. Sherman would go at: PR5887.3.S54

37.4	87.4

History, by region or country, A–Z

Literary criticism of Shelley in France: PR5437.4.F72

Literary criticism of Wordsworth in Germany: PR5887.4.G47

38	88

General works.

The Lyrics of Shelley, by Judith Chernick. PR5438.C47

The Poetry of Wordsworth, by William Frantz. PR5888.F72

39	89

Characters.

Shelley's Characters in *The Cenci*, by T.L. Farrell. PR5439.F37

Wordsworth's Characters in *The Borderers*, by J. Adler. PR5889.A45

40	90

Not now in use. Formerly, this number was used for works on individual characters, while the previous number was for groups of characters.

41	91

Techniques, plots, scenes, time, etc.

The Development of plot in Shelley's *The Cenci*, by Laurel Harbin. PR5441.H27

The Development of plot in *The Borderers*, by J. Adler. PR5891.A45

42	92

Treatment and knowledge of special subjects.

L3	Law	M3	Marriage
L4	Liberty	R4	Religion
L6	Love	S3	Science

Use of Allegory in Shelley, by Jones. PR5442.A4J66

Vegetarianism in Shelley, by Wilson. PR5442.V4W55	Love in Wordsworth, by B. Jones. PR5892.L6J66

These numbers are always used in conjunction with a subject cutter. The above is an excerpt from an extensive list of dedicated subject cutters provided in the table. One may cutter for a subject not on the list, so long as the number fits into the sequence established there. Note that treatment of a subject within an individual work is classed with that work.

43	93
Textual criticism, commentaries.	
The Early Collected Editions of Shelley's Poems: A Study in the History and Transmission of the Printed Text, by Charles H. Taylor. PR5443.T39	A study of rare editions of Wordsworth's poems, by K. Walters. PR5893.W25

44	94
Language, style, etc.	
A study of Shelley's style by F. Dawson. PR5444.D38	A study of Wordsworth's style by J. Wilson. PR5894.W56

45	95
Dictionaries, concordances.	
A Shelley Concordance, by Robert Travesty. PR5445.T72	Concordance to Wordsworth, by S. Eckard. PR5895.E35

46	96
Grammar. Use of words.	
A Study of the use of Verbs in Shelley's Poetry, by Mark Langtree. PR5446.L36	A Study of the use of Adverbs in Wordsworth, by L. Paulson. PR5896.P38

47	97
Versification, meter, rhythm.	
A Study of the Metrical schemes in Shelley's Lyrical poetry, by Albert Dancey. PR5447.D36	A Study of the Metrical schemes in the Poetry of Wordsworth, by R. Farnsworth. PR5897.F38

48	98
Dialect, etc.	
PR5448	PR5898

Here would be classed books dealing with a dialect the author generally uses, or employs in some specific work, or for some specific purpose.

Again, there is room for debate regarding the most appropriate category for a given work. We admonish you *not* to be guided solely by a work's title, which can be misleading. Instead, you must make an effort to determine the true subject of the work.

Concluding comments

The procedures and mechanisms used in the P tables we have demonstrated apply also to those for authors with number spans between 1 and 49. The tables in question may be thought of as either reductions of Table XXXI or expansions of Table XL or XXXIX. Again, if you primarily handle new books, you will find yourself using Table XL most often.

Facility in the use of the H and P tables will aid you in learning to use those from other schedules, which work on similar principles. You will best learn how to use the tables by attempting to do so. Remember that the purpose of any table is to arrange many groups of numbers in the same way. Therefore, when using a certain table repeatedly, you may predict the results, and thus verify the accuracy of the number you have built.

Review questions for Chapter 11

1. Explain the relationship between the tables of geographic locations attached to the H schedules and the "form" tables appearing within those schedules.

2. When the H schedules provide a range of numbers to be used in conjunction with an area table, why do they instruct you to add the numbers from that table to a base number which is one less — or sometimes ten less — than the first number in the range?

3. Why do the P schedules provide a larger number span for certain lesser known authors than they do for other better known authors?

4. Describe the arrangement of works by and about an author in Class P.

5. Why is the cutter number for a 20th century author built on the second letter of the author's name?

Review questions for Chapters 6-11

Based on what you have learned about both the Dewey and Library of Congress Classification schemes, list:

(a) Three types of collections which you feel should be arranged by the Dewey Decimal Classification.

(b) Three types of collections which you feel should be arranged by the Library of Congress Classification.

We have no right or wrong answers in mind, although you must be more specific than "the collection of a public library," or "the collection of an academic library."

Also, the determining factor might be the nature of the users as well as the nature of the materials. What type of patron might find the one system or the other easier to use?

Sources cited and suggestions for further reading or study

Chan, Lois Mai. *Immroth's Guide to the Library of Congress Classification*, 4th ed. Englewood, Colo.: Libraries Unlimited, 1990.

Library of Congress Classification Schedules Combined with Additions and Changes through 1989: Class H, Subclasses H-HJ. Rita Runchock and Kathleen Droste, editors; Victoria A. Coughlin, associate editor. Detroit: Gale Research, 1990.

Library of Congress Classification Schedules Combined with Additions and Changes through 1989: Class H, Subclasses HM-HX. Rita Runchock and Kathleen Droste, editors; Victoria A. Coughlin, associate editor. Detroit: Gale Research, 1990.

Library of Congress Classification Schedules Combined with Additions and Changes through 1987: Class P, Language and Literature, Subclasses PN, PR, PS, PZ. Helen Savage, editor; Kathleen Droste and Rita Runchock, associate editors. Detroit: Gale Research, 1988.

Library of Congress Classification Schedules Combined with Additions and Changes through 1988: Class P, Subclasses P-PZ, Language and Literature Tables. Rita Runchock and Kathleen Droste, editors. Detroit: Gale Research, 1989.

Material from *Library of Congress Classification Schedules Combined with Additions and Changes*, copyright ©1989 by Gale Research Inc., reproduced by permission of the publisher.

12

The Organization of Nonbook Materials

Up to this point, our discussion of cataloging, classification, and subject analysis has emphasized printed documents. However, if you are a cataloger in today's library or information center, you will likely have to deal also with items such as music scores, maps and sound recordings. You are also likely to encounter increasing amounts of computer software, video recordings and microforms. If you own a collection of records, tapes, CD's, movies on videotape, or computer software, you are probably aware already of certain problems involved in organizing and storing these materials. In this chapter, we will discuss these issues in greater detail.

What do we mean by "nonbook materials"?

Before going any further with our discussion, we should give you a comprehensive list of the categories of items we have in mind when we talk about "nonbook materials." The chapters in Part I of AACR2R88 which cover these materials provide such a list:

3. Cartographic Materials
4. Manuscripts (Including Manuscript Collections)
5. Music [in print form]
6. Sound Recordings
7. Motion Pictures and Videorecordings
8. Graphic Materials

9. Computer Files

10. Three-Dimensional Artefacts and Realia [AACR2R88 defines realia as "An artefact or a naturally occurring entity, as opposed to a replica."]

11. Microforms

It is only relatively recently that nonbook materials have been covered in detail by the rules, as we shall demonstrate in the next section.

Past and present treatment of nonbook materials

The 1967 *Anglo-American Cataloging Rules, North American Text* gave relatively little attention to nonbook materials. These rules generally discussed only the physical description in any detail, leaving catalogers to handle the rest of the cataloging process as they saw fit. Catalogers were free to apply and adapt the rules and principles for books, but were also free to decide against doing so.

Chapters 12, "Audiovisual Media and Special Instructional Materials," and 14, "Sound Recordings," of the 1967 rules were later revised to incorporate those I.S.B.D. (International Standard Bibliographic Description) principles applicable to nonprint works. Further, such investigators as Weihs (1989) realized that the same cataloging principles should apply to all media and that a practical solution to the proliferation of files and diversification of cataloging rules among nonbook media would be to enter and describe the latter according to the rules already prescribed for books.

However, the general tendency was to treat nonbook materials as what Massonneau (1980) called "second class citizens in the world of books," and, as Massonneau points out, to catalog and classify such works locally, often deliberately avoiding any connection with traditional cataloging. As a result, patrons were often unaware that libraries had any items in their collections other than books; many libraries tended to exclude bibliographic records for nonbook materials from their main catalogs.

There are two probable reasons for librarians' past reluctance to devote much time and energy to nonbook materials:

(1) Library patrons have traditionally seen libraries as sources of *books*. If patrons are not even going to think of looking for sound

recordings, motions pictures, computer software, etc., in a library, why put a great deal of effort into cataloging and classifying these items?

(2) The hitherto-mentioned effort is often of a quite significant amount; nonbook items present special problems which a library's staff may be unable or unwilling to deal with.

We shall discuss both (1) and (2) in the following two sections.

Libraries' reluctance to grant nonbook materials high priority

It is likely that libraries have, in the past, concentrated their efforts on books, believing them to be the only items truly worthy of attention. It is only recently that library workers and patrons have recognized the importance of other media. While we question the opinion of Lancaster (1980) that the book is on its way out, we do recognize the special contribution certain nonbook media can make in the dissemination of knowledge. Collections of nonbook media have, however, tended to grow in a relatively haphazard fashion, being stored in various obscure corners and indexed in a cursory — or at least idiosyncratic — manner.

Consider, for example, the handling of sound recordings. University libraries have tended to house and index these in the music library, if one exists, or in some type of "media center" or "audiovisual room." Any patron who knows that the collection of sound recordings exists can go to its catalog and determine whether it includes a specific item. However, a patron can only *discover that the collection exists* if bibliographic records for the items therein appear *in the library's main catalog*. Furthermore, if bibliographic records for only some of the items appear in the main catalog, the patron is likely to think those are the only sound recordings in the collection.

Also, even if every sound recording has a bibliographic record in the main catalog, crucial information may remain inaccessible. Many sound recordings consist of several selections, each of which may have a different composer and be performed by a different individual or group. Several examples come from the *Music of Our Time* series, which Columbia released on its Odyssey label some time ago. Following are the collective titles of several recordings in that series, along with the selections appearing on each:

New Sounds in Electronic Music
Reich, Steve. *Come Out.*

Maxwell, Richard. *Night Music.*
Oliveros, Pauline. *I of IV.*

Extended Voices
Cage, John. *Solos for Voice 2.* Electronic realization by Gordon Mumma and David Tudor.
Oliveros, Pauline. *Sound Patterns.*
Lucier, Alvin. *North American Time Capsule, 1967.*
Ashley, Robert. *She Was a Visitor.*
Ichyanagi, Toshi. *Extended Voices.*
Feldman, Morton. *Chorus and Instruments (II).*
Feldman, Morton. *Christian Wolff in Cambridge.*

New Music in Quartertones.
Ives, Charles. *Three Quarter-tone Pieces*: Largo, Allegro, Chorale.
Macero, Teo. *One-three Quarters.*
Hampton, Calvin. *Triple Play.*
Lybbert, Donald. *Lines for the Fallen.*
Hampton, Calvin. *Catch-Up.*

Any library which owns these recordings, or others like them, must perform analytics in order to provide access to the individual pieces. We will return to the subject of analytics further on in this chapter.

Smaller libraries may have begun their collection of sound recordings with a few dozen records, tapes, or CD's, stored in an appropriate bin or holder, with no cataloging access to them whatsoever. As the collection grew, continuous *ad hoc* decisions as to housing and indexing may have been made, without consideration of the importance of integrating these materials into the general collection, or even maintaining consistent practice within the collection. Local cataloging may have been done with little regard for established codes.

In sum, inadequate housing and indexing of nonbook items has probably caused many of them to stand unused. It is precisely this state of affairs that AACR2R88 seeks to ameliorate. The preface of AACR2R88 (page xix) states that:

> The introduction into most libraries of increasing numbers of the new media that have established themselves in the same period as having a parallel importance, for many library users, with the paper-based and printed documents traditionally the staple of the processing and cataloguing department, has created or intensified integrative problems on a scale unpredictable by those who wrought the 1967 texts.

The fourth guideline used in the original development of AACR2 is cited (page xxi) as "Determination of the treatment of nonbook materials primarily from a consideration of the published cataloguing rules of the Canadian Library Association, the Library Association, and the Association for Educational Communications and Technology; and of the ALA revision of chapter 12 of the 1967 text." The authors of AACR2R88 intend (page xxi) "the achievement of an integrated and standardized framework for the systematic description of all library materials . . . being also the first such comprehensive systematization to be related to the goals of international standardization." In other words, *all* materials, published in whatever medium, are to be dealt with by *one* overriding set of cataloging principles.

In this section, we have focused on why librarians may not want to give nonbook materials equal priority with books. We have also discussed how AACR2R88 seeks to change librarians' attitude toward these materials. In the next section, we shall discuss the second reason that librarians have given so little attention to nonbook materials — even when they have wanted to.

Physical nature of nonbook materials

While some books are difficult to catalog, most are easy to handle. A person can hold a book in one hand. Books can be stood up on end and placed against each other on shelves. Most of these shelves can be of uniform dimensions because of the standardized size and shape of most books. Even oversize books, such as unabridged dictionaries, can usually stand together on slightly higher and deeper shelves because they have the standard rectangular shape. Library employees can write coded location symbols on books' spines, or on labels affixed to the spines. Furthermore, a book is a self-contained medium, usable without auxiliary equipment.

Most of the nonbook materials listed so far lack these virtues, and are thus difficult to integrate with a library's book collection. When handling nonbook materials, libraries must deal with the following problems:

1. *Space and location requirements:* Materials such as dioramas, models, globes, statuary, and many types of realia are large enough that one of them may require as much space as 5, 10, or 50 books. Furthermore, when housing these items, a library must give only secondary consideration to efficiency. Unless an item is prominently displayed and easily reached, patrons will be reluctant to use it and may not even know the library has it.

2. *Assorted disparate shapes and sizes:* A library might face this problem when handling a collection of wood carvings, pottery, or sculptures. For example, imagine a collection of ceramic animals—a cat, a bird, a turtle, and a snake. Each of these four sculptures might be small but is of an irregular shape. More importantly, each is of a shape quite different from the others.

3. *Vulnerability to adverse conditions:* Items such as ceramic sculptures or hard rubber 78 rpm phonograph records from the early days of recording are extremely fragile. However, these are the least problematic of the nonbook media, several of which require carefully controlled environments. Excessive heat will warp phonograph records, CD's, and the plastic casings of videocassettes. Heat will also melt microfilm and motion picture film, or at least, in conjunction with humidity, cause them to deteriorate. Magnetic fields, generated by such common appliances as vacuum cleaners, will erase audio and videotapes and destroy data on computer disks and tapes. If dust or smoke particles settle on the exposed surface of a 5¼ inch computer diskette, they can render it unreadable. They can even work their way into a disk drive and cause it to damage other diskettes.

4. *Need for special storage accommodations:* To some extent, this is related to **2** above. The sculptures listed therein would require a special table or cabinet. Also, maps, blueprints, manuscripts, and similar materials must be laid flat, requiring special drawers or bins.

5. *Auxiliary equipment and controlled ambience requirements:* Many nonbook items are useless without a specific piece of equipment. You need a VCR and television or monitor to watch a videotape. You need a projector and screen to view a motion picture or set of slides. You can see the contents of a microfilm or microfiche only with the correct type of reader. You must have a record, tape, or CD player—and probably a set of earphones—in order to listen to a sound recording. To use software, you must have a compatible computer at your disposal. Many of the above pieces of equipment display information on a screen, and this information will be difficult to see in a room with too much ambient light. All of the above pieces of equipment require electricity, and perhaps extension cords and adapters.

6. *Rarity:* For security reasons, items such as manuscripts must be kept in a location subject to limited access.

Where and how a library houses nonbook materials affects not only patrons but classifiers, who must add to each item's call number a location symbol. The more separate facilities the library creates for nonbook materials, the more distinct symbols it must devise. A location symbol is particularly important when it distinguishes a microform reproduction of a printed book, serial, etc., from the original. The symbol used in this situation should also allow a patron to locate the item *within* the microform collection.

We shall not further discuss methods of housing and protecting nonbook materials because these issues lie outside this textbook's scope. The remainder of this chapter will discuss each element of the bibliographic record in turn, showing how catalogers may adapt principles originally intended for books to nonbook materials.

Entry headings for nonbook materials

The authorship of nonbook materials is often difficult to determine. The creation of an audiovisual work may involve one or more composers, performers, artists, arrangers, photographers, corporate bodies, cartographers, surveyors, engravers, directors, producers, and other artists and technicians. Therefore, principle responsibility for such a work is often debatable.

You can handle cases of diffuse authorship by entering the works in question under title. In fact, title main entry has found favor in the second edition of *Anglo-American Cataloging Rules*, both in the 1988 revision and the original 1978 version. The AACR2R88 also addresses this particular difficulty with its decreased emphasis on main entry. Rule 0.5 recognizes that "many libraries do not distinguish between the main entry and other entries," which makes excellent sense in the case of nonbook materials. Online catalogs should eventually remove all need for the distinction, since a computer can use any piece of data in the bibliographic record as a search element.

However, it is still standard practice to index every bibliographic description by some type of "main entry heading." Furthermore, as we explained in Chapter 2, there are valid reasons for continuing this practice, even in a totally automated catalog. Since, therefore, catalogers will often be called upon to decide on main entries for nonbook items, we shall now discuss in more detail the issues involved in doing so.

Choice of main entry for nonbook materials

Clearly, the only sensible choice of main entry for a work such as the typical motion picture is the title, since hundreds of individuals and corporate bodies are involved. Granted, viewers, reviewers, critics, and film scholars often attribute a given motion picture to a single person. For example, most people probably think of *Vertigo* as an Alfred Hitchcock film, *Dr. Strangelove* as a Stanley Kubrick film, and *Manhattan* as a Woody Allen film. However, such attributions cannot determine main entries for four reasons:

(1) Not everyone makes these attributions for every movie. For many movies that enjoy brief popularity but do not attain the status of "classic," no one gives the matter much thought. Even some more famous movies, such as *Casablanca* or *The Miracle Worker* are not known for their makers. (We discuss the issue of principle actors under 4 below.)

(2) The function of the person whom most people consider principally responsible for one film often differs from the function of the person considered principally responsible for another. While *Vertigo* is known for its director, Alfred Hitchcock, *Amadeus* tends to be known for its writer, Peter Shaffer, who adapted his own stage play for the screen.

(3) People differ among themselves as to whom they consider principally responsible for some films. Some attribute *Gone with the Wind* to its director, Victor Fleming, while others attribute it to its producer, David O. Selznick.

(4) In many cases, the person most strongly associated with a film cannot, by even the most liberal interpretation of the rules, be considered principally responsible for it. The most common example of this is probably the lead actor. While *Casablanca* is often called a Humphrey Bogart film, you could not justify choosing him as the main entry, since he was not involved in the actual creative aspects of the making of the film.

A different type of example is that of a film adaptation of a work by a well-known author. Many people are apt to refer to *The Shining* as "a Stephen King movie," even though King had nothing to do with the making of that film — which, furthermore, differs significantly from the novel.

Therefore, given the inconsistent and subjective nature of these attributions, you must not use them to determine any work's main entry. Rather, you must be guided by a consistent set of rules and principles such as those in AACR2R88, Chapter 21, "Choice of Access Points."

Principle responsibility for a nonbook work need not be diffuse to be debatable. While the *Eroica* symphony is clearly the work of Beethoven, should the electronic version of Handel's *Water Music* on *The Well-Tempered Synthesizer* be attributed to Handel or Wendy—a.k.a. Walter—Carlos?

This electronic version of *Water Music* is one of many works which fall along a continuum at one end of which is the set of works which clearly possess a single creator, and at the other end of which is the set of works whose authorship is clearly diffuse and must, therefore, receive a title main entry.

Between the two extremes lie works for which the choice of author versus title main entry is difficult to make. They are artifacts constituting an adaptation or reproduction of an original work. When the adaptation/reproduction contains no substantial change, you should enter the work under the heading for the creator of the original. We are deliberately introducing the question of what constitutes substantial change, because it is one you must face each time you deal with adaptations or reproductions.

Furthermore, in the case of such media as slides and photographs, the primary interest of the user may be in the *subject* of the photograph, regardless of the creator. In another instance, a patron of a music library may request, "something for the guitar that's easy." What composer would you, as a music librarian, recommend?

The AACR2R88 devotes major portions of Chapter 21 to the choice of main entry for some nonbook materials. For example, Section 21.23 covers sound recordings, and sections 21.18–21.22 cover musical works which are adaptations of other works. However, Chapter 21 explicitly discusses other nonbook media only in short passages. The only mention of cartographic materials in this chapter, for example, is in a portion of Rule 21.1B1. The rule provides a list of works that may be entered under corporate body, and includes "cartographic materials emanating from a corporate body other than a body that is merely responsible for their publication or distribution." If Chapter 21 makes little or no explicit reference to the specific type of nonbook material you are cataloging, you must apply whichever rules you judge to be appropriate. In many cases, you may find your judgment differing from that of another cataloger.

Description of nonbook materials

A major problem you will face when creating both headings and descriptions for nonbook items is what should serve as the chief source of information; what is the analogy of the title page for each of the nonbook media? Answers to that question appear at the beginnings of the chapters from AACR2R88 listed earlier. We have gathered them together into columns 2 and 3 of Figure 14. Column 2 lists the parts of the various nonbook materials which you are instructed to use as chief sources of information. Column 3 lists substitutes acceptable when information is not available from the chief source.

Examining these columns, you will see that, in many cases, you must obtain the needed information from an item's container or accompanying material; many of these items lack a clear title page analogy. There are also several types of nonbook media whose title page analogies are accessible only by means of auxiliary equipment. To catalog a motion picture or videorecording, you must screen the opening and closing credits (unless you can obtain a copy of the screenplay which includes them). To catalog a microform reproduction, you must use the appropriate microform reader to view (or make hard copies of) the title frames.

We will now discuss in more detail the various parts of the bibliographic record for a nonbook item. Columns 4–8 of Figure 14 list each nonbook material's prescribed sources for most portions of its bibliographic description. We have omitted the physical description, notes, and standard number and terms of availability areas from the figure because AACR2R88 directs you to take the information for these from "any source" in all cases.

Title: As columns 2 and 3 of Figure 14 show, nonbook items have various labels, captions, covers, containers, and or accompanying materials which serve as title page analogies. Multiple titles may appear, forcing you to choose one as the "title proper." The "order of preference" in which AACR2R88 lists sources of information aids in making this choice. Realia are unlikely to have titles in the usual sense. As we stated above, motion pictures, videorecordings, and microforms may have to be viewed with the proper equipment. To see the title of a computer program, you may have to execute it.

General material designation: When describing a nonbook item, you must answer the question, "What type of nonbook material is this?" The AACR2R88 requires you to answer this question according

Figure 14. Sources of Information for Nonbook Materials

Column 1 Medium	Column 2 Chief Source	Column 3 Allowable Substitutes for Chief Sources	Column 4 Title and Statement of Responsibility	Column 5 Edition	Column 6 Material or Type of Publication	Column 7 Publication, Distribution	Column 8 Series
Cartographic Materials	For printed atlas, title page or whatever serves as substitute for it. Otherwise, item itself, container, case, cradle, stand.	Any accompanying printed material	Chief source of information	Chief source of information, accompanying printed material	Mathematical data. Chief source of information, accompanying printed material.	Chief source of information, accompanying printed material	Chief source of information, accompanying printed material
Manuscripts	Manuscript itself; use, in this order of preference: title page; colophon; caption; heading; content of ms.	In this order of preference: another ms. copy; published edition; reference; source; other source	Chief source of information, published copies of manuscript	Chief source of information, published copies of manuscript	Does not apply to this material	Chief source of information, published copies of manuscript (For manuscripts, this is actually called the "date area.")	Does not apply to manuscripts
Music	Title page, unless it consists of list of items. In that case, use whichever gives fullest info. — "list" title page, cover, caption.	In order of preference: caption; cover; colophon; other preliminaries; other sources	Chief source of information	Chief source of information, caption, cover, colophon other preliminaries	Musical presentation. Chief source of information.	Chief source of information, caption, cover, colophon, other preliminaries.	Series title page, caption, cover, title page, colophon, other preliminaries

Material							
Sound recordings	For disc, open-reel, and cartridge tapes, item and label; for rolls, label; for sound recordings on film container and label	In this order of preference: accompanying textual material container (sleeve, box, etc.) other sources	Chief source of information	Chief source of information, accompanying textual material, container	Does not apply to this material	Chief source of information, accompanying textual material, container	Chief source of information, accompanying textual material, container
Motion Pictures and Videorecordings	In this order of preference: item itself (e.g., title frames) container—along with its label—which is an integral part of the item	In order of preference: accompanying textual material (e.g., scripts, shot lists, publicity material) container not integral part of item other sources	Chief source of information	Chief source of information, accompanying material	Does not apply to this material	Chief source of information, accompanying material	Chief source of information, accompanying material
Graphic Materials	Item itself, including permanently affixed labels and container which is an integral part of item, unifying container of multipart item if only it has collective title	In this order of preference: container (e.g., box, frame) accompanying textual material (e.g., manuals, leaflets) other sources	Chief source of information	Chief source of information, container, accompanying material	Does not apply to this material	Chief source of information, container, accompanying material	Chief source of information, container, accompanying material

Medium	Chief Source	Allowable Substitutes for Chief Sources	Title and Statement of Responsibility	Edition	Material or Type of Publication	Publication, Distribution	Series
Computer Files	Title screen, or, if none, main menus, program statements, etc.	In order of preference: physical carrier or its labels; documentation; information on publisher's container; other published descriptions; other sources	Chief source of information, carrier or its labels, info. issued by publisher, creator, etc., container	Chief source of information, carrier or its labels, info. issued by publisher, creator, etc., container	File characteristics. Any source	Chief source of information, carrier or its labels, information issued by publisher, creator, etc., container	Chief source of information, carrier or its labels, information issued by publisher, creator, etc., container
Three-Dimensional Artefacts and Realia	Object itself, along with any accompanying textual material or container issued by manufacturer	None given; cataloger instructed to prefer object itself to accompanying material or container	Chief source of information	Chief source of information	Does not apply to this material	Chief source of information	Chief source of information
Microforms	Title frame/card. If none use header or accompanying material if fuller form of title appears here.	In order of preference: rest of item, container which is part of item; Container not part of item; accompanying eye–readable material; any other source	Chief source of information	Chief source of information, rest of item, container	Special data. Chief source of information, rest of item, container. This area applies only to microform reproductions of items of a type that uses this area.	Chief source of information, rest of item, container	Chief source of information, rest of item, container

to a controlled vocabulary (defined in Chapter 5), choosing a term from one of the two lists which appear on page 21. The term chosen is known as the *General material designation* (GMD). List 1 is for British cataloging agencies; those in the United States should use List 2.

The GMD appears in brackets *immediately* after the title proper — before any parallel titles or subtitles:

> Lulu [sound recording] : an opera in three acts / by Alban Berg.

In a MARC record, the GMD is entered in subfield h. The brackets may be omitted, because many online systems will supply them:

> Lulu ‡h sound recording : ‡b an opera in three acts / ‡c by Alban Berg.

The GMD may be adjacent to another element which must receive brackets. In every such case, the GMD receives its own set of brackets:

> [Nursing dissertation collection] [Microform].
>
> (The title of the above work had to be supplied by the cataloger.)
>
> Macbeth [motion picture] : [a critical analysis of various film treatments]
>
> A tour of Philadelphia [motion picture] / [narrated by] Ronald Smith.

For two of the nonbook media, music scores and sound recordings, the uniform title is particularly important, since it may be the primary search key. We shall discuss uniform titles in our final chapter.

Statement of responsibility: This area is especially important to nonbook materials' descriptions, since it may be the only way to justify added entries for all individuals and corporate bodies who contributed to the work. These added entries are important because (a) there may be many such contributors, all of whom played an equally important role in creating the work, and (b) the work's main entry must often be its title.

Edition: The question of whether or not a new release of a work qualifies as a new *edition* can be especially difficult to answer in the case of nonbook materials. It can also be difficult to distinguish between a new edition of a work and a different, albeit related, work.

The AACR2R88 addresses these questions with both the appropriate rules in each chapter and definitions in Appendix D. For all nonbook materials except computer files and manuscripts, AACR2R88 defines "edition" as "all copies produced from essentially the same master copy and issued by the same entity. A change in the identity of the distributor does not mean a change of edition." The definition for manuscripts — "unpublished items" — is "all copies made from essentially the same original production (e.g. the original and carbon copies of a manuscript)." For computer files, the definition is "all copies embodying essentially the same content and issued by the same entity."

These definitions force catalogers to rethink their concepts of "edition." Also, even with these definitions to guide them, catalogers must rely on their own judgment in many situations.

Consider, for example, a sound recording that appeared first on the DECCA label, and was later rereleased on the MCA label — with exactly the same content and cover. Should the MCA rerelease be considered a new edition? To answer this question, you must first ask yourself, "Is this really a new *version* of the DECCA recording?" You must also determine the nature of the relationship between DECCA and MCA. Are they different entities or simply different distributors?

By way of a related problem, would you treat the monaural and stereo releases of a sound recording as separate editions? Assume they both appear on the same label, and were both made from the same master tape.*

For a more complicated example, consider a software package which is available for both the IBM PC and Apple Macintosh computers. Should you treat the two versions as two editions, two copies of the same edition, or two separate works? In trying to answer this question, examine both the above definition and Rule 9.7B1, which discusses notes for systems requirements. Also, assume that the Macintosh version has special provisions for using a mouse, while the IBM version does not.†

Material (or type of publication) specific details: This area is never part of a book's bibliographic description. It appears in descriptions of only four of the nonbook media (and serials). The AACR2R88 refers to this area by the above name only in Chapter 1. Each chapter which includes this area gives it a name specific to the type of data involved. These names and the data this area includes are as follows:

---

*We are aware that much of this technology described has been superseded by CD's (compact discs). However, problems of provenance remain. New "editions" of CD's may be difficult to determine.

†Macintosh and IBM are moving toward compatibility. New IBM versions will provide for the use of a mouse. Computer technology changes overnight.

MATERIAL	AREA
Cartographic material	Mathematical data: the item's scale, type of projection, and, optionally, coordinates.
Music	Musical presentation: statement, in chief source of information, of item's physical presentation. Area is optional.
Computer files	File characteristics: type of file — program or data — and number of records or program statements or bytes in file.
Microforms	Special data for cartographic materials, music, serials: contains whatever data would have gone in this area of the original item's description.

Publication, distribution, etc.: Generally speaking, the problem of determining publisher, place, and date of publication requires the same kind of decision making as for books. However, the information may be harder to find, or in a sense, be nonexistent. In the case of 3-D materials, for example, the "publisher" may be a grammar school third grade, which has also served as the "author." For motion pictures, "publisher" is likely to be somewhat diffuse; AACR2R88 Rule 7.4D1 states, "Give the name of the publisher, etc., and *optionally* of the distributor, releasing agency, etc., and/or production agency or producer not named in the statement of responsibility." There is some tendency in nonbook works for "author" and "publisher" to be the same.

Physical description: Here is where you list an item's significant physical characteristics — elaborating on them, if necessary, in notes further on. (We have discussed certain details which you must relegate to notes in Chapter 4.) These characteristics fall into four categories: extent of item, other physical details, dimensions, and details of accompanying material. The extent of an item is given in both physical and temporal terms wherever appropriate. Following is a set of specific examples:

Cartographic Materials:
1 map : col. ; 30 ×30 cm.
1 atlas (iv, 200 p.) : 100 col. maps ; 32 cm.
1 globe : col., plastic, on metal stand + 1 v. (x, 30 p. : ill. ; 18 cm.)

Manuscripts:
132 leaves : ill. ; 25 cm.

202 leaves, bound ; 26 cm.
15 boxes ; 25 × 35 × 35 cm.

Music:

1 score (100 p.) ; 35 cm.
1 miniature score (130 p.) : port. ; 18 cm.
1 score (60 p.) ; 21 cm. + 4 parts ; 26 cm. + 1 booklet

Sound Recordings:

1 sound disc (45 min.) : analog, 33⅓ rpm., stereo. ; 12 in.
1 sound disc (5 min.) : analog, 78 rpm., microgroove, mono. ;
10 in.
1 sound disc (65 min.) : digital, stereo ; 4¾ in.
on side 1 of 1 sound disc (13 min.) : analog, 33⅓ rpm., stereo ;
12 in. [For the description of a separately titled part of a sound
recording]
1 sound cassette (60 min.) : analog, 1 7/8 ips., stereo.
1 sound tape reel (15 min.) : analog, 7½ ips., stereo ; 5 in. +
1 booklet (9 p. ; 15 cm.)

Motion Pictures:

3 film reels (120 min.) : sd., col. ; 35 mm.
1 film cassette (20 min.) : sd., col. ; standard 8 mm. + 1 v. (40
p. ; 20 cm.)

Videorecordings:

1 videocassette (90 min.) : sd., b&w ; ½ in.
1 videoreel : sd., col. ; ½ in.
1 videodisc (ca. 60 min.) : sd., col. ; 12 in.
1 videodisc (44,653 fr.) : si., col. ; 12 in. + 1 booklet

Graphic Materials:

23 slides : b&w and col.
1 filmstrip (50 fr.) : col. ; 35 mm. + 1 sound disc (10 min :
analog, 33⅓ rpm., mono. ; 7 in.)
21 photographs : b&w ; 13 × 15 cm.
1 art original : oil on canvas ; 28 × 50 cm.
1 art print : lithograph, col. ; 30 × 30 cm.

Computer Files:

1 computer disk : col. ; 5¼ in.
1 computer disk : sd., col., single sided, single density, soft sec-
tored ; 5¼ in.
1 computer disk : col. ; 3½ in. + 1 v. (50 p. : ill. ; 23 cm.)
1 computer cassette : col : 3 7/8 in × 2½ in.
3 computer tape reels : 6,250 bpi.

Three-Dimensional Artefacts and Realia:
1 sculpture : wood ; 120 cm. high
7 models : col. ; in box 40 × 30 × 30 × 30 cm. + 1 teacher's guide (3 v. ; 30 cm.)
1 game (1 board, 10 role cards, 2 dice) ; in box 30 × 30 × 5 cm.

Microforms:
1 microfilm reel : negative, ill. ; 35 mm.
2 microfiches (140 fr.) : negative, ill. ; 11 × 15 cm. [Note: AACR288 Rule 11.5D3 instructs you to give dimensions only when they are nonstandard. The Library of Congress Rule Interpretations (1982–) omits this condition from the rule.]
7 micro-opaques ; 8 × 13 cm.

Note that you must sometimes make judgments as to what constitutes an item *per se* and what constitutes accompanying material. Is a given item a book with an accompanying sound recording or a sound recording with an accompanying book? Although this question concerns the entire bibliographic description, it is particularly important with respect to the physical description.

Before leaving the subject of physical description, we wish to offer the following warning. *Do not* attempt to apply any of the rules for books — those in Section 2.5 — to any of the nonbook media. Record the physical details of a nonbook item *strictly* according to the rules in the chapter which applies to it. We believe that you might be tempted to apply book rules to other media for two reasons. First, since many people still see libraries as sources of *books*, there is a good chance they might believe book rules should apply to all media. Second, we have found records in the OCLC database which contain errors of the type we are describing. (This is an example of how a record's presence in the database does not guarantee its correctness.)

Following is an example of the misapplication of a rule from section 2.5. Rules 2.5B2 and 2.5B4 instruct you to record the last numbered page of a sequence *as printed*, supplying a correction if this number "gives a completely false impression of the extent of the item." Under these two rules, statements such as these are permissible:

50 [i.e. 100] p.
42 [i.e. 420] p.
619 [i.e. 691] p.

However, if you are cataloging a set of 30 microfilm reels numbered 1–5, 5A–5E, 6–10, 10A–10E, 11–20, you are *not* permitted to do this:

> 20 [i.e. 30] microfilm reels

Rule 11.5B1 simply tells you to state the numbers of reels in the set. There are no provisions for recording and correcting the last number printed on the reels or their boxes. Therefore, the correct statement of extent in this case is:

> 30 microfilm reels

You must deal with the discrepancy between the actual number of reels and the number given for the last reel in a note.

Statements such as:

> 20 [i.e. 30] microfilm reels

are not permitted, according to our reasoning, because they draw the wrong analogy between books and microforms. If you read Rule 11.5B2, you will see that the pages in a book are analogous to the *frames of a microfilm or microfiche*; the actual microfilm reels are analogous to *entire printed volumes*.

Series: Most of the problems and issues concerning series statements apply to both book and nonbook materials. Therefore, we shall not discuss them in detail here, but rather refer you to our earlier chapter on the subject.

We will, however, mention one particular type of nonbook item to which the series statement is particularly important. This is the video-recording which contains one or more episodes of a dramatic television series, such as *Star Trek*, or *The Twilight Zone*. Library patrons are likely to search for these by the series title first.

Notes: Nonbook materials often have attributes which cannot be covered within the body of a proper AACR2R88 description. The place to list and describe such attributes, as we stated in Chapter 4, is in notes. Certain notes, such as those listing variations in title, intended audience, the library's holdings, and contents, are applicable to all nonbook materials.

Other notes apply only to one or two of the nonbook media. For example, music scores and sound recordings should receive a "medium of performance" note listing the musical instruments for which the piece in question is scored. Two notes which apply specifically to music scores are: (1) Publishers' numbers and plate numbers. If these are provided for an item, they are given, preceded by either "Publisher's no.:" or "Pl. no:". and (2) Notation. This should be given "if it is not the notation normally found in that type of item." In most cases, this would be anything other than modern staff notation. However, it could apply to a work composed before the invention of the modern system, then re-scored using present-day notation. This note could also apply to a score in which the parts for transposing instruments, such as the B-flat clarinet, alto flute, or French horn, are written at concert pitch.

Another important media-specific note is that listing the system requirements of a computer file. These requirements include the make and model of the computer on which the file will run, the amount of memory required, and various other hardware and software requirements.

Certain notes apply to all nonbook media, but have different specific meanings for each. The most obvious example of this is the listing of additional details of the physical description. These will, of course, vary with the type of nonbook item being described. For videorecordings, notes in this category provide details such as whether a videocassette is Beta or VHS. For sound recordings, a note of this type can provide a term such as "Compact disc." A physical description note can also indicate that a digital compact disk was made from an analog master tape, or that a 33⅓ rpm analog LP was made from a digital master tape.

Another general note which has one important specific application is that providing for additions to the statement of responsibility. This note is particularly important to the description of a motion picture—or videorecording of one—which is a film version of a novel. Earlier, we provided one example of this, *The Shining*. The actual statement of responsibility for such a work must include only those persons involved in the *making of the film*. The author of the original novel, Stephen King, in this case, must appear in a note.

Analytics: In Chapter 4, we discussed the need to provide access to portions of some works published under collective titles. In that chapter, we gave the series as one example. Each of the sound recordings listed earlier in this chapter is another. There are many sound recordings, videorecordings, and other nonbook items which consist of two or more complete works. Patrons must be able to locate the individual works if the items within which they appear are to be of any use. You may provide access to these works through the various types of analytics—descriptions of individual parts of an item also described as a whole—discussed in AACR2R88, Chapter 13. The descriptions of separate works on a sound recording, motion picture, and videorecording, which AACR2R88 allows for in Rules 6.1G4 and 7.1G4, are analytics if they are linked with a description of the complete item.

Added entries: The many and varied users of nonbook materials will have a diversity of reasons for wanting a given work. These many reasons may lead users to search for a given work under many potential access points. For example, a music student who is just beginning to study 20th century music might be more likely to search for the opera *Wozzeck* under Alban Berg. On the other hand, the listener who is familiar enough with the opera to seek out a specific performance might search for it under Pierre Boulez. A person studying the films of Stanley Kubrick would search under his name for *Dr. Strangelove*, while someone who wanted to see Peter Sellers' portrayal of the president would search under that actors' name.

An example of a different type concerns the spoken recordings of books available from the Library for the Blind and Physically Handicapped. Patrons of the Library—persons who either cannot see to read print or cannot hold a printed volume—will often develop a preference for a specific reader. In particular, the Library receives numerous requests for any book read by the late Alexander Scourby. Scourby, whose recordings include the Bible, various works of Dostoevsky, and Joyce's *Ulysses*, is generally considered to be one of the Library's all time best readers.

Library patrons may also approach slides, photographs, and other reproductions by any of a number of avenues. For example, one user may want to see examples of photographs by a particular photographer regardless of content, a second user may be interested in the social significance of the same photographs, and a third, just in their beauty as art objects. How would you, as a cataloger, take care of all these users' needs?

In view of the considerations just cited, and also because of AACR2R88's increased emphasis on title main entry, you must be certain to give sufficient attention to added entries. Otherwise, works can remain inaccessible to any user who does not know what the library in question has used as entry elements. In the case of maps, for example, entry under title (particularly in cases where several possible titles appear on the map or container) may give little indication of the authenticity or even the coverage of the map. Listed below, for the various media, are types of added entries which catalogers should consider:

> *Cartographic materials:* Cartographer; subtitle; corporate author; locale.
> *Music:* Uniform title; arranger; adapter; instrument or ensemble; author of libretto; composer of accompaniment.

Sound recordings: Performers; producers, directors and the like; writers; analytic added entries for individual works on the recording; record company. (This could be important in the case of a company such as Deutsche Grammophon, whose recordings many listeners find superior. However, note that the Boulez recording of *Wozzeck*, which we mentioned earlier, is *not* on Deutsche Grammophon, but on Columbia. A listener who cannot recall Boulez's name might be able to remember the record company.)

Motion pictures and videorecordings: Performers; producers, directors and the like; writers; analytic added entries for individual works on the film or videorecording; author of literary work on which motion picture is based; for science-fiction and horror movies in which special effects play an important role, the person or corporate body responsible for them — e.g., Rick Baker, Tom Savini, Industrial Light and Magic.

Graphic arts: Adapter; person responsible for reproduction; artist.

Computer files: Corporate body; programmer.

Microforms: Creator of original; since many other nonbook materials may be reproduced in microform, the same problems of entry headings will apply to the microform reproduction. The general problem of describing microforms leads us to the final section of this chapter.

Description of microform reproductions — advantages and drawbacks of LC policy

Many items published in microform are actually reissues of existing eye-readable publications. Examples are microform editions of various journals and newspapers, which many libraries choose over print editions to save space. Items which are deteriorating and cannot be saved may be microfilmed to preserve their content. Rare items may be microfilmed so that the original can be kept out of circulation, and thus protected from damage.

When cataloging these microform reissues, as the *Library of Congress Rule Interpretations* (1982–) explains, the Library of Congress places details of the *original version* in the body of the description. Details of the reproduction appear in a formal note thus:

Microfilm. Ann Arbor, Mich. : University Microfilms International, 1989. 23 microfilm reels : negative ; 35 mm.

In a MARC record, this note belongs in the 533 field, with subfield tags as follows:

> 533 Microfilm. ‡b Ann Arbor, Mich. : ‡c University Micro-
> films International, ‡d 1989. ‡e 23 microfilm reels : negative ; 35
> mm.

The Library of Congress does this, as Maxwell (1989) explains, to emphasize the connection between the original item and the microform reproduction. This connection is particularly important to the Library of Congress, which, in many cases, owns both the original and the reproduction. If the details of the microform reproduction appeared in the body of the description, a patron might not realize that it was, in fact, a reproduction of an existing work.

You might also argue that the details of the original better serve to identify the item and distinguish it from others with which it might be confused. Consider, for example, two books on medicine. A book published by Academic Press will probably treat this subject much differently than one published by Time-Life Books. However, University Microfilms International might reproduce both of these. Also, a 50-page paper will probably discuss Einstein's Theory of Relativity more extensively than a three-page pamphlet. Either of these, however, could fit on one microfilm reel.

On the other hand, if you wish to read a book, would you settle for a microfilm reproduction? If your library has two works on a subject, and you judge both to be of equal quality, would you prefer the one available in book form to the one available only on microfilm? You could argue that, because of issues like these, a bibliographic description should emphasize details of the actual physical item in hand. (Note, however, that even descriptions which emphasize the original contain the GMD "[microform]" immediately following the title proper.)

There is one final point to consider with respect to the handling of microforms. One of AACR2's major goals, both in the original 1978 version and the 1988 version, is to treat all media with the same respect and meticulousness as books. To put it another way, AACR2, rather than treating nonbook materials as "second class citizens in the world of books," seeks to grant them equal rights to a thorough and accurate description. The practice of relegating details of a microform's description to a secondary position, treating it as if it were a new printing of a book, is at odds with this goal.

In any case, since many American libraries follow Library of Congress policies, you will, if you work with microforms, probably be required to handle them as the Library of Congress does. Unfortunately, you will not always have a copy of the original at hand to provide such details as size. In such situations, you may omit the element of the description which is unavailable.

In certain instances, this Library of Congress policy may force you to make a difficult judgment call. Many microform publications are collections of documents that originally existed in eye-readable form. The *Library of Congress Rule Interpretations* states that when a publisher of microforms assembles such documents in order to produce an original microform collection, the collection is described in terms of the reproduction.

Consider, however:

> Microform of the Mary Smith papers : a collection assembled by and housed in the New York Public Library.

You would have to treat this as a reproduction, since the actual collection existed *as an entity* before the microfilming agency published it; it was the New York Public Library, not the microfilming agency, who assembled the collection. It may be difficult to determine whether a certain collection is an original microform publication or a reproduction of an existing collection. The crucial question is whether the microfilming agency which published the collection also assembled the documents therein.

Conclusion

Our overview of the cataloging and classification of nonbook materials can only hint at the complexity of the problems involved in their bibliographic description. It is apparent that knowledge of the specific subject areas involved — geography, music, photography, computer science, cinema, and so on — is almost obligatory for an understanding of the optimum manner of indexing, storage, and retrieval of many of the nonbook media. Since it is very likely that such materials will play an increasingly important role in the library of the future, we urge you to become familiar with these potentially excellent sources of information.

Review questions for Chapter 12

1. Cite two examples, each, of nonbook works which should: (a) be entered under "author" (b) be entered under title. Give your reasoning in all cases.

2. Give two examples of works for which there are good reasons to enter under either title or author. Give the reasons.

3. Give an example of a work which should be entered under performer. State why.

4. Select six works requiring different GMDs, and write out the first two elements of the title area.

5. Construct a physical description for:

    (a) a motion picture

    (b) a videorecording

    (c) a compact disc

    (d) a 33⅓ rpm analog disc

    (e) a diorama or model

    (f) 20 colored slides

    (g) a filmstrip with an accompanying sound recording and booklet

6. What are the arguments in favor of describing a microform reproduction in terms of the original? What are the arguments against this practice?

Sources cited and suggestions for further reading or study

Anglo-American Cataloging Rules: North American Text. Chicago: American Library Association, 1967.

Anglo-American Cataloging Rules, 2nd ed., 1988 revision, edited by Michael Gorman and Paul W. Winkler. Ottawa: Canadian Library Association; Chicago: American Library Association, 1988.

Bierbaum, E.G. "Beyond Print: Object Collections in Academic Libraries." *Collection Building* 10, nos. 1–2 (1989): 7–11.

Crawford, Walt. *MARC for Library Use: Understanding Integrated USMARC*, 2nd ed. Boston: G.K. Hall, 1989.

Daniel, Evelyn H., and Carol I. Notowitz. *Media and Microcomputers in the Library: A Selected Annotated Resource Guide*. Phoenix, Ariz.: Oryx Press, 1984.

Frost, Carolyn O. *Cataloging Nonbook Materials: Problems in Theory and Practice*. Littleton, Colo.: Libraries Unlimited, 1983.

_____. *Media Access and Organization*. Englewood, Colo.: Libraries Unlimited, 1989.

Graham, C. "Definition and Scope of Multiple Versions." *Cataloging and Classification Quarterly* 11 (1990): 5–32.

Holzberlein, D. and D. Jones. *Cataloging Sound Recordings: A Manual with Examples.* Binghamton, N.Y.: Haworth Press, 1988.

Intner, S.S. "Writing Summary Notes for Films and Videos." *Cataloging and Classification Quarterly* 9 (1988): 55–72.

Lancaster, F. Wilfred. "The Future of the Librarian Lies Outside the Library." *Catholic Library World* 51 (April 1980): 388–391.

Library of Congress Rule Interpretations for AACR2: A Cumulation from Cataloging Service Bulletin Numbers 11–, compiled by Lois Lindberg, Alan Boyd, and Elaine Druesedow. Oberlin, Ohio: Oberlin College Library, 1982–.

Massonneau, Suzanne. "Bibliographic Control of Audiovisual Materials: Opportunities for the 1980's." *Catholic Library World* 51 (April 1980): 384–387.

Maxwell, Margaret F. *Handbook for AACR2: Explaining and Illustrating the Anglo-American Cataloguing Rules*, 1988 revision. Chicago: American Library Association, 1989.

Morse, H., and M. Holland. "Cataloging of AV Materials on DOBIS/LIBIS." *Audiovisual Librarian* 15 (August 1989): 134–141.

Olson, N.B., and E. Swanson. "The Year's Work in Nonbook Processing, 1988." *Library Resources and Technical Services* 33 (October 1989): 335–343.

Schroeder, John R. "AACR2 Abandonment of Corporate Body Main Entry." *Western Association of Map Libraries Information Bulletin* 10 (1978): 78–81.

Selmer, Marsha L. "Map Cataloging and Classification Methods: A Historical Survey." *Special Libraries Association Geography and Map Division Bulletin* 103 (1976): 7–12.

Weihs, Jean Riddle. *Accessible Storage of Nonbook Materials.* Phoenix, Ariz.: Oryx Press, 1984.

————, Shirley Lewis, and Janet Macdonald. *Nonbook Materials: The Organization of Integrated Collections*, 3rd ed. Ottawa: Canadian Library Association, 1989.

13

The Shelf List

A "shelf list" is an arrangement by classification number of the bibliographic records of the items in a collection. It is, therefore, a record of the cataloged materials in a library reflecting the order in which the individual items stand on the shelves. The book number by which each record is filed will consist of the full classification code — i.e., the Dewey number or the "class" portion of the LC number — the item number and any special symbols which distinguish among various editions or multiple copies of the same work. The shelf list can take any form that reflects the holdings of a library in the order in which the materials stand on the shelves. Two possible forms are:

1. A set of catalog cards.
2. A computer printout sorted by call number.

(In one sense, an online display of partial holdings by call number, however limited, can be thought of as a mini–shelf list.)

The uses of the shelf list

There are many uses, actual and potential, for a shelf list:

As an inventory record and catalog editing tool. When a library wishes to take account of every copy of a work in the collection, the shelf list can help determine what is missing or misfiled. Works charged out, lost, being mended or being bound can thus be singled out. Similarly, portions of the collection can be edited using a partial shelf list.

For purposes of insurance. In the case of a catastrophe, such as fire, theft or sabotage, the shelf list can serve as a record for insurance claims.

To show what kinds of items, and how many items, the library holds in a given classification number.

To show how many copies of an individual work are held by the library.

To assist the acquisitions librarian, therefore, by demonstrating what materials the library already holds in a given class.

As a check of item numbers. As you classify a new work, you should consult the shelf list to be sure that the item number which you either constructed or found in a MARC record for the work fits into the established sequence. For example, an OCLC member library which acquires Steve Reich's *Writings About Music* might catalog this work by editing the LC record OCLC #1106824. The Library of Congress Classification system number appearing in this record is ML60.R35. If the "ML60.R _ _" portion of this library's shelf list contains:

> ML60.R36 Randall, Thomas.
> Essays on music.
>
> ML60.R4 Renfield, William.
> Thoughts about music.

you must assign a new item number. This situation is know as a *shelf list conflict.* So as not to conflict with "Renfield," the new item number must fall within the range R361–3999...; "R388" reflects reasonably well the distance between each pair of adjacent names. (In line with our earlier discussion of Library of Congress item numbers, this hypothetical library should change the item number *only* in the case of a conflict, since OCLC #1106824 is an LC record.)

To reveal information, such as author and title, for a work for which only the call number is known.

To provide data on such matters as date purchased, cost, source and accession number, if the library does not keep other accession records.

To provide guidance on the choice of a class number. When working as a cataloger, you must often deal with items for which several class numbers may be appropriate. For instance, you may encounter a book on homing pigeons which gives equal emphasis to the breeding of these birds and their use by the military. Should this book receive the class number SF469 or UH90? The shelf list can answer this question by showing what precedent your library has set. The shelf list may reveal that the library has classed all books dealing equally with breeding and military use of homing pigeons at SF469. In this case, you should place the new book there to maintain uniformity and consistency.

In an academic library, you are also likely to encounter many books on psychology. In the Library of Congress classification, this discipline is divided among classes B, H and R. In this situation, you may find the shelf list to be an essential tool in determining which books should stand together.

As a "picture" of the entire collection, to demonstrate strengths, weaknesses and imbalances in the collection and thus to aid in collection development.

To serve as a history and allocation record for the collection. If a shelf list card includes such data as date purchased, source, price, and copies held (total, by the main library, by branch libraries), it can be used as a means of generating collocations of information on any such points: e.g., how many books have been lost, how many copies of title X were purchased, how many titles are shelved in branch library Y, and so on.

To serve as a "union list" in large research libraries. The several copies of a work may appear in various branch libraries. The shelf list brings together all the information about all the copies of a work, despite their separate physical allocations.

To furnish a subject bibliography based on classification number. A list of all titles bearing a given class number, while it may exclude other works on the subject classified elsewhere, does give a useful bibliography of at least representative titles dealing with the subject in question. A shelf list arranged according to the Dewey Decimal Classification system would probably be more useful for this purpose than one arranged by the Library of Congress Classification system. This is because the Dewey Decimal Classification system's notation reflects the hierarchical relationship which the system creates among topics.

To serve as a classed catalog. Those libraries still maintaining manual card catalogs (as, for example, for older works in the collection) use one of three arrangements: (1) All author, title and subject entry cards are arranged in a single alphabetic sequence; (2) Author, title and subject cards each have their own sequence; (3) Author and title entries are combined into one sequence while subject cards have their own.

Only the shelf list serves as a classed catalog, bringing together entries arranged by classification number. Again, the Dewey Decimal Classification system will probably produce a more useful arrangement than the Library of Congress Classification system. In fact, as we demonstrated in our introduction to the Dewey Decimal Classification, Dewey numbers are potentially powerful and versatile search tools in an automated catalog. For this reason, libraries using the Library of Congress Classification system may wish to consider adding Dewey numbers to their records, and making these numbers available as search elements.

To serve as a teaching and research tool. Many technical services librarians view the shelf list solely as a tool for their use in performing their duties. It is possible that many library patrons are not even aware of the shelf list's existence, since it is usually housed in the cataloging department, and is thus inaccessible to the public.

For this reason, it is likely that the faculty member or researcher seldom considers the potential assistance of the shelf list in planning course materials or in seeking out information. There is no reason why a library user could not employ the shelf list to make an organized search of all the material the library has on a given subject, since, presumably, the sophisticated researcher would be the best judge of the potential value of the items listed under any given class number. Such a search, personally conducted by the faculty member or researcher, might be not only informative but heuristic.

Of course, such researchers would have to be trained in the use of their library's classification system. At the very least, they would have to become aware that classification numbers are not simply location symbols. They would also have to learn the difference between numbers denoting broad, general topics and those denoting more specific subjects.

Granted, the shelf list, assuming it exists in card form, must be protected from damage by either careless handling or vandalism. Also, since most shelf list users will be library personnel from either the cataloging or acquisitions departments, the positioning of the shelf list must suit the specialists' convenience.

All constituencies could be served, however, if the shelf list file remained in the cataloging department, but was located in such a manner that other than technical services personnel could have access to the list without having to travel through that department. Further, as suggested above, allowing call number searching in the online catalog will obviate such difficulties.

The manual shelf list — form and content

A manual shelf list is one which exists in print form rather than in any type of computer file. A library whose public catalog is online may still wish to maintain a manual shelf list, as suggested above. While, as we noted previously, a manual shelf list may take several forms, it usually exists as a set of catalog cards. To be maximally useful, shelf list cards should contain such data as price, date purchased, accession number and notation of loss. A library using an online shared cataloging system, such as OCLC, may choose to have some of this information printed on shelf list cards. However, any data subject to change, such as copy holdings or loss notations, should be written on the cards in pencil. Needless to say, corrections of this sort can be made much more easily in an online shelf list.

In either case, data should be entered in a consistent manner. For example, acquisition information might be listed in that portion of the card normally given over to notes. Furthermore, the coding of the acquisition data should be consistent, easily understood and in chronological order. Figure 15 shows examples of possible shelf list cards. We intend these examples to be illustrative, but not necessarily prescriptive.

Notice the kind of information that will appear only on the shelf list card. The card shows the number and allocation of copies, together with comments about the loss of copies and attempts to reclaim such.

The call number labels affixed to the copies of a work will include the copy number on its own line. They will also contain the symbol for the appropriate branch library above the call number. For example, the three labels for *Management of Addictions* will look like this:

```
        U.L.  BA/SS
RC    RC    RC
565   565   565
.P6   .P6   .P6
c. 1  c. 2  c. 3
```

We are assuming that the institution places the first copy of a work in the main library. This is, however, a matter of local policy. It is also any library's prerogative to omit "c. 1" from the label for the first copy.

A library will often note in its shelf list the date of purchase, source and price of an item. Had either of the works in our example been a gift, the library would have noted this as well. If by chance, the third copy of either work had been printed in another city because of the publisher's

Figure 15. *Sample shelf list cards*

```
U.L.
PR2638   Knoll, Robert E
.K5          Ben Jonson's plays : an introduction / by
         Robert E. Knoll. -- Lincoln : Univ. of
         Nebraska Press, 1964.
             xvii, 206 p. : ill. port. ; 24 cm.
c.1, ul lost
c.2, ul
c.3, main
             1.  Jonson, Ben, 1573?-1637.  I.  Title.

         7-1-65 U. of Neb.  $25.


PR2638.K5
4/29/65  PJNjg 10          O           SL 64-17220
Library of Congress       822.3            NcU
```

```
H.S.
RC 565   Podolsky, Edward, 1902-          ed.
.P6          Management of addictions. -- New York :
         Philosophical library, 1955.
Also         413 p. : ill. ; 22 cm.
in
Main         1.  Alcoholism.  2.  Narcotic habit.
         I.  Title.
c. 3 BA/SS

         2-27-56 - BU  $12.50



RC 565.P6    616.861
                              O
recl. repl. 6/24/78 mg 5                55-14403
```

changing locations, this could also be noted. (The book would have to be considered a different edition if there were any other major changes. It would also have to be so considered if it had been printed in another country.) The information included on a shelf list card will vary from library to library, depending on each institution's needs.

To file shelf list cards — or shelve the items they represent — correctly, one must know where to place a call number with respect to others in the same scheme. Dewey Decimal classification numbers, for example, represent principles of number building different from Library of Congress classification numbers and are to be "read" differently. Dewey numbers are to be understood as proceeding from the general to the specific as one "reads" from left to right. The numerical sequence has the same meaning as any decimal number and will file accordingly. For example, "616.861" (of the *Podolsky* example) will file between "616.86(0)" and "616.862," while "RC 565.P6," on the other hand, will file between "RC 565.M6" and "RC 565.R6." In the latter case, it is the modifying *cutter* number which determines the sequence.

Actually, a Dewey library must use some type of item numbers since it will likely give many works the same class number. Many Dewey collections use some variation on the "item" cutters numbers we discussed in conjunction with the Library of Congress Classification. Again it is each library's prerogative, although the system any institution chooses must place works in a logical order.

The precise method of filing is not so important as establishing a policy of *consistent* filing practices. Notice, for example, that the call numbers in Figure 15 contain the symbols "H.S." and "U.L." for two branch libraries. Another frequently used symbol is "REF," indicating that a work is located in the library's reference department and does not circulate. A library may handle cards bearing this type of call number in one of three ways:

(1) File all branch library shelf list cards after those for items in the main library. Place all cards for a given branch library together and arrange these groups of cards alphabetically by symbol.

(2) Ignore all branch library symbols, filing all cards strictly by call number.

(3) File all cards strictly by call number except those representing items in certain collections. Place cards denoting such items in a separate sequence.

Again, a library is free to select any of these methods, but must apply the one it chooses in all cases.

The online list—form and content

As we have said earlier, an online catalog can effectively arrange a set of bibliographic records in order by title, author, subject, or some other element instantly on demand. (For a more detailed discussion of how a computer accomplishes this, see Appendix III.) Therefore, any online catalog is an online shelf list if you can search it by call number. Following is an example of how you might use such a system.

You are a cataloger in a library which uses the Library of Congress Classification. You have in hand a book on music history written by Thomas Gray. You have assigned it the class number ML200.5, and need to add an item number which will fit into your library's sequence. This, as we explained earlier, requires you to check the shelf list. Rather than searching through a drawer of catalog cards, you go to a computer terminal and type:

cl = ML200.5

On the screen appears:

1. ML200.5.A33   10. ML200.5.R63
2. ML200.5.A47   11. ML200.5.T36
3. ML200.5.A64   12. ML200.5.T38
4. ML200.5.B55   13. ML200.5.T46
5. ML200.5.G32   14. ML200.5.T87
6. ML200.5.G45   15. ML200.5.W36
7. ML200.5.G48   16. ML200.5.W66
8. ML200.5.G57   17. ML200.5.W86
9. ML200.5.G84

If, instead, you had typed,

cl = ML200.5.G

you would have gotten only this portion of this list:

1. ML200.5.G32   4. ML200.5.G57
2. ML200.5.G45   5. ML200.5.G84
3. ML200.5.G48

By typing a line number from the screen display, you can see the complete record for the item with that call number. This includes bibliographic description, holdings information, and any other data available on that item. In this situation, all you need is the main entry. You find main entries as follows:

G57: Glutz, Ezra.
G84: Gunn, Joseph.

Therefore, if you assign "G73" to the book by Gray, it will fit. (Note: The commands and screen displays in this example are not intended to represent any particular existing system. Rather, they are examples of how such commands and displays can look.)

The above example assumes a library's holdings are completely on-line. What happens when a library acquires an online system after having cataloged a large part of its collection manually? In fact, most American libraries are facing this situation, since they existed long before online catalogs did. For a library that has only been in existence since the 1960s, the answer is *retrospective conversion*, often termed "retrocon." Retrospective conversion is the act of keying the data from manual catalog records into an online cataloging system. A library can use essentially the same procedure to perform retrospective conversion as is does to catalog new acquisitions. We have described those procedures in Chapter 2.

However, a large institution that has existed for over a century must seek another solution. One such institution is the library system of the University of Pennsylvania. At the time of this writing, the University uses an online catalog for recent acquisitions while retaining its manual catalog for older works. (The University's manual catalog contains many old cards of great historical value.)

However a library handles the above situation, it must answer another question: when we go online, should we continue to assign items numbers that reflect manual filing practices or should we begin using numbers that reflect the way a computer sorts data? As any reader who is also a computer user knows, a computer cannot apply any qualitative measures when placing items in order. It cannot equate

> *2001: A Space Odyssey* with *Two Thousand and One: A Space Odyssey*
> or McDonald with MacDonald

Instead, it places all titles beginning with digits before those beginning with *A*. It also places all names beginning with *Mc* after *all* names beginning with *Ma* — i.e., Mather, Matheson, etc. (For a more detailed description of why this happens, see Appendix IV.)

The Library of Congress has begun assigning item numbers which reflect a computer's sorting of data. A book with a title such as *50 Hints for Better Health*, if it is entered under title, will now receive a number beginning ".A1," rather than ".F5." Libraries should establish policies regarding situations like this *before* a cataloger encounters them and has to make a decision on the spot.

In this chapter, we have tried to explain the nature and the use of the shelf list. We have also tried to demonstrate that the shelf list can be an invaluable tool not only for the cataloger, but for the researcher or other library user who is willing to make the effort to learn to use it.

Review questions for Chapter 13

1. Using examples, explain the process of ascertaining that a given item number will fit into your library's shelf list.

2. Do the same for a subject cutter and a "reserved" cutter.

3. Explain how a researcher or other library patron may use the shelf list as a classed catalog.

4. Assuming that a library maintains a manual shelf list, what types of information will appear on shelf list cards, but not on records in the public catalog?

5. What do you think a library's policy should be on the computer sorting issue? Do you feel that a library should assign item numbers which reflect the manner in which a computer will sort the corresponding main entries? Should a library assign such item numbers in some cases but not others? Why or why not?

14

Advanced Problems: Corporate Bodies, Serials, and Uniform Titles

Throughout this book, we have dealt almost entirely with works having the following characteristics:

1. They are *monographs*. They are self-contained, having a specific and finite number of physical parts and a definite date of completion.

2. They have been created by one or more individual authors.

3. Each has either a single title or one clearly preferred title.

4. Each such title clearly refers only to one specific item.

However, there also exist many works of which one or more of the following are true:

1. The author of part or all of the work is a group of individuals acting as an entity with its own name.

2. The work is an ongoing publication, having no projected date of completion, and a potentially infinite number of physical parts, each of which may differ in significant respects from any other.

3. The work is known by many titles, no one of which is clearly preferred over the others. Often, this is because there exist a large number of differing manifestations of such a work.

4. The work's title is also the title of one or more other items.

To a large extent, the problems associated with such items are beyond the scope of this introductory textbook. However, we feel that you should be aware of the issues such items raise. Therefore, we shall focus, in this chapter, on these issues, rather than on step-by-step instructions for handling the materials in question.

Corporate bodies as authors

Definition of a corporate body

The AACR2R88 defines a corporate body as "an organization or group of persons that is identified by a particular name and that acts, or may act, as an entity." This includes organizations and groups as diverse as IBM, the Juilliard String Quartet, the Rolling Stones, the Humanities-Communications Department of Drexel University, the United Church of Christ, a scientific expedition to the Antarctic, or the U.S. Internal Revenue Service.

Past attitudes toward the concept of corporate bodies as authors

Whether or not a group such as those named above can truly be an "author" has been a subject of debate throughout the 20th century. Cutter, in 1904, criticized the practice of German libraries, which considered all work issued by corporate bodies as anonymous. Cutter stated that "bodies of men are to be considered as authors of works published in their name or by their authority." Cutter also identified the two main problems associated with the concept of corporate body: "The chief difficulty with regard to bodies of men is to determine (1) what their names are, and (2) whether the name or some other words shall be the heading."

Half a century later, in 1949, the American Library Association, in its "red book," *ALA Cataloging Rules for Author and Title Entries* clearly recognized and defined "corporate entry" as true authorship, stating: "Governments and their agencies, societies, institutions, forms, conferences, etc. are to be regarded as the authors of publications for which they, as corporate bodies, are responsible. Such material . . . is entered under the heading for the corporate body, even though the name of the individual preparing it is given."

In 1961, the International Conference on Cataloging Principles was held in Paris, under the direction of Seymour Lubetsky. The conference marked a major accomplishment in international cooperation in the field of cataloging and bibliography, and led to the development of the "Paris Principles," indicating the proper rules for making entries in catalogs and bibliographies. A new cataloging code was published in 1967, called *Anglo-American Cataloging Rules*, which was, unfortunately, not a complete amalgamation of British and American rules, the American version being subtitled, "North American Text." The preface to this 1967 AACR, page vi, states: "It is regrettable that, because of the great size of many American catalogs, it was necessary for the Catalog Code Revision Committee to agree to the suggestions of the Association of Research Libraries that certain incompatible American practices be continued in the present rules."

There was, on the whole, substantial agreement among the representatives of the various countries on the proper rules for making entries in catalogs. The British and American texts differed mainly in certain specific rules and spellings—for instance, "cataloguing" versus "cataloging." Both 1967 texts, however, clearly accepted the "corporate author" concept. The AACR67 Rule 1A states: "enter a work, a collection of works, or selections from works by one author under the person or corporate body that is the author, whether named in the work or not." The AACR67 defines the corporate body as, "an organization or group of persons that is identified by a name and that acts, or may act, as an entity."

The orientation of AACR2 toward the concept of corporate bodies as authors

An about-face occurred in 1978, with the publication of AACR2'78. The new rules so restricted entry under corporate body that many works formerly entered thus now had to be entered under title. Consider the wording of AACR2'78 Rule 21.1B2: "Enter a work emanating from one or more corporate bodies under the heading for the appropriate corporate body if it falls into one or more of the following categories." The categories, which we present here in paraphrased and condensed form, are: (a) Works dealing with the corporate body's administrative policies and procedures; (b) Some types of legal and governmental works—e.g., laws, court decisions; (c) Works that "record the collective thought of the body"; (d) Conference proceedings; and (e) Certain nonbook items created by a performing group.

The rule also directs you *not* to enter the work under the corporate body if you have any doubt as to whether it falls into one of these categories.

However, before you attempt to determine whether the work falls into one of these categories, you must first deal with the issue of emanation. There are works that fall into the above categories but which you must still enter under title because they do not emanate from the corporate body. The word "emanating" is not wholly definitive. An AACR2'78 footnote to Rule 21.1B1 instructs you to "consider a work to have emanated from a corporate body if it is issued by that body or has been caused to be issued by that body or if it originated with that body." This does not clear up the situation, partly because a footnote immediately following states: "Some legal and governmental works are entered under headings for bodies other than the body from which they emanate."

Furthermore, the wording of Rule 21.1B1, along with the page layout of that rule, in both the 1978 edition and the 1988 revision, belie the importance of the emanation issue. The phrase "emanating from" appears within a sentence whose main purpose is to introduce the five categories listed above. In addition, those categories appear prominently in the main text while the criteria for emanation appear in a footnote. For a more extensive discussion of the emanation issue than either AACR2'78 or AACR2R88 provides, see the Library of Congress (1982).

Another difficult question is that of what constitutes collective thought, and the manner in which you should handle works that combine statements of collective thought with reports of collective activity. The *Library of Congress Rule Interpretations* (1982–) discusses this question in detail.

An important point to keep in mind regarding the newer approach is that AACR2—in both its 1978 and 1988 incarnations—in its criteria for main entry under corporate body, makes the degree of responsibility for the work's content a secondary consideration.

The present approach to the issue of corporate bodies as authors

The AACR2R88 takes, fundamentally, the same position as the 1978 edition, except that it has readmitted the following categories of works as having corporate authorship: constitutions, court rules, religious laws (e.g. canon law), liturgical works, and cartographic materials.

Consider some of the implications of title versus corporate author main entry. Many works for which corporate bodies are responsible have titles which are generic and nondescriptive, such as *Proceedings, Transactions, Annual Report, Conference on . . ., Journal of . . .*, etc. Most online systems designate the generic terms appearing in such titles as *stop-words*—words which the computer disregards when indexing, and which users must disregard when searching, in the same manner as initial articles. Manual catalogs often ignore these words as well, thus creating a kind of "default" corporate entry. The danger of overusing full title main entry in such situations is that it may effect collocations which are tedious for a library patron to use. The similarity of many of these titles can also cause a patron to confuse two or more items: *American Journal of...* versus *Journal of the American....*

As we have said in previous chapters, the online catalog enables users to search on any element of the bibliographic record, thus diminishing the importance of the "main entry" concept. However, a work "emanating" from a corporate body, whether entered under title or not, requires one or more added entries, meaning, as suggested in the previous paragraph, that if you are cataloging such a work, you cannot avoid a "corporate body" entry. Therefore, you must deal with the question: what is the corporate body's name?

Determining the correct form of a corporate body's name

In general you are to follow the same rule when constructing headings for corporate bodies that you follow when constructing headings for personal authors: Select the name by which the body is commonly identified. You will determine the "common" form of the name in the same manner as you would for a personal author — from works issued by the corporate body in its own language, selecting the name by which the body identifies itself.

However, a corporate body is different from a personal author in many ways. A personal author is an unique entity, living within a defined period of years, and remaining the same person even under changes of name. A corporate body, on the other hand, has the following attributes.

1. A corporate body is a *group* of individuals acting as a unit.

2. A corporate body may have a lifetime of hundreds of years.

3. The name of the corporate body often changes.

4. The individual members or the structure of the corporate body may change.

5. The discrete existence of the corporate body may change or even disappear as with mergers, takeovers, reorganizations, or evolution over time from simplicity to complexity — or, in some cases, the reverse.

6. The corporate body, while acting autonomously, may itself be a subordinate part of a larger unit, as, for example, the U.S. Bureau of Census is a part of the U.S. Department of Commerce.

Furthermore, when trying to establish headings for corporate bodies, you will be dealing with such diverse *types* of entities as:

- Governments, and their subordinate and related bodies
- Conferences, congresses, meetings, etc.
- Exhibitions, fairs, festivals
- Radio and television stations
- Heads of state
- Armed forces
- Religious bodies and their officials
- Commercial institutions
- Societies and associations
- Performing groups in the fields of arts and entertainment

Your chief authority for the proper form of the corporate body's name will be, as stated previously, works which that body has issued. When the body has not actually authored any works or portions of works, you must use, as your authority, an appropriate reference source.

We shall not attempt, in this discussion, to analyze or solve each of the problems you will encounter in trying to select the "commonly identified" name of a particular corporate body. We shall, instead, discuss three very common problems in corporate entry headings: (1) How to select among variant names, (2) What to do about name changes, and (3) When to enter a work under a subordinate body.

How to select among variant names

Initials versus spelled-out names: A corporate body may call itself by different forms of its name in different publications, sometimes using initials or acronyms, and sometimes spelling out the whole name. Patrons used to initials may actually not know the terms the initials stand for. You will need to make references from all names you decide against to the one you adopt.

Names in nonroman scripts: You will have to transliterate these for American libraries, even though they were published only in a nonroman script. Use a consistent transliteration table for all such works.

Differing usages made by the corporate body itself, sometimes in a single publication: Several forms of a corporate body's name may appear in one work. Use the form of the name found on the chief source of information for that work — see Figure 14 on page 218 — or the closest equivalent to a title page that you can find.

What to do about name changes

Rule 24.1C1 of the AACR2R88 states: "If the name of a corporate body has changed (including change from one language to another) establish a new heading under that name. Refer from the old heading to the new and from the new heading to the old." Unfortunately, this can lead to the dispersion of material throughout the catalog, forcing patrons to follow a set of "see also" references from one point to another.

In many cases, the name change results from an actual disappearance or absorption of a former corporate body. Here, a simple "see" or "see also" reference will be insufficient. You must make explanatory notes as comments on your catalog record, and a "history" tracing on your authority record. The public catalog notes may be brief, but must be explicit enough for the library user to find needed older materials.

When to enter a work under a subordinate body

Many large institutions, such as governments, universities and religious bodies, are organized in a hierarchical structure with many subdivisions. If the name of the lesser body implies subordination — "Department," "Section," "Division," "Branch," etc. — or is general in nature — "Research Institute," "Friends of the...," "Bureau of the...," "School of...," etc. — enter the name as a subheading of the larger body.

On the other hand, many subordinate bodies have distinctive names under which patrons are likely to search. When this is the case, enter directly under the name of the subordinate body, with a reference from the overarching institution. Be governed in your choice, as always, by (1) the name used in the body's publications, and (2) the name commonly listed in reference sources.

Although corporate bodies are, as a rule, groups of individuals, there exist several interesting exceptions — individual persons classed as corporate bodies. When a religious official or head of state acts in an official capacity, he or she will be entered in the following manner:

United States. *President (1981–1989) : Reagan*
Catholic Church. *Pope (1963–1964) : Paul VI*

In creating authority records for headings such as these, you will have to consult reference sources other than those you would use in constructing a heading for a personal author. For example, you may start with such a general source as *The Encyclopedia of Associations*, but will probably need, in the end, very specific sources dealing only with a particular kind of body. You will find a number of possibilities in this chapter's bibliography, and in Appendix II.

Serials

Definition of a serial

A serial can be a scholarly journal, such as the *Journal of Applied Psychology*, or a magazine aimed at the general public, such as *Good Housekeeping*. A serial can also be a nonbook item. As we mentioned in Chapter 4, the home video release of the original *Dark Shadows* is a serial.

For an item to be a serial, it must first of all be intended to continue indefinitely, so that you may include in its description neither a closing date nor a definite number of physical units — unless you are describing a serial which ceased publication before you cataloged it. We shall discuss description of serials in more detail further on.

Secondly, for an item to be a serial means that its various issues are not bibliographically independent. A given issue may be devoted to a single topic, and will contain complete units — articles, short stories, etc. — but is still part of a whole. Three examples of the interdependence among issues are:

1. Letters from readers which comment on material in a previous issue.

2. A regular column in which the author refers to something he or she has written in a previous issue, or will cover in a subsequent issue.

3. Details of an episode of a television serial — including the entire episode — which you are unable to understand unless you have seen the entire serial from the beginning.

As we said in Chapter 4, you must keep in mind the distinction between a serial and a *series*. The various members of a series are bibliographically independent, and are usually cataloged separately, each with a series statement. Also, keep in mind also the distinction between a serial and a *set* or *multipart item*, such as a multivolume encyclopedia, which has a finite number of physical units and a definite completion date.

As we pointed out in Chapter 4, the distinction between the series, the serial, and the set is not always easy to make. A case in point is the television serial drama. *Dark Shadows* is clearly a serial; while you may buy or rent each videocassette of the home video edition separately, the material on each is clearly part of a larger whole. In contrast, *Star Trek* and the *National Geographic Society* documentaries are definitely series. Not only may you buy or rent videocassettes of each episode separately, you can understand each episode without ever having seen any of the others.

Consider, however, a group of nine videocassettes, each containing an episode of a nine-part "miniseries" or *Masterpiece Theater* presentation. Furthermore, assume that whichever television network presented the drama informed viewers how many episodes it was to contain. On the one hand, each videocassette is dependent on the others, since it contains only a portion of the drama. On the other hand, the nine tapes together constitute a complete unit. For more discussion of this matter, see Chapter 4.

Special problems with serials

You will encounter many of the same problems in attempting to determine the proper form of a serial's title then you will when trying to establish a corporate body's name. In fact, serials whose titles begin "Transactions of . . .," "Annual Report . . .," "Proceedings of . . .," and the like are usually products of the corporate body whose voice they express. Like a corporate body, a serial may change its name, change its purpose, or merge with another serial during the course of its existence.

The main challenge you will face in attempting to catalog a serial is that key pieces of bibliographic data, such as title, publisher and size, will often change from issue to issue. Furthermore, some serials will change their scope, making it more difficult for you to assign subject headings.

Access points for serials

The fact that a serial's title can change is particularly problematic because of the limitations AACR2R88 places on corporate entry. Under these limitations, many serials formerly entered under corporate body now *must* be entered under title. The AACR2R88 gives no clear direction for the choice of access points to serials except by default, or, in some cases, by implication. For example, AACR2R88 Rule 21.1B2d allows entry under corporate body "for those works that report the collective activity of a conference (e.g. proceedings, collected papers) or an expedition (e.g. results of exploration, investigation) or of an event (e.g. an exhibition, fair, festival) falling within the definition of a corporate body (see 21.1B1) provided that the conference, expedition, or event is prominently named (see 0.8) in the item being cataloged."

(Again, remember that the item must emanate from the corporate body. In trying to determine if this is true for a given set of conference proceedings, you might ask whether the agency responsible for the conference held it wholly or partly *for the purpose of producing the document you are cataloging.*)

To have a corporate body main entry, therefore, a work must not merely be sponsored by that body but must be a product of the collective activity of the body as a whole. Few serials can meet these criteria.

Maxwell (1989) recognizes AACR2R88's lack of direction to catalogers regarding what they are to use as access points in the absence of allowable corporate entries. Both the 1949 and 1967 codes had permitted corporate entry headings for serials if the title included the name of the corporate body or consisted solely of a generic, nondefinitive term. Pages 219–228 of Maxwell's *Handbook* describe the evolution of rules for serial cataloging that resulted in the 1978 restrictions. If you consider the term "restrictions" too judgmental, consider the following problems which result from title main entry.

- The title may be generic or nondescriptive.
- The title may be initials or an acronym for a corporate body.
- The title may change.
- Since titles cannot be copyrighted, more than one serial can, and does, have the same title.
- Titles may remain constant but represent an entirely new entity. One such example is *Life*, a title purchased by one magazine from another magazine of a totally different type.

Description of serials

In deciding what title to use for the serial you are cataloging, remember that the cardinal principle of the AACR code is to describe the *work in hand*. This means that, if the title of a serial changes, you must make a separate main entry under the new title. Rule 21.2C1 of AACR2R88 instructs: "If the title proper of a serial changes, make a separate main entry for each title." You will need to make notes and references showing the relationship between the old and the new title.

The directive to describe what you have in hand obtains throughout all of the elements of a serial's bibliographic description. The chief source of information is the title page of the *first* issue of the serial. This is often the last page of the first completed volume of the serial, which may not be available to you. You may have to use the cover or masthead of the first issue, or consult reference works dealing with serials.

A serial's description may include a statement of responsibility, but often does not. Remember that you may only take a statement of responsibility from those parts of an item covered by AACR2R88's definition of "prominently." Usually, all persons or corporate bodies named in those areas are editors, and Rule 12.1F3 explicitly instructs you *not* to list these in the statement of responsibility. The only other candidate for inclusion in this area is the publisher, which you are ordinarily not to consider an author.

In deciding whether to include the next area, the edition statement, remember that any information appearing here must apply to the serial *as a whole*. A statement such as "Southeastern Pennsylvania ed.," or "English language ed.," would belong in this area. See Section 12.2B for a more complete listing of what you must place in a note.

Serials also use the "Material (or type of publication) specific details area," which we have already discussed with respect to nonbook materials. The version of this area used for serials is termed the "Numeric and/or alphabetic, chronological, or other designation area." This contains the number, date, and other significant details of the serial's first issue. An example is *Rodale's Food and Nutrition Letter*, for which this area would read:

Vol. 1, no. 2 (October 1990) —

For more detailed information, see Section 12.3.

Record the place of publication and publisher's name as you would for a monograph. For the date of the publication, use the date of first issue, followed by a hyphen and four spaces. If you are describing a serial that has definitely and permanently ceased publication, record the dates of the first and last issues, with a hyphen between them.

Since a serial may take the form of any of the print or nonprint media, AACR2R88 instructs you to handle most aspects of the physical description according the rules for the medium of the serial you are cataloging. This includes such details as the names and dimensions of the physical units which comprise the serial, and the nature of any illustrations the serial may contain. If you are cataloging a serial whose issues differ in size, indicate this according to the rules, from the various other chapters of AACR2R88, which cover size differences in multipart items in whichever medium the serial is issued.

The most distinctive feature of a serial's physical description is that the number of physical units is left unspecified. Record the extent of the item as "v.," "microfilm reels," etc., preceded by three spaces. If, however, you are describing a serial that has definitely and permanently ceased publication, include the total number of physical units.

If a printed serial contains illustrations, note them as you would for a printed monograph. If you are cataloging a serial issued in a nonbook medium, record whatever additional physical details are provided for in the AACR2R88 chapter covering that medium. See Rule 12.5C1 for more details.

Observe that the open date and unspecified number of physical units together indicate that the item has no known ending point. Any catalog record which uses these two devices in this manner is termed an *open entry*. Not every open entry, however, is a serial record; an open entry may also designate an incomplete set.

Notes are an important part of a serial's bibliographic description. The first is always the frequency with which the serial is published. This note should be as succinct as possible. Use a single word, such as "Quarterly," if this will suffice. You may use "Irregular," or "Frequency varies," if either of these is true of the serial you are cataloging.

The AACR2R88 lists 23 possible notes for a serial's description. Include any you may need to give your potential user information not apparent from the body of the description, such as:

- Language of the serial, if not obvious
- Variations in title

• Statements of responsibility, including an editor whose name may be better known than the title of the serial
• Relationships with other serials—e.g., translations, continuations, mergers, absorptions, supplements, etc.
• Complex or irregular numbering
• Accompanying material
• Indexes
• Contents
• Library holdings—e.g., "Library has: 1976–1983," "Not currently received."

From the above list, you can infer that serials cataloging requires a great deal of sheer housekeeping. For example, "Library holdings," may change, as may any attribute of an ongoing serial.

When a serial ceases publication, "close" its bibliographic description. That is, note its closing date and the final number of volumes, or other physical units. (This is the purpose of the leading and trailing spaces you are to include in an open entry.) If the serial will reappear under another title, add a note reading:

Continued by: [New title].

Concluding remarks on serials

There are many small publications, geared to a very specific audience, many of which are "desktop" publications. That is, they are produced by one person, or a small group of people, working with a personal computer, printer, and the appropriate desktop publishing software. Some examples are:

• Religious publications, such as *Guideposts*
• College and university-based literary magazines, such as *Appalachian Heritage*, and *The Antigonish Review*
• Small press magazines specializing in science-fiction, fantasy, and horror, such as *After Hours, 2AM*, or the now-defunct *Horror Show*

These serials may not make it to your library, being listed only in one of the *Writer's Market*s or a similar type of annual. Since these publications have a unique and valuable purpose, you may wish to try and provide clues to your library's patrons that these materials exist.

As we noted earlier, with respect to corporate bodies, this chapter's bibliography and Appendix II list reference sources which you may consult for further information on all of the points we have raised.

Uniform titles

Definition of and need for uniform titles

In Chapter 3, we introduced the concept of authority control as it related to personal names. In Chapter 5, we explained that you must also apply authority control to subject headings. Earlier in this chapter, we briefly discussed authority control for corporate bodies. In certain cases, it is desirable, or even necessary, to apply authority control to titles as well. These are cases in which the title proper of an item — the title which appears in the chief source of information, and which, therefore, you must place in the title area — fails to identify that item or distinguish it from others with which it might be confused. In general, such cases are of three types:

(1) A work is known by several titles, none of which is clearly identifiable as the "preferred" title:

> Beethoven's third symphony
> Beethoven's symphony no. 3
> Third symphony / Ludwig van Beethoven
> Symphony no. 3 / Ludwig van Beethoven
> Eroica

(2) There exist numerous portions, versions or manifestations of a work, each published separately under its own title. Each such title may identify the individual item but does not identify it *as a manifestation/portion of the work in question*:

> Bible   Acts
> Living Bible   Book of Acts
> Holy Bible   Acts of the Apostles
>
> Old Testament   Arabian nights
> New Testament   Ali Baba
> Good News for Modern Man   Sinbad the sailor
>
> Messiah
> He shall feed His flock

(3) The work has a title which is also the title of another work:

Life
> See the discussion under *Serials.*

Lecture notes in mathematics
> Two different publishers have a series by this name.

Ninth symphony
Symphony no. 9
> Both of these could refer to the work of Beethoven, Mahler, or any composer who wrote nine or more symphonies.

Batman
> This is the title of two significantly different movies. The first (1966) is essentially a feature-length episode of the humorous television series of the time. It presents Batman as a good-natured buffoon, and, although not originally intended as such, is often regarded as a children's movie. The second (1989), although it contains an element of dark humor, is intended as a serious treatment of the subject matter. It presents Batman as a frightening and not entirely benevolent character. Many reviewers have pointedly stated that it is *not* suitable for children.

The fly
> Both the 1958 and 1986 movies with this title chronicle the disastrous results of an experiment in teleportation gone awry. However, the nature of those results is quite different in the two movies.

From the examples above, you may note that the three categories are not mutually exclusive and the need for title authority control is not limited to esoteric or scholarly works.

In situations such as those described above, you will need to add to the work's description an authoritative form of that work's title, analogous to the authoritative form of an author's name used as a heading. This special form of a given work's title is termed a *uniform title.*

Rule 25.2A of AACR2R88 provides a list of situations in which you should use uniform titles—a list on which we have loosely based the three categories presented above. However, AACR2R88 does not actually require you to use a uniform title in any given situation. Instead, it provides a list of guidelines, instructing you to use these and your library's policy to make a decision. In most libraries or other cataloging agencies, it is standard procedure to include uniform titles in descriptions of musical works and manifestations of the Bible or any portion thereof.

The uniform title's location in a bibliographic description

One way to approach uniform titles is to divide them into two categories — those attached to works for which the author is known and those attached to works of unknown authorship.

When including a uniform title in the description of a work with a known author, construct the description as you otherwise would, but place the uniform title, in brackets, on its own line between the author main entry and the title, thus:

> Dickens, Charles, 1812–1870.
> [David Copperfield]
> The history of David Copperfield / by Charles Dickens.

In a MARC record, place such a uniform title in field 240. Omit the brackets, because most online systems will supply them on catalog cards and in online public catalog displays.

When adding a uniform title to the description of a work without an author, place the uniform title in the position that the author main entry would have occupied, thus:

> Arabian nights.
> The thousand and one nights : the tales told by Scheherazade.

In this case, you have the option of recording the title without brackets. In a MARC record, place a uniform title appearing as a main entry in field 130.

There are also cases in which you will need to make a uniform title added entry. When cataloging a separately titled part of a work, you are to use the title of the part as the uniform title and make an added entry for the title of the whole work with the part as a subdivision:

> Main entry: Sinbad the sailor.
> Added entry: Arabian nights. Sinbad the sailor

The MARC field for a uniform title added entry is 730.

For more information on the above procedure, see Rules 25.6A1 and 26.4B2.

Note that you must *not* use this procedure for either sacred scriptures or musical works, both of which we shall discuss further on.

Choice and form of a uniform title

Whether or not you use a uniform title as a main entry, you must construct, or locate, in whatever authority file you are using, an authority record to justify your choice. This will be a list of the various titles which have been used for the work, establishing that the one chosen appears most frequently in reference sources:

>Swift, Jonathan, 1667–1745.
> [Gulliver's travels]
> Travels into several remote nations of the world / by Lemuel Gulliver.

Works created before 1501 are often anonymous classics. Use the title, or form of title, in the original language, by which such works are identified in modern sources. Examples are:

>Beowulf
>Chanson de Roland
>Nibelungenlied
>Arabian nights

When you are cataloging a collection of the complete works of an author, use *Works* as the uniform title:

>Wodehouse, P.G. (Pelham Grenville), 1880–1975.
> [Works]
> The autograph edition of the complete works of P.G. Wodehouse.

For a selection of three or more works, use *Selections*.

>Wodehouse, P.G. (Pelham Grenville), 1880–1975.
> [Selections]
> The most of P.G. Wodehouse.

For further discussion, see AACR2R88 Rules 25.8A and 25.9A.

Certain types of work fall under special rules. For Incunabula, Rule 25.14 states: "Use as the uniform title for an incunabulum the title found in standard reference sources for incunabula." (This is a case in which you will need very specialized reference sources.) In the case of laws and treaties, the uniform title will be either the phrase *Laws, etc.*, or the phrase, *Treaties, etc.* For further information, see Rules 25.15 and 25.16.

The uniform titles for both sacred scriptures and musical works are of a more formal nature, consisting of a list of elements set down in prescribed order. We shall now discuss each in turn.

Uniform titles for sacred scriptures

The Bible, and other sacred scriptures, require formally constructed uniform titles. These begin with the name of the scripture in question — *Bible, Talmud, Vedas,* and numerous others. Following is a labeled display of a uniform title for a portion of a sacred scripture — the Bible, in this case:

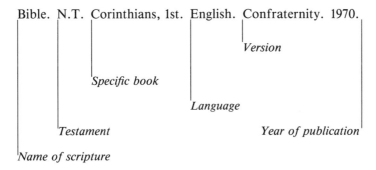

Bible. N.T. Corinthians, 1st. English. Confraternity. 1970.

Version

Specific book

Language

Testament   *Year of publication*

Name of scripture

The uniform titles for other sacred scriptures follow a similar plan of listing successively narrower subdivisions of the work.

You must make an added entry for, and a reference from, the individual portions of the scripture named at each point in the uniform title. This is because library patrons may have problems understanding the arrangement which these uniform titles produce. For example, the patron, looking for *Psalms* may not understand the necessity to read through entries for Bible as a whole, the Old testament as a whole, then the books of the Old Testament with titles preceding *Psalms* in the alphabet. Note that this contrasts with the general rule of using the title of a separately cataloged part as the uniform title for that part's description.

Uniform titles for music

You should have a reasonably good working knowledge of music theory, music history, and music bibliography if you plan to construct uniform titles for music. In fact, most cataloging agencies will hire someone only with such knowledge for a position which involves a significant amount of music cataloging. The following discussion will give you a sense of the level of musical knowledge you should have before attempting to catalog music.

There are a number of situations you will encounter as you attempt to construct uniform titles for various musical works. Below are several labeled displays which will illustrate the more important of these. Following the displays, we shall list a few general rules applying to all or most uniform titles for music.

Berg, Alban, 1885–1935.
  [Lulu]

Initial title element. Since this is a work with a true title, you should add nothing to the initial title element if you are cataloging a score of sound recording of the opera in its original form.

Beethoven, Ludwig van, 1770–1827
  [Sonatas, piano, no. 21, op. 53, C major]

Key. Give this for all works written before 1900.

Opus number

Serial number

Medium of performance. In most cases, this simply means the instruments for which the work is written.

Initial title element. Here, the title is merely the name of a type of musical composition. It is because of this that you must add all of the following information. Note that the initial title element is plural. You should make it so whenever the composer has written more than one work of the type in question.

Mozart, Wolfgang Amadeus, 1756–1791.
  [Concertos, violin, orchestra, K. 218, D major]

Key

Thematic index number. Use this if no serial or opus numbers are available. Use it in addition to or instead of serial and opus numbers if it better serves to identify the work.

Medium of performance. "Orchestra" is one of a set of terms you may use to designate a specific group of instruments.

Initial title element.

Beethoven, Ludwig van, 1770–1827.
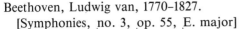
[Symphonies, no. 3, op. 55, E. major]

Key

Opus number

Serial number

Initial title element. Since the type of composition named here implies the medium of this work's performance, the orchestra, you are to omit the medium of performance.

Bartók, Béla, 1881–1945.
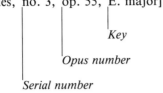
[Quartets, strings, no. 1, op. 7]*

Opus no.

Serial no.

Medium of performance. Each instrument is not listed individually because the initial title element implies a specific set of stringed instruments — two violins, one viola, and one cello.

Initial title element.

*Note that this does not include a key. Since many works composed during the 20th century are not in any key, you are to omit the key designation from the uniform titles for such works unless it "is stated prominently in the item being cataloged."

Schubert, Franz, 1797–1828.
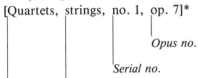
[Octet, woodwinds, horn, strings, D. 803, F major]

Key

Thematic index no.

Medium of performance. Here, the category names "woodwinds" and "strings" take the place of a list of all individual instruments for a different reason than in the preceding example; the term "Octet" does not imply any specific set of instruments. Rather, you must use category names here because the medium of performance must not include more than three elements. There is one exception to this, shown in next example.

Initial title element. You must use the singular form in this case because Schubert wrote only one octet.

Schubert, Franz, 1797–1828.
[Quintets, piano, violin, viola, violoncello, double bass, D. 667, A major]

> *Medium of performance. As stated in the previous example, there is one case in which you are permitted, in fact required, to include more than three elements here if it should prove necessary. This is when a work is written for a group of instruments other than that which would be implied if you were to name only a category of instruments in conjunction with the initial title element. In this uniform title, "Quintets, piano, strings," would have implied that Schubert wrote the piece for piano, two violins, viola, and cello.*

Whenever the medium of performance includes a list of instruments, list them in the following order:

1. Voices
2. Keyboard instruments if there is more than one *non*-keyboard instrument.
3. All other instruments in score order.
4. Continuo

If the piece is written for two or more of any instrument, place the appropriate number in parentheses after that instrument's name:

flutes (2), violins (2), . . .

You must use prescribed names for all instruments. You may use either *cello* or *violoncello*, but you must use *double bass*, rather than *contrabass*, and *horn*, rather than *French horn*.

Another important restriction on names concerns families of instruments, each member of which has the same name with a modifier added to designate its range or key. Examples are the soprano, alto, tenor, baritone, and bass saxophones, and the B-flat, A, C, E-flat, and bass clarinets. When listing these instruments, you are to omit the modifiers. (You should, however, provide the information in a note.)

There are other provisions for designating arrangements, particular types of scores, and other important pieces of information. Also, the general rules for the use of *Selections* apply in certain instances. Sections 25 through 35 of AACR2R88 cover uniform titles for music. For further discussion of this topic, see Smiraglia (1987) or Spalding (1979).

Although the reference tools listed in this chapter's bibliography and in Appendix II will help you, many of the advanced problems set out above require you to use your own judgment to a much greater extent than in any other area of cataloging.

Review questions for Chapter 14

1. Compare and contrast the criteria for main entry under personal author with those for main entry under corporate body.

2. Why must you enter certain works under title even though they fall into one of the five categories listed in Rule 21.1B2, a–e?

3. Springer-Verlag has published many conference proceedings as volumes of its *Lecture Notes in Mathematics* series. From examining several of these volumes, we have conjectured that Springer-Verlag solicited the proceedings in each case. Assuming you also believed this to be the case, would you enter one of these works under the conference heading or under title? How would you enter the work if you believed that those in charge of the conference had requested that Springer-Verlag publish the proceedings?

4. Contrast a serial with a monograph.

5. Contrast a serial with both a series and a set. Be sure to distinguish between serial/*series* differences and serial/*set* differences. As an aid to doing this, you might want to also consider the *similarities* between the serial and the other two types of publications.

6. Why will a serial's description rarely contain a statement of responsibility?

7. Where do you obtain instructions for giving the dimensions of a serial whose issues vary in size?

8. In what situations do you need uniform titles?

9. Using the appropriate examples under Rule 25.5B1 as a model, and taking Rule 25.2C1 into account, construct uniform titles for the two movies entitled *The Fly*.

10. Construct a uniform title for a 1970 edition of *The Living Bible*.

11. How do you decide whether to include a key designation in the uniform title for a piece of 20th century music?

12. Why do you omit the medium of performance in the uniform title for a Beethoven symphony?

13. When may you — must you, in fact — list more than three elements in the medium of performance?

14. You are cataloging a musical work written for the following

ensemble: Flute, Alto flute, B-flat clarinet, E-flat clarinet, Alto saxophone, Tenor saxophone. What is the correct form for the medium of performance?

Sources cited and suggestions for further reading or study

American Library Association. *Cataloging Rules for Author and Title Entries*. Chicago: American Library Association, 1949.

Anglo-American Cataloging Rules: North American Text. Chicago: American Library Association, 1967.

Anglo-American Cataloguing Rules, 2nd ed., edited by Michael Gorman and Paul W. Winkler. Chicago: American Library Association; Ottawa: Canadian Library Association, 1978.

Anglo-American Cataloguing Rules, 2nd ed., 1988 revision, edited by Michael Gorman and Paul W. Winkler. Ottawa: Canadian Library Association; Chicago: American Library Association, 1988.

Cook, C. Donald. "Headings for Corporate Names: International Standardization under AACR2." *Library Resources and Technical Services* 28 (July/September 1984): 239–252.

Clack, Doris Hargrett. *Authority Control: Principles, Applications, and Instructions*. Chicago: American Library Association, 1990.

Crawford, Walt. *MARC for Library Use: Understanding Integrated USMARC*, 2nd ed. Boston: G.K. Hall, 1989.

Cutter, Charles Ammi. *Rules for a Dictionary Catalog*, 4th ed., rewritten. Washington, D.C.: U.S. Gov. Printing Office, 1904.

Directory of European Associations. Pt. 1 (1971-). Detroit: Gale Research, 1971-.

Downing, Mildred Harlow. *The World of Daytime Television Serial Drama*. Philadelphia: Dissertation, Ph. D. University of Pennsylvania, 1974.

Encyclopedia of Associations. Detroit: Gale Research, 1956– Biennial.

International Federation of Library Associations. *Liste Internationale de Vedettes Uniformes pour les Classiques* = International List of Uniform Headings for Anonymous Classics, edited by Roger Pierrot. Paris: IFLA, 1964.

International Federation of Library Associations. *Statement of Principles Adopted at the International Congress on Cataloguing Principles, Paris, October 1961*, annotated ed. with commentary and examples by Eva Verona, assisted by Franz Georg Kaltwasser, P.R. Lewis, Roger Pierrot. London: IFLA Committee on Cataloguing, 1971; pp. 6–7.

Leong, Carol L.H. *Serials Cataloging Handbook: An Illustrative Guide to the Use of AACR2 and LC Rule Interpretations*. Chicago: American Library Association, 1989.

Library of Congress. *Cataloging Service Bulletin*, Robert M. Hiatt, ed. 18 (fall 1982). pp. 31–32.

Library of Congress Rule Interpretations for AACR2: A Cumulation from Cataloging Service Bulletin Numbers 11-, compiled by Lois Lindberg, Alan Boyd, and Elaine Druesedow. Oberlin, Ohio: Oberlin College Library, 1982-.

Maxwell, Margaret F. *Handbook for AACR2: Explaining and Illustrating the Anglo-American Cataloguing Rules*, 1988 revision. Chicago: American Library Association, 1989.

Smiragli, Richard. *Cataloging Music*, 2nd ed. Lake Crystal, Minn.: Soldier Creek Press, 1987.

Spalding, C. Summer. "Music Authority Files at the Library of Congress." *Music Cataloging Bulletin* 10 (October 1979): 4–6.

Ulrich's International Periodicals Directory: A Classified Guide to Current Periodicals, Foreign and Domestic. New York: Bowker, 1931– Biennial.

United States Government Organizational Manual. Washington, D.C., 1935– Annual.

World of Learning. London: Europa Publications, 1947– Annual.

Appendix I

Sample Catalog Records

*Bibliographic Description in Accordance with AACR2R (1988)
and MARC Field Codes*

```
x
x
12345678Lastname, Firstname Middlename, date-date.
123456789012Title proper [general material designation]
12345678= parallel title : other title information /
12345678first statement of responsibility ; each
12345678subsequent statement of responsibility. --
12345678Edition statement / first statement of
12345678responsibility relating to the edition. --
12345678First place of publication, etc. :
12345678first publisher, etc., date of publication,
12345678etc. --
12345678    132 p. : ill. ; 45 cm. --

                              (continued on next card)
```

1. *Paradigm of basic catalog card-type display*

```
x
x
12345678Lastname, Firstname Middlename, date-date.
123456789012Title proper...date of publication
12345678(Card 2)

                                        (Title
      proper of series / statement of respons-
      ibility relating to series, ISSN of series ;
      numbering within the series. Title of
      subseries, ISSN of subseries ; numbering
      within subseries)


                        (continued on next card)
```

2. *Continuation of paradigm display*

```
x
x
12345678Lastname, Firstname Middlename, date-date.
123456789012Title proper...date of publication
12345678(Card 3)

123456789012Note(s).

        ISBN 0-0000-0000-0

123456789012First tracing (1. Subject).
12345678Further added entries.
12345678901234Third indention
```

3. *Continuation of paradigm display*

USMARC Field	Indicator	Data with Delimiters and Subfield Codes
020		‡a 0-0000-0000-0 (ISBN number)
100	10	‡a Last name of author, First name, Middle name, ‡d date
245	10	‡a Title proper ‡h general material designation = ‡b parallel title : other title information / ‡c first statement of responsibility; each subsequent statement of responsibility
250		‡a Edition statement / ‡b first statement of responsibility relating to the edition
260	0	‡a First place of publication : ‡b First publisher, ‡c date of publication
300		‡a Extent : ‡b ill., ‡c date of publication
440	0	‡a Title proper of series
500		‡a Note
650	0	‡a Subject (topical) added entry
700	10	‡a Added entry, personal name

For definitions of fields see next page.

4. *Elements of paradigm catalog display shown listed according to USMARC fields*

---

x
x

     Carlyle, Thomas, 1795-1881.
       Sartor resartus = the tailor restored :
    the life and opinions of Herr Teufelsdrockh /
    by Thomas Carlyle ; with biographical
    introduction by J. Holloway. -- Large
    print ed. -- Boston : Classics Press, 1975.
     xxv, 379 p. : ill. ; 45 cm.

     ISBN 0-7131-1646-3

     I. Title. II. Title : The tailor restored.
   III. Title: The   life and opinions of
   Herr Teufels-   drockh.

---

5. *Author main entry card-type display*

020		‡a 0-7131-1646-3
100	10	‡a Carlyle, Thomas ‡d 1795–1881
245	10	‡a Sartor resartus = ‡b the tailor restored : the life and opinions of Herr Teufelsdrockh / ‡c by Thomas Carlyle ; with biographical introduction by J. Holloway
250		‡a Large print ed.
260	0	‡a Boston ; ‡b Classics Press, ‡c 1975
300		‡a xxv, 379 p. : ‡b ill.; ‡c 45 cm.

6. *USMARC coding for above exhibit*

Definitions:

USMARC Field – Three-digit code for elements of catalog record developed by Library of Congress; "tag"
Indicator – Numerals which further describe the field
Subfield – Smaller logical unit of field
Delimiter – Double dagger (‡) preceding a lower case letter (a,b,c, etc.) which is the subfield code

12345678Dethier, Vincent Gaston, 1915--
     Animal behavior : its evolutionary and
neurological basis / by V. G. Dethier and
Eliot Stellar. -- Englewood Cliffs, N. J. :
Prentice-Hall, 1961.
     118 p. : ill. ; 23 cm. --- (Prentice-Hall
foundations of modern biology series)

     Bibliography: p. 116-118.
     ISBN 0-8389-3156-1

     1. Animals -- Habits and behavior.
I. Stellar, Eliot,   1919-   joint author.
II. Title.   III. Series.

7. Card-display format for two authors and series note

     Stellar, Eliot, 1919-   joint author.
Dethier, Vincent Gaston, 1915-
     Animal behavior : its evolutionary and
neurological basis / by V. G. Dethier and
Eliot Stellar. -- Englewood Cliffs, N. J. :
Prentice-Hall, 1961.
     118 p. : ill. ; 23 cm. -- (Prentice-Hall
foundations of modern biology series)

     Bibliography: p. 116-118.
     ISBN 0-8389-3156-1

     1. Animals -- Habits and behavior.
I. Stellar, Eliot,   1919-   joint author.
II. Title.   III. Series.

8. Added entry card for second author

020		‡a 0-8389-3156-1
100	10	‡a Dethier, Vincent Gaston, ‡d 1915–
245	10	‡a Animal behavior : ‡b its evolutionary and neurological bases / ‡c by V.G. Dethier and Eliot Stellar
260	0	‡a Englewood Cliffs, N.J. : ‡b Prentice-Hall, ‡c 1961
300		‡a 118 p. : ‡b ill. ; ‡c 23 cm.
440	0	‡a Prentice-Hall foundations of modern biology
504		‡a Bibliography: p. 116–118
650	0	‡a Animals ‡x Habits and behavior
700	10	‡a Stellar, Eliot, ‡d 1919–

9. *USMARC-tagged display for two authors, series note, and series tracing*

Cheney, Sheldon, 1886–
    A new world history of art / by Sheldon
Cheney. -- Completely revised edition with
additional text / by J. Hubert Marlow. --
New York : Viking Press, 1956.
    xxvi, 676 p. : ill. (some col.), 9 maps
(on lining paper) ; 26 cm.

    "First published in 1937 under title: A
world history of art."
                    (continued on next card)

10. *Edition statement and statement of responsibility, with "continued on next card" at bottom.*

```
Cheney, Sheldon, 1886-
    A new world history of art...1956
  (Card 2)

    Bibliography: p. 660-664.

    1.  Art -- History.   I. Marlow, J. Hubert, ed.
II. Title.
```

11. *Edition statement and statement of responsibility with tracing for editor on continuation card*

100	10	‡a Cheney, Sheldon, ‡d 1886–
245	12	‡A new world history of art / ‡c by Sheldon Cheney
250		‡a Completely revised edition, with additional text / ‡c by J. Hubert Marlow
260	0	‡a New York : ‡b Viking Press, ‡c 1956
300		‡a xvii, 676 p. : ‡b ill. (some col.), maps; ‡c 26 cm.
500		‡a Nine maps on lining papers
504		‡a Bibliography: p. 660–664
650		‡a Art ‡x History
700	10	‡a Marlow, J. Hubert, ‡e ed.

12. *USMARC coding for bibliographic elements displayed in previous card-type catalog display*

```
Whitwell, W. L.  (William Langley)
    Readings for introduction to art / by
W. L. Whitwell. -- Berkeley, Calif. : McCutchan,
1968.
    v, 107 p. ; 28 cm.


ISBN 0-340-16427-1

1. Art -- Study and teaching.  I. Title.
```

13. *Heading using initials with full name in parentheses*

020		‡a 0-340-16427-1
100	10	‡a Whitwell, W.L. ‡q (William Langley)
245	10	‡a Readings for introduction to art / ‡c by W.L. Whitwell
260	0	‡a Berkeley, Calif. : ‡b McCutchan, ‡c 1968
300		‡a v, 107 p. ; ‡c 28 cm.
650	0	‡a Art ‡x Study and teaching

14. *USMARC coding for bibliographic elements of above display*

Cranston. Henry Bellamy, 1901–1976.
Flower gardens of the last century /
by Henry B. Cranston. -- 2nd ed. -- London :
Macmillan ; New York : McGraw-Hill, 1978.
x, 374 p. : col. ill. ; 28 cm.

1. Gardens. I. Title.

15. *Two publishers with the foreign publisher first or prominently displayed*

100	10	‡a Cranston, Henry Bellamy, ‡d 1901–1976
245	10	‡a Flower gardens of the last century / ‡c by Henry B. Cranston
250		‡a 2nd ed.
260	0	‡a London : ‡b MacMillan; ‡a New York : ‡b McGraw-Hill, ‡c 1978
300		‡a x, 374 p. : ‡b col. ill. ; ‡c 28 cm.
650	0	‡a Gardens

16. *USMARC coding for bibliographic elements of above display*

William Hayes Ackland Memorial Art Center.
  A guide through the collections / The William
Hayes Ackland Memorial Art Center. -- Chapel
Hill, N. C. : Old South Press, 1972.
      27 p. : ill. (some col.) ; 26 cm.

   1. North Carolina -- Galleries and museums.
I. Ackland Art Museum.   II. Title.

17. *AACR2 corporate entry*

110	20	‡a William Hayes Ackland Memorial Art Center
245	12	‡a A guide through the collections / ‡c The William Hayes Ackland Memorial Art Center
260	0	‡a Chapel Hill, N.C. : ‡b Old South Press, ‡c 1990
300		‡a 27 p. : ‡b ill. (some col.) ; ‡c 26 cm.
651	0	‡a North Carolina ‡x Galleries and museums
710	20	‡a Ackland Art Museum

18. *USMARC coding for corporate entry display shown above*

```
Hessel, Hanlon Cornwell, 1870-1936.
   Canoe travel in little-known rivers /
by H. C. Hessel. -- [S.l. : s.n.], 1911.
   x, 125 p. : ill. ; 27 cm.


   Privately printed.


   1. Boats and boating.  I. Title.
```

19. *Place of publication and name of publisher unknown*

100	10	‡a Hessel, Hanlon Cornwell, ‡d 1870–1936
245	10	‡a Canoe travel in little-known rivers / ‡c by H.C. Hessel
260	1	‡a [S.l. : ‡b s.n.] , ‡c 1911
300		‡a x, 125 p. : ‡b ill. ; ‡c 27 cm.
500		‡a Privately printed
650	0	‡a Boats and boating

20. *USMARC coding for unknown publisher and place of publication*

Saurois, Pierre Gaston, 1901-1973.
  The court of Marie Antoinette / by
Pierre Gaston ; translated by Constance
Downs. -- Spartanburg, S. C. : Advance Press,
1962.
    375 p. : col. ill. ; 51 cm. -- (Courts
of Europe series)

    Translation of: Sous le règne de Louis
XVI.

    1. Marie Antoinette, Queen of France,
1755-1793.   I. Downs, Constance,
1920-   tr.   II. Title. III. Series.

21. *Tracing for translator*

100	10	‡a Saurois, Pierre Gaston, ‡d 1901-1973
245	14	‡a The court of Marie Antoinette / ‡c by Pierre Gaston ; translated by Constance Downs
260	0	‡a Spartanburg, S.C. : ‡b Advance Press, / ‡c 1962
300		‡a 375 p. : ‡b col. ill. ; ‡c 51 cm.
440	0	‡a Courts of Europe series
500		‡a Translation of: Sous le règne de Louis XVI
600	00	‡a Marie Antoinette, ‡c Queen of France, ‡d 1775-1793
700	10	‡a Downs, Constance, ‡d 1920-

22. *USMARC coding for bibliographic elements displayed above*

Willingham, Howard Justin, 1929–
   King Philip's War, 1675–1676 / by
H. Justin Willingham. -- New York :
Archival Press, 1963.
   234 p. ; 23 cm.

   1. King Philip's War, 1675–1676.

23. *Tracing for subject entry; title same as subject; subject entry supersedes*

100	10	‡a Willingham, Howard Justin, ‡d 1929–
245	10	‡a King Philip's War, 1675–1676 / ‡c by H. Justin Willingham
260	0	‡a New York : ‡b Archival Press, ‡c 1963
300		‡a 234 p. ; ‡c 23 cm.
650	0	‡a King Philip's War, 1675–1676

24. *USMARC coding for bibliographic elements displayed above*

Perrault, Charles, 1628-1703.
    Tales of long ago / Charles Perrault ;
pictures by Maraja. -- New York : Maxton
House, 1939.
    32 p. : ill. ; 20 x 26 cm. -- (A Maxton
picture book ; 25)

    I. Kolesnik, Maraja, 1912-   ill.
II. Title.

25. *Publisher's series, no tracing; Two dimensions included (book wider than high)*

100	10	‡a Perrault, Charles, ‡d 1628–1703
245	10	‡a Tales of long ago / ‡c Charles Perrault; pictures by Maraja
300		‡a 32 p. : ‡b ill. ; ‡c 20 × 26 cm.
260	0	‡a New York : ‡b Maxton House, ‡c 1939
490	0	‡a A Maxton picture book; ‡v 25
700	10	‡a Kolesnik, Maraja, ‡d 1912– ‡e ill.

26. *USMARC coding for bibliographic elements displayed above*

Murray, John Thomas, 1915-1970.
Short stories of the nineteenth century /
by John T. Murray. -- Philadelphia :
Lippincott, 1953.
2 v. ; 22 cm.

Contents: v. 1. Rip Van Winkle / Washington
Irving -- Wandering Willie's tale / Sir
Walter Scott -- Young Goodman Brown / N.
Hawthorne -- v. 2. Dr. Heidigger's experiment /
N. Hawthorne -- William Wilson / E. A. Poe --
The celestial railroad / N. Hawthorne.

I. Title.

27. *Contents note*

100	10	‡a Murray, John Thomas, ‡d 1915–1970
245	10	‡a Short stories of the nineteenth century / ‡c by John T. Murray
260	0	‡a Philadelphia : ‡b Lippincott, ‡c 1953
300		‡a 2 v.; ‡c 22 cm.
505	0	‡a V. 1 Rip Van Winkle / Washington Irving -- Goodman Brown / N. Hawthorne -- V. 2 Dr. Heidigger's experiment / N. Hawthorne -- William Wilson / E.A. Poe -- The celestial railroad / N.Hawthorne

28. *Contents note displayed according to USMARC*

Aspenwell, Jeffrey, 1895-1960.
    The city of Paris / by J. Aspenwell. --
New York : Archival Press, 1950.
    xx, 202 p. : ill. ; 24 cm.

    With: A cultural excursion through Paris /
Frances Aspenwell. New York, 1950.

    1. Paris -- Description. I. Title.

29. *"With" note*

100	10	‡a Aspenwell, Jeffrey, ‡d 1895-1960.
245	14	‡a The city of Paris / ‡c by J. Aspenwell
260	0	‡a New York : ‡b Archival Press, ‡c 1950
300		‡a xx, 202 p. : ‡b ill. ; ‡c 24 cm.
501		‡a With: A cultural excursion through Paris / Frances Aspenwell. New York : Archival Press, 1950
651	0	‡a Paris ‡x Description
700	10	‡a Aspenwell, Frances ‡t A cultural excursion through Paris
740	21	‡a A cultural excursion through Paris

30. *Bibliographic elements displayed above coded for USMARC*

Representative American plays : from 1767 to
the present day / edited with introductions
and notes by Arthur Hobson Quinn. -- 7th ed.,
rev. and enl. -- New York : Appleton-
Century-Crofts, c1953.
xii, 1248 p. ; 25 cm.

Partial contents: Pocohantas, or The
settlers of Virginia / G. W. P. Curtis --
Rip Van Winkle / as played by J. Jefferson --
Madame Butterfly / D. Belasco and J. Long --

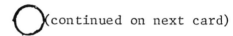(continued on next card)

31. *Partial contents note*

Representative American plays...c1953.
(Card 2)

The faith healer / W. V. Moody -- Beyond the
horizon / E. O'Neill -- Winterset / M. Anderson

1. American drama -- Collections. I. Quinn,
Arthur Hobson, 1875-1960, ed. II. Title.

32. *Continuation card for contents note*

245	10	‡a Representative American plays : ‡b from 1767 to the present day / ‡c edited with introduction and notes by Arthur Hobson Quinn.
250		‡a 7th ed., rev. and enl.
260	0	‡a New York : ‡b Appleton-Century-Crofts, ‡c 1953
300		‡a xii, 1248 p. ; ‡c 25 cm.
505	2	‡a Pocohantas, or The settlers of Virginia / G.W.P. Curtis -- Rip Van Winkle / as played by J. Jefferson -- Madame Butterfly / D. Belasco and J. Long -- The faith healer / W.V. Moody -- Beyond the horizon / E. O'Neill -- Winterset / M. Anderson
650	0	‡a American drama ‡x Collections
700	10	‡a Quinn, Arthur Hobson, ‡d 1875–1960, ‡e ed.

33. *USMARC coding for exhibits 31 and 32*

Webster, John, 1578-1632.
    Webster and Tourneur : four plays / John Webster and Cyril Tourneur ; with an introduction and notes by John Addington Symonds. -- New York : Hill and Wang, 1956.
    381 p. ; 18 cm. -- (The mermaid series of English dramatists)

"A Mermaid Dramabook".
    Contents: The white devil / John Webster -- The duchess of Malfi / John Webster -- The atheist's tragedy / Cyril Tourneur --

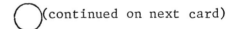(continued on next card)

34. *Analytical tracing without creating added or separate records*

Webster, John, 1578-1632.
   Webster and Tourneur...1956
(Card 2)

The revenger's tragedy / Cyril Tourneur.

   I. Webster, John, 1578-1632. The white
devil (1612) II. Webster, John, 1578-1632.
The duchess of Malfi (1623) III. Tourneur,
Cyril, 1575-1626. The atheist's tragedy (1611)
IV. Tourneur, Cyril, 1575-1626. The revenger's
tragedy (1607)   V. Series.

35. *Continuation card for analytical tracing*

100	10	‡a Webster, John, ‡d 1578–1632
245	10	‡a Webster and Tourneur : ‡b four plays / ‡c John Webster and Cyril Tourneur ; with an introduction and notes by John Addington Symonds
260	0	‡a New York : ‡b Hill and Wang, ‡c 1956
300		‡a 381 p. ; ‡c 18 cm.
440	4	‡a The mermaid series of English dramatists
500		‡a "A Mermaid Dramabook"
505	0	‡a The white devil / John Webster -- The duchess of Malfi / John Webster -- The atheist's tragedy / Cyril Tourneur -- The revenger's tragedy / Cyril Tourneur
700	12	‡a Webster, John, ‡d 1578–1632. ‡t The white devil ‡f 1612
700	12	‡a Webster, John, ‡d 1578–1632. ‡t The duchess of Malfi ‡f 1623
700	12	‡a Tourneur, Cyril, ‡d 1575–1626. ‡t The atheist's tragedy ‡f 1611
700	12	‡a Tourneur, Cyril, ‡d 1575–1626. ‡t The revenger's tragedy ‡ 1607

36. *USMARC coding for Exhibits 34 and 35 showing analytical tracing*

Corneille, Pierre, 1606–1684.
    Three plays by Corneille and Racine / edited
and with an introduction by Paul Landis. -- New
York : The Modern Library, 1959.
    xiii, 372 p. : 18 cm.

    Contents: The Cid / Pierre Corneille --
Cinna / Pierre Corneille -- Athaliah / Jean Racine

    I. Corneille, Pierre, 1606–1684.   The Cid.
II. Corneille, Pierre, 1606–1684.   Cinna.   III.
Racine, Jean, 1639–1699.   Athaliah.   IV. Title.

37. *Name-title added entry; catalog card-type display compared to MARC*
name-title coding

100	10	‡a Corneille, Pierre, ‡d 1606–1684.
245	10	‡a Three plays by Corneille and Racine / ‡c edited and with an introduction by Paul Landis
260	0	‡a New York : ‡b The Modern Library, ‡c 1959
300		‡a xiii, 372 p. ; ‡c 18 cm.
505	0	‡a The Cid / Pierre Corneille -- Cinna / Pierre Corneille -- Athaliah / Jean Racine
700	12	‡a Corneille, Pierre, ‡d 1606–1684. ‡t The Cid.
700	12	‡a Corneille, Pierre, ‡d 1606–1684. ‡t Cinna.
700	12	‡a Racine, Jean, ‡d 1639–1699. ‡t Athaliah

38. *MARC coding for name-title added entry*

Arabian nights。
　　Songs of Scheherazade / by Sir Richard
Burton ; with drawings by George M. Stott. --
London : Dent, 1969.
　　xvii, 389 p。 ; ill. : 23 cm.

　　I. Burton, Richard, 1594-1659.
II. Title。

39. *Uniform title as main entry*

130	00	‡a Arabian nights
245	10	‡a Songs of Scheherazade / ‡c by Sir Richard Burton; with drawings by George M. Stott.
260	0	‡a London : ‡b Dent, ‡c 1969
300		‡a xvii, 389 p. ; ‡b ill. : ‡c 23 cm.
700	1	‡a Burton, Richard, ‡d 1594-1659.

40. *Uniform title as main entry, USMARC coding*

Shakespeare, William, 1564–1616.
   [Hamlet]
      The tragedy of Hamlet / commentary by Robert
Harbage. –– Student edition. –– Philadelphia :
University of Pennsylvania Press, 1948.
      xvii, 109 p. ; ill. : 18 cm.

      I. Harbage, Robert,   ed.
   II. Title.

41. *Uniform title interposed*

100	10	‡a Shakespeare, William, ‡d 1564–1618.
240	10	‡a Hamlet
245	14	‡a The tragedy of Hamlet / ‡c commentary by Robert Harbage
250		‡a Student edition
260	0	‡a Philadelphia : ‡b University of Pennsylvania Press, ‡c 1948
300		‡a xvii, 109 p. ; ‡b ill. : ‡c 18 cm.
700	10	‡a Harbage, Robert, ‡e ed.

42. *USMARC Coding for uniform title interposed*

Beethoven, Ludwig van, 1770-1827.
   [Symphonies. no. 3, op. 55, E-Flat Minor]
   The Eroica symphony [score] / by L. van
Beethoven. -- New York : Plantagenet Press,
1899.
   1 score (iv, 138 p.) + 24 parts ; 32 cm.

   I. Title.

43. *Uniform title with a musical score*

100	10	‡a Beethoven, Ludwig van, ‡d 1770–1827
240	10	‡a Symphonies ‡n no. 3, op. 55, ‡r E-flat minor
245	14	‡a The Eroica symphony ‡h score / ‡c by L. van Beethoven.
260	0	‡a New York : ‡b Plantagenet Press, ‡c 1899
300		‡a 1 score (iv, 138 p.) + ‡e 24 parts ; ‡c 32 cm.

44. *USMARC Coding for uniform title with a musical score*

AUTHOR	Watson, Georgia B.
TITLE	Doses of humor to be taken regularly by citizens of mature age / Georgia B. Watson.
IMPRINT	Moore Haven, FL : Rainbow Books, c1988.
DESCRIPT	244 p. ; 23 cm.
SUBJECT	Aged --Conduct of life --Anecdotes. Retirement --Anecdotes.

	LOCATION	CALL #	STATUS
1	Main Collection	158.1024 Wat	AVAILABLE

AUTHOR   Trollope, Anthony, 1815–1882.
TITLE   The Eustace diamonds / with a preface by Michael
              Sadleir. Illustrations by Blair Hughes-Stanton.
IMPRINT   Oxford : Oxford Univ., [1973]
DESCRIPT   384 p. : illus.
SERIES   The Palliser Novels.

	LOCATION	CALL #	STATUS
1	Main Collection	Fiction	AVAILABLE

AUTHOR   Taylor, Shelley E.
TITLE   Positive illusions : creative self-deception and the healthy
              mind / Shelley E. Taylor.
IMPRINT   New York : Basic Books, [1989]
DESCRIPT   xv, 301 p. ; 25 cm.
NOTE   Bibliography: p. 265–291.
              Includes index.
SUBJECT   Mental health.
              Self-deception --Therapeutic use.
              Medicine and psychology.

	LOCATION	CALL #	STATUS
1	Main Collection	158.1 Tay	AVAILABLE

45. *Computer terminal displays from public library catalog. (Reproduced with the kind permission of Gerald M. Kline, President, Innovative Interfaces, Inc., Berkeley, California.)*

Appendix II

A Sampling of Reference Sources for Establishing Entry Headings for Personal and Corporate Names

There are thousands of potential sources of information, in many languages and from many countries. The following works are representative, not inclusive. *Begin* your search by examining a broad, comprehensive source, such as those listed in the first category below. This will save you time and effort.

1. Comprehensive guides and indexes.

Library of Congress *Name headings with references*, compiled and edited by the Catalog Management and Publication Division, Library of Congress, 1974–1980. Superseded by:

Library of Congress *Name authorities cumulative microform edition*, 1977– Quarterly, with a fifth issue consisting of multi-year cumulations of the entire file. Includes personal and corporate names, conference headings, geographical names of political and civil jurisdictions, uniform titles, and series. Also, gives sources for identification of the heading.

National union catalog: a cumulative author list. Washington, D.C., Library of Congress, Card Division. Monthly, with quarterly and annual cumulations. Beginning in 1983, issued in microform as:

National union catalog. Books microform Jan. 1983– Washington, D.C.: Library of Congress, 1983– Monthly. Microfiche.

Sheehy, Eugene E. *Guide to reference books.* 10th ed. Chicago: American Library Association, 1986.

Subject guide to books in print. 1990–91. New York: Bowker.

2. General biographical indexes (personal author)

Almanac of famous people [formerly *Biography almanac*]: *a comprehensive reference guide to more than 25,000 famous and infamous newsmakers, from Biblical times to the present.* 4th ed. Susan L. Stetler, ed. Detroit: Gale Research. 1989. 3 vol.

Biography index: a cumulative index to biographical material in books and magazines. Vol 1– Jan. 1946/ July 1949– New York: Wilson, 1947– Quarterly. Current issues unbound.

Contemporary authors: a bio-bibliographical guide to current writers in fiction, general nonfiction, poetry, journalism, drama, motion pictures, television and other fields. Detroit: Gale Research, 1967–1988. See also *Contemporary authors: new revision series,* 1981–1988.

Current biography, v. 1– 1940– New York: Wilson, 1940– ill. Monthly, except December. Annual cumulation, *Current biography yearbook.*

International who's who. 1935– London: Europa Publications and Allen & Unwin. Annual.

McNeil, Barbara, ed. *Biography and genealogy master index.* 3rd ed. Detroit: Gale, 1989.

Marquis Who's who publications: index to all books. 1974– Chicago: Marquis. Biennial. An index to the names of all persons whose biographical sketches appear in current editions of 11 Marquis biographical directories, with reference to the work in which the biography appears.

New York Times index for the published news. New York: New York Times. For obituaries, see also *New York Times obituaries index.*

Slocum, Robert B. *Biographical dictionaries and related works.* 2nd ed. Detroit: Gale, 1986– 1056 p.

3. Special group and field-oriented biographical titles

American men and women of science. Ed. by Jacques Cattell Press. New York: R.R. Bowker, 1971–1973, 1976–1978, 1979, 1982, 1986.

Encyclopedia of computer science and engineering. 2nd ed. Anthony Ralston, ed. New York: Van Nostrand Reinhold, 1983. 1664 p.

Notable American women, 1607–1950: a biographical dictionary. 3 vols. Ed. by Edward T. James. Cambridge, Mass.: Harvard University Press, Belknap Press, 1971.

Notable American women: the modern period; a biographical dictionary. Ed. by Barbara Sicherman and Carol Hurd Green. Cambridge, Mass.: Harvard University Press, Belknap Press, 1980.

Dictionary of American Negro biography. Ed. by Rayford W. Logan and Michael R. Winston. New York: W.W. Norton, 1982.

Who's who in world Jewry, 1955– New York: Pitman, 1955– Frequency varies. Fourth edition (1978) included Jews living in the Soviet Union for the first time.

Interesting athletes: a newspaper artist's look at blacks in sports. By George L. Lee. Jefferson, N.C.: McFarland, 1990.

American artists: an illustrated survey of leading contemporary Americans. Ed. by Les Krantz. New York: Facts on File publications, 1985.

Dictionary of women artists: an international dictionary of women artists born before 1900. By Chris Petteys. Boston: G.K. Hall, 1985.

A biographical dictionary of film. By David Thomson. 2nd ed. New York: Morrow, 1981.

International motion picture and television almanac, 1929– New York: Quigley. Annual.

International index to television periodicals: an annotated guide 1979/ 80– London: International Federation of Film Archives. Biennial. Section 3 is devoted to biography.

New Grove dictionary of music and musicians. Ed. by Stanley Sadie. London: Macmillan, 1985. 2 vols. ill.

American Society of Composers, Authors and Publishers. *ASCAP biographical dictionary.* 4th ed. Comp. for the American Society of Composers, Authors and Publishers. New York: Jacques Cattel Press/Bowker, 1980.

Baker, Theodore. *Biographical dictionary of musicians.* 7th ed. New York: Schirmer, 1984.

Bull, Storm. *Index to biographies of contemporary composers.* Metuchen, N.J.: Scarecrow Press, 1964-74. 2 vols.

Greek and Latin authors, 800 B.C.-A.D. 1000: a biographical dictionary. By Michael Grant. New York: H.W. Wilson, 1980.

Ancient writers: Greece and Rome. T. James Luce, ed. in chief. New York, Scribner's, 1982. 2 vols. 1148 p.

Albert, Walter, ed. *Detective and mystery fiction: an international bibliography of secondary sources.* San Bernardino, Calif.: Brownstone, 1985. 800 p.

Hubin, Allen J. *Crime fiction 1749-1980: A comprehensive bibliography.* (Garland Reference Library of the Humanities, v. 371.) New York: Garland, 1984. 712 p.

Twentieth-century crime and mystery writers. 2nd ed. Ed. by John M. Reilly. New York: St. Martin's, 1985. 1568 p.

Whodunit? Ed. by H.R.F. Keating. New York: Van Nostrand Reinhold, 1982.

Science fiction writers: critical studies of the major authors from the early nineteenth century to the present day. R.F. Bleiler, ed. New York: St. Martin's, 1981. 642 p.

4. Religious biography

American Jewish Yearbook, 5660- Sept. 5, 1899- Philadelphia: Jewish Publication Society, 1899- v. 1- Annual.

Annuario pontifico. 1716- Rome: Tipografia Poliglotta Vaticana. Annual.

Atwater, Donald. *The Penguin dictionary of saints.* 2nd ed. rev. & updated by Catherine Rachel John. Harmondsworth, England, and New York: Penguin, 1983.

Biographisch-bibliographisches Kirchenlexicon Bearb. u. hrsg. von Friedrich Wilhelm Bautz. Hamm (Westf.) Verlag. Traugott Bautz 1975-78. V. 1-2 (Lfg. 1-15) In progress.

Bowden, Henry Warner. *Dictionary of American religious biography.* Edwin S. Gaustad, advisory ed. Westport, Conn.: Greenwood Press, 1977.

Crockford's clerical directory. 1958- Oxford University Press. Annual.

Delaney, John J. *Dictionary of American Catholic biography.* Garden City, N.Y.: Doubleday, 1984.

Rosenbloom, Joseph R. *A biographical dictionary of early American Jews: Colonial times through 1800.* Lexington: University of Kentucky Press, 1960.

Who's who in religion. Ed. 1-2. 1975/76-77. Chicago: Marquis 1975-77.

Women religious history sources: a guide to repositories in the United States. Ed. by Evangeline Thomas, CSJ. New York: Bowker, 1983.

5. Corporate bodies

Encyclopedia of Associations. 1956- Karin Kock, Deborah Burek and Susan B. Martin. Detroit: Gale. Annual.

Directory of European Associations. 1971- London, Europa Publications, Annual.

Directory of historical organizations in the United States and Canada. 14th ed. Edited by Mary Bray Wheeler. Nashville: American Association for State and Local History, 1990.

The world of learning. 1990. 40th ed. London: Europa. Annual.

Yearbook of international organizations. 1948- Brussels: Union of International Associations. Biennial.

Political handbook and atlas of the world 1975- New York: McGraw-Hill, 1975- Annual.

Foundations grants to individuals. 6th ed. Ed. by Stan Olson. New York: Foundation Center, 1988.

The official museum directory. 1989. Washington, D.C., and Wilmett, Ill.: American Association of Museums and National Register Publishing Co., Directory Division, Macmillan, 1988. 1279 p. + guides and indexes.

Yearbook of American and Canadian Churches. 1916– New York: National Council of Churches of Christ in the U.S.A. Annual. Includes all faiths.

Foundation directory. 10th ed. Comp. by the Foundation Center. New York: Foundation Center, 1985. 885 p.

Federal/State and Municipal/County executive directory. 1985– Washington, D.C.: Carroll Publishing Co. Annual. Government officials at all levels.

United States Government Manual. 1935– Washington, D.C. 1935– Annual.

Weinberger, Marvin J., Greevy, David, and Gore, Chadwick R. *The PAC directory: a complete guide to political action committees.* 2nd ed. Cambridge, Mass.: Ballinger, 1984.

Moody's municipal and government manual. Vol. 1 (1977)– New York: Moody's Investor's Service. Updated semiweekly.

Business firms master index. Jennifer Mossman and Donna Wood, eds. Detroit: Gale, 1985. 1124 p.

Standard & Poor's register of corporations, directors and executives. New York: Standard & Poor's, 1928– Annual.

Europe's 15,000 largest companies, 1975– Oslo, etc.: A.S. Økonomisk Literatur; Bowker, 1975– Annual.

Directory of corporate affiliations ["Who owns whom"]. Skokie, Ill.: National Register Pub. Co., 1968– Annual.

Business organizations and agencies directory. Ed. 1– Detroit: Gale, 1980– Irregular. Supplement published 1985.

6. Anonyms and pseudonyms

Atkinson, Frank. *Dictionary of literary pseudonyms.* 4th ed. Chicago: American Library Association, 1987.

Clarke, Joseph F. *Pseudonyms: the names behind the names*. Nashville: T. Nelson, 1977.

Cushing, William. *Anonyms: a dictionary of revealed authorship*. Reprint of 1889 ed. Evanston, Ill.: Adlers Foreign Books, 1968.

Halkett, Samuel, and Laing, John. *Dictionary of anonymous literature*. 7 vols. (Reference Series, No. 44.) Brooklyn: Haskell, 1971. (Reprinted.)

LeFontaine, Joseph Raymond. *The collector's bookshelf: a comprehensive listing of authors, their pseudonyms, and their books*. Buffalo, N.Y.: Prometheus Books, 1991. Lists 33,000 works of fiction written since the mid–1800s by 931 authors who published under 1,764 names.

Sharp, Harold S. *Handbook of geographical nicknames*. Metuchen, N.J.: Scarecrow Press, 1980.

Sharp, Harold S., comp. *Handbook of pseudonyms and personal nicknames*. Metuchen, N.J.: Scarecrow Press, 1972. 2 vols.: Volume 1 A–J, Volume 2 K–Z, 1395 p. First supplement 1975; second supplement 1982.

Taylor, Archer and Mosher, Fredric J. *The bibliographical history of anonyma and pseudonyma*. Chicago: University of Chicago Press for the Newberry Library, 1951.

Appendix III

How a Computer Stores Bibliographic Records

The purpose of the following discussion is to explain how an online catalog can retrieve and effectively arrange all of its records by any element of their descriptions on demand. For a more detailed description of the MARC format, see Crawford (1989).

Consider the following five bibliographic records, shown here as an online catalog's public terminal might display them:

RECORD #1

Rhodes, William, 1945–
  A history of America in the 19th century / by William Rhodes. -- New York : Historical Books, 1980.
  x, 239 p. : ill., facsims., maps ; 25 cm.

SUBJECT HEADINGS:
  United States -- History -- 19th century.

RECORD #2

Rhodes, William, 1945–
  A history of America from 1900 to the present / by William Rhodes. -- New York : Historical Books, 1981.
  xi, 220 p. : ill., facsims., maps ; 25 cm.

SUBJECT HEADINGS:
  United States -- History -- 20th century.

RECORD #3

Carter, Frank, 1934–
America from 1800 to 1900 / by Frank Carter. -- Chicago : Humanities Press, 1979.
x, 239 p. : ill., facsims., maps ; 26 cm.

SUBJECT HEADINGS:
United States -- History -- 19th century.

RECORD #4

Carter, Frank, 1934–
America from 1900 to today / by Frank Carter. -- Chicago : Humanities Press, 1980.
xii, 240 p. : ill., facsims., maps ; 26 cm.

SUBJECT HEADINGS:
United States -- History -- 20th century.

RECORD #5

Jones, Roger, 1950–
Twentieth-century music, twentieth-century America : how new sounds reflect modern history / Roger Jones and Frank Carter. -- London : Historical International ; New York : Humanities Press, 1990.
viii, 300 p. : ill., facsims., maps, music ; 30 cm. -- (Fine arts and history series ; 4)

SUBJECT HEADINGS:
Music -- United States -- 20th century -- History and criticism.
United States -- History -- 20th century.

ADDED ENTRIES:
Carter, Frank, 1934–

What happens when a user performs a subject search? Intuition might lead you to believe that if a user types

s United States -- History -- 20th century

the computer will examine all of the master records in turn, looking for that subject heading in each. Such an approach would be extremely inefficient and time consuming, since the online catalog might contain hundreds of thousands of records.

Instead, the online catalog maintains a set of what are called *inverted files*. These are indexes to the catalog, in which each author, title, subject heading, etc., is listed *once*, along with some type of pointers to all records containing that title, author, or subject. The author and subject files of our hypothetical five-record database might look like this:

AUTHOR FILE

1: Rhodes, William, 1945–
(1, 2)

2: Carter, Frank, 1934–
(3, 4, 5)

---

3. Jones, Roger, 1950–
(5)

SUBJECT FILE

1: United States -- History -- 19th century.
(1,3)

2: United States -- History -- 20th century.
(2, 4, 5)

3: Music -- United States -- 20th century -- History and cricitism.
(5)

Therefore, when a user types

    s United States -- History -- 20th century

the online catalog finds that heading in the subject index, then retrieves records 2, 4 and 5.

The computer does not search sequentially through the subject index either. If the file contained a large number of subjects—as many as are in the *Library of Congress Subject Headings*, for example—this would be almost as inefficient as searching the master file. Rather, it uses one of several mechanisms which allow it to go directly to the correct heading. We shall not discuss these mechanisms here, since they involve computer algorithms, which are beyond the scope of this textbook. We will say only that they take advantage of the fact that every letter of the alphabet or sequence of letters has a numeric value inside the computer.

Although few online catalogs do this at present, they could index all elements of their bibliographic records. For example, they could index the places of publication and publishers of our five records:

PLACE FILE

1: New York
(1, 2, 5)

2: Chicago
(3, 4)

3: London
(5)

PUBLISHER FILE

1: Historical Books
(1, 2)

---

2. Humanities Press
(3, 4, 5)

---

3. Historical International
(5)

In fact, the University of Pennsylvania's online catalog, "Franklin," does allow a type of related searching. Although you cannot search a place index or publisher index, you can search by keywords which may come from anywhere in the bibliographic record. You may also specify the MARC field in which the keyword is to appear.

In some online catalogs, there may not even be a master file as such. Rather, each master record may consist of a set of pointers to the proper spots in the various inverted files.

As you might suspect, the creation and updating of inverted files is a time consuming process, because it does require the computer to examine every record in the master file. For this reason, most libraries have their computer systems update their inverted files overnight. Therefore, you might input a record but be unable to retrieve it until the next day.

It is because of these inverted files that you may, with an online catalog, retrieve and effectively arrange bibliographic records by any element of the bibliographic description on demand. You should discover that your ability to do this makes the online catalog a much more useful tool than the manual catalog has ever been.

Sources cited

Crawford, Walt. *MARC for Library Use: Understanding Integrated USMARC*, 2nd ed. Boston: G.K. Hall, 1989.

Appendix IV

How a Computer Sorts Names and Titles

The purpose of the following discussion is to explain why a computer sorts certain names, titles, etc., quite differently from the way a human would.

A computer stores any word or phrase in a storage area called a *character string*. This is a row of alphabetic, numeric, or other characters, each of which has a specific numbered location in the string. A computer would store the name heading

Smith, John, 1954–

in a character string as follows:

S	m	i	t	h	,		J	o	h	n	,		1	9	5	4	–
1	2	3	4	5	6	7	8	9	10	11	12	13	14	15	16	17	18

A computer will store the title

Lulu : an opera.

in a character string as follows:

L	u	l	u		:		a	n		o	p	e	r	a	.
1	2	3	4	5	6	7	8	9	10	11	12	13	14	15	16

Note that the computer considers the comma, the dash, the colon, and the blank space to be characters; each of these has its own numbered location in the string.

The numbers appearing in conjunction with each character in the two character strings above are ordinal values specific to those strings. The letter *o* has a positional value of 9 in the first string and 11 in the second. The letter *u* has a positional value of 2 the first time it appears in the second string and 4 the second time it appears.

However, each each character also has its own numeric value independent of its position in any string. Most computers in the United States assign these values according to the American Standard Code for Information Interchange (ASCII, pronounced "AS-kee"). The ASCII value for *A* is 65, the value for *B* is 66, and so on through *Z*, which has a value of 90. The lowercase letters have ASCII values running sequentially from 97, for *a*, to 122, for *z*.

Here are the two character strings shown above with the ASCII values for each character added:

83	109	105	116	104	44	32	74	111	104	110	44	32	49	57	53	52	45
S	m	i	t	h	,		J	o	h	n	,		1	9	5	4	–
1	2	3	4	5	6	7	8	9	10	11	12	13	14	15	16	17	18

76	117	1	117	32	58	32	97	110	32	111	112	101	114	97	46
L	u	l	u		:		a	n		o	p	e	r	a	.
1	2	3	4	5	6	7	8	9	10	11	12	13	14	15	16

By combining the positional and ASCII values of all characters in a string, the computer can assign it a numeric value relative to any other string. Because the computer does this automatically, computer programmers can write statements which include "greater than" and "less than" comparisons between strings. Furthermore, because the letters *A–Z* and *a–z* have sequential ASCII values, computer programmers can take for granted that if String 1 is greater than String 2, then String 1 should appear later in an alphabetically sorted list than String 2; the computer will always place

> Aaron

before

> Abbott

which it will, in turn, place before

> Ackley

Any sorting algorithm assumes that a computer will function as we have just described.

Unfortunately, there is one type of character string which a computer will *not* automatically place in the proper alphabetical sequence. This is the string which, according to traditional filing rules, you must sort on the basis of data other than the actual sequence of letters or numbers it contains. Three such strings which occur frequently in bibliographic records are:

(1) A title beginning with any of the initial articles, *A, An,* or *The,* which are always ignored in filing;

(2) A proper name beginning with *Mc*; such names and those beginning with *Mac* have traditionally been interfiled;

(3) A title beginning with a number, which needs to be filed as if the number were written out in words:

> 2001 : a space odyssey
> 101 checklists

When a computer encounters any of these three types of character strings, it cannot "know" that it must read them as something other than what they are. The computer cannot, for example equate

> 2001

with

> Two thousand and one

It is relatively easy to "teach" a computer to ignore initial articles. A programmer can precede a sorting algorithm with one to remove all instances of

> T h e [space]
> A [space]
> A n [space]

from all strings before sorting them.

(This algorithm, and all others we discuss below, does not actually alter the text of any field in a bibliographic record. Rather, it creates a copy of the string, alters the copy, determines its proper place in the sorting sequence, then placing the original string in that position. Alternatively, it could alter the original string, then reverse the alteration after sorting.)

The programmer can write a similar algorithm to change every instance of *Mc* to *Mac* in any field containing, a proper name, but this

involves considerable risk, because *Mc* at the beginning of a name may
or may not be an alternative form of *Mac*.

An algorithm to change numbers written as digits into numbers
written as words would not be so easy to write. One that could handle
only cardinal numbers is definitely within the bounds of possibility, but
would be rather complicated nonetheless. However, it may or may not
be possible to write an algorithm that would successfully translate the
digital portions of all of the titles in the left column below into the
proper words in the right column.

2001 : a space odyssey	Two thousand and one : a space odyssey
1984	Nineteen eighty-four
976 rules for better writing	Nine hundred and seventy-six rules for better writing
976 numbers : a national directory	Nine seven six numbers : a national directory
Fahrenheit 451	Fahrenheit four fifty-one

At present, the designers and users of many online systems have
decided that the best solution to the problem of computer sorting is to
allow the computer to sort strictly on the basis of a character string's
contents. That means that all names beginning with *Mc* will sort after
every name beginning with *Ma*. Since the digits *0* through *9* have ASCII
values of 48-57, which are below that of *A*, all titles beginning with
digits will sort before all titles beginning with *A*.

As we stated earlier, the Library of Congress has begun to assign
cutter numbers based on the computer sorting sequence. Therefore,
you may be in the position of deciding how to integrate these new cutter
numbers with older ones.

Index